T0344427

Technology-Enhanced Human Interaction in Modern Society

Francisco Vicente Cipolla-Ficarra
*Latin Association of Human-Computer Interaction, Spain &
International Association of Interactive Communication, Italy*

Maria Valeria Ficarra
*Latin Association of Human-Computer Interaction, Spain &
International Association of Interactive Communication, Italy*

Miguel Cipolla-Ficarra
International Association of Interactive Communication, Italy

Alejandra Quiroga
Universidad Nacional de La Pampa, Argentina

Jacqueline Alma
Electronic Arts - Vancouver, Canada

Jim Carré
University of The Netherlands Antilles, Curaçao

A volume in the Advances in Human
and Social Aspects of Technology
(AHSAT) Book Series

IGI Global
DISSEMINATOR OF KNOWLEDGE

Published in the United States of America by
IGI Global
Information Science Reference (an imprint of IGI Global)
701 E. Chocolate Avenue
Hershey PA, USA 17033
Tel: 717-533-8845
Fax: 717-533-8661
E-mail: cust@igi-global.com
Web site: http://www.igi-global.com

Library of Congress Cataloging-in-Publication Data

Names: Cipolla-Ficarra, Francisco V. (Francisco Vicente), 1963- editor.
Title: Technology-enhanced human interaction in modern society / compiled by
   Francisco Vicente Cipolla-Ficarra, Maria Valeria Ficarra, Miguel
   Cipolla-Ficarra, Alejandra Quiroga, Jacqueline Alma, and Jim Carr?e.
Description: Hershey, PA : Information Science Reference, [2018]
Identifiers: LCCN 2017016638l ISBN 9781522534372 (hardcover) l ISBN
   9781522534389 (ebook)
Subjects: LCSH: User interfaces (Computer systems)--Evaluation. l Information
   technology. l Telecommunication--Social aspects. l Medical telematics. l
   Commercial correspondence.
Classification: LCC QA76.9.U83 T44 2018 l DDC 005.4/37--dc23 LC record available at https://
lccn.loc.gov/2017016638

This book is published in the IGI Global book series Advances in Human and Social Aspects of Technology (AHSAT) (ISSN: 2328-1316; eISSN: 2328-1324)

British Cataloguing in Publication Data
A Cataloguing in Publication record for this book is available from the British Library.

For electronic access to this publication, please contact: eresources@igi-global.com.

Advances in Human and Social Aspects of Technology (AHSAT) Book Series

ISSN:2328-1316
EISSN:2328-1324

Editor-in-Chief: Ashish Dwivedi, The University of Hull, UK

MISSION

In recent years, the societal impact of technology has been noted as we become increasingly more connected and are presented with more digital tools and devices. With the popularity of digital devices such as cell phones and tablets, it is crucial to consider the implications of our digital dependence and the presence of technology in our everyday lives.

The **Advances in Human and Social Aspects of Technology (AHSAT) Book Series** seeks to explore the ways in which society and human beings have been affected by technology and how the technological revolution has changed the way we conduct our lives as well as our behavior. The AHSAT book series aims to publish the most cutting-edge research on human behavior and interaction with technology and the ways in which the digital age is changing society.

COVERAGE

- Human Rights and Digitization
- Cultural Influence of ICTs
- Gender and Technology
- Activism and ICTs
- Digital Identity
- ICTs and human empowerment
- Cyber Behavior
- Computer-mediated communication
- Human Development and Technology
- Cyber Bullying

IGI Global is currently accepting manuscripts for publication within this series. To submit a proposal for a volume in this series, please contact our Acquisition Editors at Acquisitions@igi-global.com or visit: http://www.igi-global.com/publish/.

Titles in this Series

For a list of additional titles in this series, please visit:
https://www.igi-global.com/book-series/advances-human-social-aspects-technology/37145

HCI Challenges and Privacy Preservation in Big Data Security
Daphne Lopez (VIT University, India) and M.A. Saleem Durai (VIT University, India)
Information Science Reference • ©2018 • 275pp • H/C (ISBN: 9781522528630) • US $215.00

Handbook of Research on Human Development in the Digital Age
Valerie C. Bryan (Florida Atlantic University, USA) Ann T. Musgrove (Florida Atlantic University, USA) and Jillian R. Powers (Florida Atlantic University, USA)
Information Science Reference • ©2018 • 526pp • H/C (ISBN: 9781522528388) • US $275.00

Optimizing Human-Computer Interaction With Emerging Technologies
Francisco Cipolla-Ficarra (Latin Association of Human-Computer Interaction, Spain & International Association of Interactive Communication, Italy)
Information Science Reference • ©2018 • 471pp • H/C (ISBN: 9781522526162) • US $345.00

Designing for Human-Machine Symbiosis Using the URANOS Model...
Benjamin Hadorn (University of Fribourg, Switzerland)
Information Science Reference • ©2017 • 170pp • H/C (ISBN: 9781522518884) • US $125.00

Research Paradigms and Contemporary Perspectives on Human-Technology Interaction
Anabela Mesquita (School of Accounting and Administration of Porto, Polytechnic Institute of Porto, Portugal & Algorithm Research Centre, Minho University, Portugal)
Information Science Reference • ©2017 • 366pp • H/C (ISBN: 9781522518686) • US $195.00

Solutions for High-Touch Communications in a High-Tech World
Michael A. Brown Sr. (Florida International University, USA)
Information Science Reference • ©2017 • 217pp • H/C (ISBN: 9781522518976) • US $185.00

For an enitre list of titles in this series, please visit:
https://www.igi-global.com/book-series/advances-human-social-aspects-technology/37145

701 East Chocolate Avenue, Hershey, PA 17033, USA
Tel: 717-533-8845 x100 • Fax: 717-533-8661
E-Mail: cust@igi-global.com • www.igi-global.com

Table of Contents

> *Francisco V. Cipolla-Ficarra, Latin Association of Human-Computer*
> *Interaction, Spain & International Association of Interactive*
> *Communication, Italy*
> *Jim Carré, University of the Netherlands Antilles, Curaçao*
> *Valeria M. Ficarra, Latin Association of Human-Computer Interaction,*
> *Spain & International Association of Interactive Communication,*
> *Italy*

> *Francisco V. Cipolla-Ficarra, Latin Association of Human-Computer*
> *Interaction, Spain & International Association of Interactive*
> *Communication, Italy*
> *Jim Carré, University of the Netherlands Antilles, Curaçao*

> *Francisco V. Cipolla-Ficarra, Latin Association of Human-Computer*
> *Interaction, Spain & International Association of Interactive*
> *Communication, Italy*

Epigraph

If patience is worth anything, it must endure to the end of time. And a living faith will last in the midst of the blackest storm – Mahatma Gandhi (1869–1948)

Preface

Through the modernization of the sciences and education it can be seen how the technology-enhance human interaction in the so called modern society has disseminated progressively in the last three decades. All those who have been daily in contact with computers since that time are privileged witnesses of the switching from the use of the big computers in the government institutions, that is, universities, city halls, ministries, etc., first in the business, commercial, industrial context, etc. then in the home and finally in the personal and mobile domain (tablet PC, iPhone, etc.), whether it is individually or in a group.

In the decade of the '80s the role of each one of the members in the educational and conputer science process, for instance, were very well defined. The team or individual work allowed to surmount the limitations imposed by the hardware in the personal computers, such as was the memory limitations of the processer, in the BASIC (Beginner's All-purpose Symbolic Instruction Code) programming of the early videogames, oriented at pastime and/or education. Those were artisanal and highly creative moments, where the printed listings of the programs were gone through many times with the purpose of optimizing the final versions, that is, the executable programs, once they were compiled, and with zero mistakes. An identical procedure for other programming languages such as Cobol (COmmon Business-Oriented Language), the Fortran (Formula Translation), the C (ANSI C), among others, oriented at the management of accountancy offices, centres of analysis of statistic data, warehouses of industrial components, to mention a couple of examples. In those times, in the public and private institutions, with a certain size, for the great investments in software and hardware, as were the calculation centres, many started as computer operators switching then to programmers, systems analysts, until becoming systems engineers. That is, it could be seen in time a logical and growing evolution of the professional role in the clearly computer science domain.

In the educational context, the teachers started to develop the inclusion of computers in the teaching process. In this sense, it is to be stressed the excellent task developed by Seymour Papert, especially among children. In them he saw the need that they learned the use of the computers in an easy and entertaining way, and that at the same time they fostered the thought process. For which reason, together with Danny Bobrow and Wally Feuerzeig developed the Logo language. This programming language quickly became an exceptional tool to teach the process of though and learning to the youngest, based on the graphics and basic geometry. A triangular cursor called turtle. The head wil show the user where the cursor will move. The movements in the screen have different direction and/or actions (turn right, turn left, forwards, backwards, etc.) drawing lines with which the neophyte user see immediately what is the result of her actions.

Synthetically speaking, a turtle that fosters the use of graphics, the notion of recursivity and the making of listings. Without any doubt, the qualitative attribute of friendly exists in the Logo, since it is related to the turtle and how to use it, as an object with which to think. Besides, from a didactic perspective and of programming, the Logo has a more structural method with regard to the first versions of BASIC. The BASIC constantly resorted to the "goto" command, which in programmes with a high number of programming lines required a long time to the programmers, systems analysts, etc., to locate the failings or programming errors derived from "goto". In other words, the birth of Logo has been a bridge product where the human pillars like Seymour Papert, Marvin Minsky, Jean Piaget, among so many others, allowed a real intersection of the formal and factual sciences. An innovating space which with the passing of time has progressively disappeared in the children education domain and the New Information and Communication Technology (NICT) in the new millennium.

The computer aided education (CAE) allowed to train in private computer science academies located in the centre or the neighbourhoods of the main cities a myriad of future users of personal computers, especially in applications related with office automation, such as texts processors, broadsheets, databases, presentations, etc. With the appearance of the clone computers, that is, built by electronics, computer science technicians, etc. starting from each one of the components. Components which were made mainly in the Asian countries in the 90s. It was so that with the arrival of those personal computers to the home it was accelerated in an exponential way. The commercial videogames colonized the homes of millions of users thanks to the multimedia hardware advances, especially in the high quality graphic cards, fast speed processors,

CD/DVD readers, loudspeakers, joysticks, among other peripheral components of input/output. First it was a family fruition, and later on it became a personal fruition. Physically, in the south of Europe, first they were in the living room and later they moved to the sleeping room or studio. All of that happened at the late '80s and early '90s.

The quality of the commercial products in the domain of the hypertext, multimedia and hipermedia systems for education, general information, pastimes, etc., mainly, was very high given the limitations in the use of dynamic media (computer animations, video, music, etc.), because of the space they took in the off-line supports. These limitations would disappear as the Internet democratized and the wideband, especially in optic fibre, was expanding geographically speaking. Now in that democratizing process the user lost his ability to program because he entered naively in a high consumption spiral of multimedia titles, as if they were multiplex movies. In this sense, the audiovisual industry did not develop to generate qualitatively and quantitatively multimedia contents to meet the demand of the market which grew vertiginously.

Oddly enough all of this happened in spite of the financial assistance that existed from Brussels, and which many representatives of the decision or power groups had been trained in industrial schools or polytechnic universities. Once again the Achilles heel of those communities was the lack of originality or creativity of the rulers in the educational domain, the opacity in the actions of the public servants of the sector, the lack of vision of the future in the power groups, and equality of chances for those professionals capable of innovating the human-interaction in the modern societies. In few words, the contents were developed thousands of kilometers away with regard to where the potential users of those interactive systems were to be found.

We are in the face of the great failure of the educational model which linked to healthcare are the two main pillars of modern societies. These failed models or rather antimodels little by little were set in other overseas communities whose students and teacher did not have the latest technological novelties, had survived for centuries, though, without the mercantilist factor, in their study plans. The failure of those models is such in the places where they originated, that currently the PhD thesis in many modern societies are tantamount to the end of study projects of the engineering degrees or graduates of the 80s, obtained in many public universities of cities in the American continent. In this reality, even the words of a same language do not have the same meaning with reality, specifically when they are compared with the professionalism of the users located in the Old World and the American continent, for example.

This linguistic gap, the division of classes in the population pyramid, the access to multimedia information, among other failures, have found in the multimedia mobile phones a kind of panacea to all the evils of regression in the quality of life inside the modernized communities or not. However, the central axis of the solutions goes through the human being.

A human being which daily sees the digital world that surrounds him grow and who starts not to distinguish at sight the real world from the virtual one. Therefore it is necessary to find a balance in this regard and for that it is necessary to know the technological evolution, that is, where we are, where we come from and where they want to take us. In this sense, our simple contribution has been to have a diachronic view (always placed in the reality of the of the time and without underrating the achievements obtained since the media or tools of that time will always be different to the current ones) and positive of the neutral technological advances applied to the development of training, health, interactive systems, free information online, social communication among others, and a very critical and denunciation perspective towards anything that damages the progressive advance aimed at fostering the common good of all humankind.

All the works that make up the current proceedings have been submitted since the start of 2014 until the end of 2016 in the following international events (conferences and/or workshop and/or symposium): ADNTIIC (Advances in New Technologies, Interactive Interfaces and Communicability), CCGIDIS (Communicability, Computer Graphics and Innovative Design for Interactive Systems), ESIHISE (Evolution of the Sciences, Informatics, Human Integration and Scientific Education), HCITISI (Human-Computer Interaction, Telecommunications, Informatics and Scientific Information), HCITOCH (Human-Computer Interaction, Tourism and Cultural Heritage), HIASCIT (Horizons for Information Architecture, Security and Cloud Intelligent Technology), MSIVISM (Multimedia, Scientific Information and Visualization for Information Systems and Metrics), RDINIDR (Research and Development in Imaging, Nanotechnology, Industrial Design and Robotics), and SETECEC (Software and Emerging Technologies for Education, Culture, Entertainment, and Commerce). The book is organized into 14 chapters. Now, a short summary of each one of them to indicate the main aspects and contributions of the work research carried out by their authors:

In Chapter 1, "UNESCO, Digital Library, Interactive Design, and Communicability: An Excellent Example Online" their authors Francisco V. Cipolla-Ficarra, Jim Carré and Valeria M. Ficarra, present a new category of interactive design called "eidomix". Besides, they submit the results of the evaluation of the communicability applied to one of the websites related to the online and free access dissemination such as the "World Digital Library". A detailed examination allows to know the mainstays of the current website, regarded by its authors as an excellent example for online information, with regard to the dissemination of cultural heritage through the UNESCO. The results obtained in the current work have allowed them to elaborate a first guideline to create interactive contents. Contents where the culture variable is a constant value, especially oriented at the era of the expansion of communicability called "quantic-nanotechnological-self-sufficient". Besides, for a better understanding of some notions, the authors have included a summary of the "UNESCO Declaration on Cultural Diversity."

In Chapter 2, under the title "Biomedical Test Instruments: Usability, Ergonomy, and Communicability Assessment" the authors Francisco V. Cipolla-Ficarra and Jim Carré reveal the results of a heuristic evaluation between ergonomics, usability and communicability applied to an instrument of worldwide use, such as sugar measurer in the blood for those people with diabetes, especially of the Melitus II type. In the study are revealed the main difficulties in the use of those instruments, as the models change with the passing of time. It is also described in the case of the elderly population the motivations why several healthcare instruments (including those related to multimedia mobile phones) oriented at the self-control of health, require the constant assistance of another person to know the results of the tests made with said instruments.

In Chapter 3, the research work "Multimedia, Scientific Information, and Visualization for Information Systems and Metrics" the author studies the importance of quality in the communication process, mainly in interactive communication. Across the text are enumerated and explained some primary keys to easily detect the presence or absence of qualitative attributes in the online and/or offline interactive systems. In this regard they work with methods and techniques to work out metrics which measure the quality attributes under the formula "Low-Cost and High Quality". Simultaneously, Francisco V. Cipolla-Ficarra presents some analysis strategies of the interactive design and the importance of making measurements, whose origins go back to the first systems of off-line multimedia, commercial, and with a world-wide dissemination, as well as the scientific information and visualization for information systems. Finally, the current research work contains a summary of the human and/or social factors which prevent a harmonious era of the expansion of communicability in the modern societies.

In Chapter 4, "An Exemplary Interface for All" is the short title chosen by the authors, Francisco V. Cipolla-Ficarra, Alejandra Quiroga, Jim Carré and Jacqueline Alma, to highlight the qualities of a videogame that has surpassed a quarter of a century of life: SimCity. A videogame thought for the whole family, for instance, that has known how to adapt to the demands of the users in all these years, as well as the evolution of the hardware and the software. It is in this last component where the authors have focused the research, specifically in the study of the interface and the incorporation of the novelties coming from the social networks. With this purpose they present in a comprehensive way the importance of the isotopies to interrelate each one of the categories of the interactive design, starting by the interface. Besides, it is stressed how the application of semiotics in the design stage is positive for the potential videogames users. The set of chosen examples makes likeable and facilitates the understanding of the main and secondary topics that have been dealt with in the research.

In the Chapter 5, "A Lisibility Assessment for Mobile Phones," Francisco V. Cipolla-Ficarra, Jacqueline Alma, and Jim Carré, stress the importance of the lisibility or readability factor in mobile phones, especially for the adult population. A series of experiments where they interrelated the notions of usability, ergonomics and communicability that are presented by abc to underline some of the main problems in the reading of contents, to which are exposed daily millions of users of mobile phones across our planet. From a theoretical point of view, the authors make a synthetic analysis of main design models of hypertextual systems, multimedia and hypermedia enunciated in the last decades. The purpose is the verification of the evolution along time of said models and whether they have been applied in our days in the field of multimedia mobile phones, for instance.

In Chapter 6, Francisco V. Cipolla-Ficarra, Alejandra Quiroga, and Valeria M. Ficarra are the authors of the research which they have called "Kernel of the Labyrinths Hypertextuals". In it are established bidirectional relationships among literature, the social sciences and programming concepts in computer science. They study the semiotics notions such as the semantemes which have already allowed them to detect negative behaviour of the users in cyberspace. A diachronic analysis where literature interacts with the basic notions of the labyrinths, and the main aspects of the hypertext, today may become valid analysis instruments such as those used by the authors in the current research. A set of real examples has allowed them to verify the hypothesis set at the start of their research. This verification is pioneer in a first approximation to detect illicit behaviour in the current social networks and the traditional Internet communication channels.

In Chapter 7, the rhetorical question "Digital Television and Senior Users: Design Evolution or Involution?" is the origin of the research work made by Francisco V. Cipolla-Ficarra, Jacqueline Alma, and Miguel Cipolla-Ficarra. Through it they activate some lab experiments to the purpose of detecting whether the triad simplicity, universality and ergonomics of the remote commands allows the access or not to the DTT in the 100% of potential viewers. The work has as a universe of study a random sample of elderly people in the south of Europe. The results obtained do not only point at the digital divide for ergonomic motivations, but also to the permanent fruition of the audiovisual contents. Finally, in the learned lessons and the conclusions there are some research lines for the immediate future tending to solve the problems detected in the current research, in the context of interactive design, ergonomics, usability and communicability among others to reduce the gap between potential users and new technologies.

In Chapter 8, the study "Computer Animation for Ingenious Revival" underlines the importance of computer graphics and especially computer animation in the historical reconstruction of ingenius, stored for centuries in paper support. Francisco V. Cipolla-Ficarra and Miguel Cipolla-Ficarra are the authors of the chapter where gradually are disclosed the advantages of the user of computer graphics notions to reproduce in 3D and animation, starting from graphics, sketches, two-way plans, belonging to mechanisms of complex accuracy of the cultural heritage of humankind, such as: machines to extract water, water clocks, musical automats, etc. Across the chapter it is also researched about the traditional importance and the differences between emulation and simulation of reality through computer graphics, when that reality is depicted in the many devices of the last generation screens. Lastly, in the study is determined the intensity of the communicability in the naturalness of the metaphor, and the reusability of the information, from which is inferred not only the informative aspect of the studied interactive system but also its didactic component.

In Chapter 9, with the title "Poiesis and Video Games for Adults: A Good Example for the Cultural Heritage" its authors, Francisco V. Cipolla-Ficarra, Jacqueline Alma, Miguel Cipolla-Ficarra, and Jim Carré, examine the Greek notion of poiesis in the creative process of the videogames. Consequently, they carry out an evaluation with adult users at the moment of interacting with a videogame, in all its versions across its history. Experiments which interrelate poiesis with communicability and usability. The distribution aspects of the basic components in the interfaces and the usability are analyzed in detail from the start. Besides, the theoretical aspects of the chapter have a wide set of references which allows the interested reader to keep on delving on the presented topics, if so wishes. The figures that accompany the text boost the presentation of the subjects that are developed gradually from the start. Also indirectly are revealed the tactics of interactive design, used in a videogame that has been adapting itself to the passing of time and the revolution of the ICTs.

In Chapter 10, the authors, Francisco V. Cipolla-Ficara and Valeria M. Ficarra respond to the question "*Quo Vadis* 'Interaction Design and Children' in Europe?" through the current work. In it is analyzed the context of interactive design aimed at the EU children in the university research. The purpose is to detect the presence of absence of neutrality of the formal and factual sciences in this kind of studies related to the human-computer interaction for children; the fostering of the digital divide in Europe: the butterfly effects in ICTs among other topics. In this sense the work is oriented mainly at the academic domain and the transfer of technologies in the south of Europe. Also is researched the genesis, constitution, promotion and realization of the international events –conferences, workshops, symposiums, etc., or the conformation of scientific publications, for instance, magazines, handbooks, etc., whose main and/or secondary topics are related to the eventual answer to the rhetorical question. Besides, the modus operandi is investigated of the members of the different committees of the events/publications in the face of the appearance of an eventual or potential competition inside the HCI sector and the new technologies. Lastly, is examined a heuristic equation for the professional activities in an autonomous way.

In Chapter 11, the authors of the work "Anti-Models for Architectural Graphic Expression and UX Education" are Francisco V. Cipolla-Ficara, Jim Carré, Alejandra Quiroga, and Valeria M. Ficarra. It is a work that examines how in certain educational environments, especially the industrial schools, depending on the universities, sometimes the creativity in the offer of courses and pedagogical solutions does not exist. The authors indicate the techniques and tactics used by power groups that act from public universities in the coast of the European Mediterranean. They also indicate how they manipulate daily public opinion, with regard to the ICTs, human-computer interaction, UX, Architectural Graphic Expression, CAD, etc., in the traditional media, such as: magazines, newspapers, radios, etc., and in the social networks, in the local, national, regional, European and international environment, with the purpose of expanding real educational antimodels within and without their national borders. Finally, the authors describe the profile of the dynamic persuader and his negative actions, which from the university website fosters wild mercantilism in education and the need of the fact checking in the educational and scientific community.

In Chapter 12, "Free Emails in Bad Portals" is the title chosen by the authors, Francisco V. Cipolla-Ficarra, Alejandra Quiroga, and Valeria M. Ficarra, to study the phenomenon of the loss of quality in the information contents of the websites where free email services are offered. The authors carry out a detailed study of the evolution of the websites, the categories of interactive design, the online news service, among other main and secondary subjects such as: "Browsers: A commercial and informatics evolution"; "Textual information news plagiarism and manipulation"; "Visual design: Topology of the information elements in the user interface and international connotations"; "An analysis of the content of the website by communicability experts", etc. The chosen universe of study in the Yahoo Spain portal. Besides, they investigate how in the new century there is a trend towards a radial and centralized structure in each one of the interactive design categories of those portals. Lastly, they present a series of examples where the objectivity of the online information does not exist as well as the first results of the evaluations made with users.

In Chapter 13, Francisco V. Cipolla-Ficarra, Valeria M. Ficarra, and Miguel Cipolla-Ficarra are the authors of an analysis strategy called "Inverted Semanteme," reason for which they have titled their work "Inverted Semanteme into Financial Information Online." It is through semiotics and linguistics from where they have been able to elaborate the strategy they explain in the chapter, accompanied by figures of real cases. It is a tool that allows them to verify the veracity of the financial information in the Spanish portals, with ISO quality certificates, with a high rate of reliability and with reduced costs. In the analysis carried out in a former firm, it denotes the lack of credibility in the ISO certification and the damage to the image of the institutions that back said portals through their logos. Simultaneously are investigated the social factors that damage the communicability and credibility of the current financial information when it is false, putting a brake on economic recovery in the modern societies after the international financial crisis initiated in the past decade.

In Chapter 14, through the notions stemming from semiotics, descriptive statistics, online interactive design and communicability, the authors, Francisco V. Cipolla-Ficarra, Alejandra Quiroga, Jim Carré and Valeria M. Ficarra, of the work "Statistics and Graphics Online: Links Between Information in Newspapers and User Experience Evaluation" have decided to establish a bridge of analysis of the iconicity of the statistic graphics belonging to the Spanish digital newspapers, and the interaction of the users with that modality of online information. In the research work the authors stress the importance of computer graphics, and the validity of the graphics with statistic data, by using funny vignettes, pictures, maps, etc., which accompany the online information texts. It is also stressed the importance of including 3D computer graphics techniques to boost the communicability of the figures among the readers of the online information. The wealth of examples which make up the current chapter is accompanied by the results of the evaluation by the readers of the newspapers.

All these research works that wouldn't have been possible without the collaboration of a human team that has known how to adapt itself to myriad adversities, originated from the outside by those who oppose the freedom of the democratization of scientific knowledge, in the great global village, and the equality of the human beings which must continue to exist in the new millennium. In the view of those exogenous factors alien to our will, we can only say that we will keep on rowing in the middle of the wonderful and universal tsunami of the new technologies and all their derivations. Once again, thanks a lot to all those who believe in foster our modest and very honest effort for over a quarter of a century.

Francisco V. Cipolla-Ficarra
Latin Association of Human-Computer Interaction, Spain & International
Association of Interactive Communication, Italy

Acknowledgment

The realization of the current book wouldn't have been possible without the valuable and highly professional collaboration of Colleen More, as well as the rest of the human team in Chocolate Ave., in Hershey (Pennsylvania), who efficiently and wonderfully have oriented us in each moment and have made our final work easy. To all of them a sentence from the soul: Endless thanks!

A deepest gratitude to Maria Ficarra, one of the human beings with a noble heart, transparency, simplicity, goodness, wisdom and infinite affability.

I would like to give special thanks to Donald Nilson, Miguel Cipolla-Ficarra, Amélie Bordeaux, Doris Edison, Giselda Verdone, Julia Ruiz, Luisa Varela, Mary Brie, Pamela Fulton, Sonia Flores, and Carlos Albert.

Chapter 1
UNESCO, Digital Library, Interactive Design, and Communicability:
An Excellent Example Online

Francisco V. Cipolla-Ficarra
Latin Association of Human-Computer Interaction, Spain & International Association of Interactive Communication, Italy

Jim Carré
University of the Netherlands Antilles, Curaçao

Valeria M. Ficarra
Latin Association of Human-Computer Interaction, Spain & International Association of Interactive Communication, Italy

ABSTRACT

We present a new category of interactive design called "eidomix". Besides, the early results of a heuristic evaluation of communicability with the purpose of highlighting the main elements of a website related to the diffusion of cultural heritage such as "World Digital Library" (www.wdl.org), from UNESCO. Finally, a first guidelines is presented for the generation of interactive contents aimed at the future era of expansion of communicability called "quantic-nanotechnological-self-sufficient."

INTRODUCTION

We have started the transition between the era of the expansion of communicability towards the era of "quantic-nanotechnological-self-sufficient" communicability (Cipolla-Ficarra, 2015), in each passing minute

DOI: 10.4018/978-1-5225-3437-2.ch001

the human being increases his dependence on the interactive systems in terms of daily business activities. In this process of the interactive design for the new era of communicability also a new category of design is needed, where the user can understand beforehand, quickly and in a summarized way the shape that the structure for the navigation has, the essence of the contents and the modalities of the presentation in the interface of the dynamic and/or static means and the kind of compatibilities with other devices through the hardware. That is to say, the mental idea of the designer with regard to the users of the multimedia systems, aimed at a new generation of them (quantic-nanotechnological-self-sufficient). This mixture of bidirectional interaction among the categories of the design of the communicability and the mental idea of the designer towards the potential users of the system is what we call "eidomix".

The term "eidos", a Greek term meaning form, essence, type already treated by the Greek philosophers, such as Plato in his theory of forms and Aristotle's in the theory of universals (Cooper & Hutchinson, 1997; Barnes, 1984). The theory of the shapes or theory of the ideas is one of the main aspects of platonic philosophy, it is, in fact, its core. It stems from a division between a world of visible things, material (sensible world) and another which cannot be perceived by the senses (intelligible world) where ideas dwell. The author contemplates such ideas as the structure, the models on which the physical things are based, which are but imperfect copies of them. Aristotle's theory of universals is one of the classic solutions to the problem of universals. Universals are types, properties or relations that are common to their various instances. The word "mix" refers to the interrelation of several categories of design in the online and offline interactive systems.

The increase of speed in the interactive communication, the decrease of the size of the computer devices, telematic, etc., with their own intelligence, etc. (Witte, et al. 2010; Bosch, Erp & Sporleder, 2010; Maiden, et al. 2007) will require in the future having a previous mental image of the eventual interrelations of the diverse categories, at the moment that they interact with these new technological devices (Goesele, et al., 2010; Shiomi, et al. 2007; Norman, 2009; Bederson & and Shneiderman, 2003). In the present chapter, we will focus on the heuristic analysis of communicability with the purpose of the diffusion of universal knowledge, such as the libraries, where we will make interact all the existing design categories and in a special way "eidomix".

EIDOMIX GENESIS

The process is similar to that used in the generation of the first methodology for the heuristic evaluation of the multimedia systems called <u>ME</u>thodology for <u>H</u>euristic <u>E</u>valuation in <u>M</u>ultimedia: MEHEM (Cipolla-Ficarra, 1999). It consists in the following stages:

- Selection of the categories of interactive design to be evaluated. In our case, the categories belong to the communicability of the online and offline multimedia systems and are layout, content, navigation, structure, panchronic, and connection:
- Assignment of the "criteria or quality attributes" to the categories selected in the previous point. Some of the quality criteria are control in the fruition, the factual function, isomorphism, the naturalness of the metaphor, motivation, orientation, the richness, the transparency of meaning, etc. The interested reader will find a description of them in the following references (Cipolla-Ficarra, 2010a; Cipolla-Ficarra, 1999; Cipolla-Ficarra, 1997; Cipolla-Ficarra, 1996).
- Application of the corresponding procedure to each one of the quality criteria, for that it is necessary to break down the quality criteria into measurement factors.
- Definition of the heuristic metrics.

It is a methodology which respects the quality models of software engineering, that is, going from the general to the particular. The four stages can be depicted graphically as an inverted pyramid, since the goals of the whole of the activities pass from being more general to more detailed during the procedure for the definition of the heuristic metrics:

In part A of the pyramid, the system is considered as a structure integrated by the basic categories which are interrelated in a bidirectional way. A quality failure in some of the categories will directly affect the communicability of the system. Some of these categories also allow to evaluate the usability of the system, however, we consider that the users of the "Z" generation, for instance, know very well how the applications work in the interactive systems, especially of the social networks (Cipolla-Ficarra, 2015).

In part B of the pyramid are established the categories which are more related to the "engine" of an application, such as the organization of the

Figure 1. Design categories and interactions

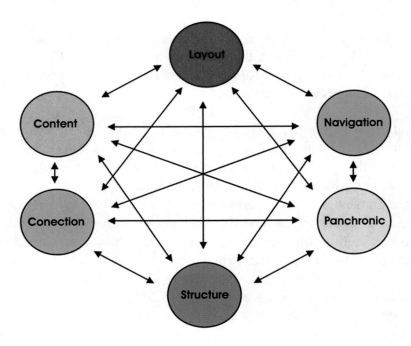

Figure 2. Stages used to obtain the metrics in the multimedia systems

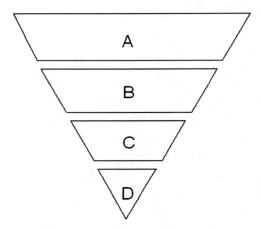

information and the behaviour of the system. Evidently, the analysis can be focused on one or more categories. We will focus mainly on the interrelation among all of them. The variables related to potential users and the idea of the designer towards them, in the stage of the inception of the system, must also be considered given the intrinsic characteristics and the interrelation with the quality criterion which is to be evaluated.

In parts B and C of the pyramid was used at first a set of quality criteria belonging to software engineering, such as reusability, accessibility, etc. Later on these criteria have been readapted and perfected for the online and offline interactive systems, thus obtaining a new set of quality criteria to be evaluated. Said process can also be depicted with another inverted pyramid, on whose base are placed those criteria belonging to software engineering and on the upper part are those criteria belonging to the multimedia systems. It is the summit of that pyramid where is represented the maximum quality for the multimedia systems. In our case, we will focus on communicability.

Part D of the pyramid is made up by the metrics which allow the heuristic evaluation of the system. Upon creating our methodology, a wide study was made of the existing metrics in the software sector, observing that most of the metrics existing in software engineering turn out to be insufficient to evaluate the multimedia systems, since in these it is necessary to measure simultaneously the active/dynamic means and the passive/static means.

In the last years, there has been observed a need of increasing the number of metrics to solve problems detected in the new multimedia systems, such as the feedback mistakes and/or absence of synchronization among the dynamic means, giving origin to a new category of interactive design such as panchronism. With the momentum of the web 2.0 and the multimedia mobile phones another category of design was created called connection.

The metrics described in the MEHEM (Cipolla Ficarra, 1999) belong to the group of direct and objective measures, according to Mario Bunge (Bunge, 1981), since the results can be quantified and compared. Besides, the measurements are direct and objective (Cipolla-Ficarra, 1999). This is a main quality in the techniques and/or methods used for the heuristic evaluation or in software engineering (Kit, 1995). For instance, to guarantee the quality in the software, aside from creating the techniques of direct and indirect measurement, it is necessary to determine a control of observation errors and of measurement (systematic errors in the execution of the measurement, and random errors). The current systems, since they are more complex, are more likely to have communicability failings, where the design requires special attention, considering the costs that they can reach to be solved (Cipolla-Ficarra, 2010a). Besides, it is feasible to come across usability failings, when theoretically, they should have been overcome since they belong to the decade of the 90s. Therefore, it is interesting to differentiate the different kinds of errors existing in keeping with those enunciated by Kit (Kit, 1995) at the moment of the evaluation, such as: mistake, a human action which brings about an incorrect result; fault, an imperfect stage, process or data definition in the computer program, for instance; failure, an incorrect result. The result (manifestation) of a fault. Error, meaning by which the result is incorrect. However, if we analyze the mistakes within the educational context, through a brief analysis of the human and social factors online, for example, we can find from xenophobia down to swindle, through projects with European subventions (Cipolla-Ficarra, 2010b; Cipolla-Ficarra & Kratky, 2011). Moreover, in the evaluation tasks the main conditions must be present:

- **Validity:** It is understood that the measurement meets such a requirement when it measures in some demonstrable way that which it tries to measure, free from systemic distortions.
- **Reliability:** That is, if it is applied several times on the object of study, similar results are obtained. The determination of reliability consists in establishing if the differences in the results are due to inconsistencies in the measurement.
- **Precision:** When it is found with accuracy, in relation with the purpose that is being sought, the place of the phenomenon that is studied.

These conditions are irrespective of the kind of sciences to which they refer, that is, factual and/or formal. An excellent example where these sciences converge and interrelate among themselves is the World Digital Library portal. The accessibility to the information was a quality attribute in our model of heuristic evaluation of the late 90s. With the passing of time, it is a common denominator with the momentum of the web 2.0 in the new millennium, for instance. However, it is not always possible to access the online databases, due to the mistakes, faults, failures, errors, etc, of the designer, programmer, user, etc. (Quinzon, 2010). Exceptionally, the World Digital Library portal can be regarded as a model for our eidomix category. Evidently, we are not applying the hardware/software for heuristic evaluation which currently exists in the scientific labs, as prototypes, and which with the passing of time, many of these software and/or hardware products will enter the international commercial market.

A simple interface with easy interactive access where the universal contents are presented through the figure such as a world map. In it can be seen how the eidomix is present since the user not only has an accurate information of the documents he/she can access in keeping with historic evolution, but can also be detected the presence of the social networks such as the link to Twitter.

Figure 3. In the interface of the universal system can be seen the presence of the eidomix

The minimalist design of the system where we have as interface a natural metaphor, boosts and motivates its use through the potential users, irrespective of the interest of the consultation of the information stored in the hyperbase. Although we are in the face of a great bulk of textual information, the image has had a great predominance in the inception phase of the current online interactive system, as it can be seen in the Figures 4 and 5. In other words, within the minimalism of the design, we find the quality attribute of wealth. Simultaneously, other attributes that are also present are the transparency of

Figure 4. The browse option allows the user to access the information stored in different ways: place, time, topic, type of item, institution

the meaning, the control in the fruition, the factual function and isomorphism. The reader interested in these attributes may look up the following references (Cipolla-Ficarra, 1997; Cipolla-Ficarra, 1999).

Another of the components which boost the wealth of the system are the different languages in which are presented all the contents (Arabic, Chinese, English, Spanish, French, Russian, Portuguese) as well as the existence of the karaoke system to listen to the text, where the user can choose some of

Figure 5. With the option type of item, the user can access all the dynamic means of the system, such as the videos

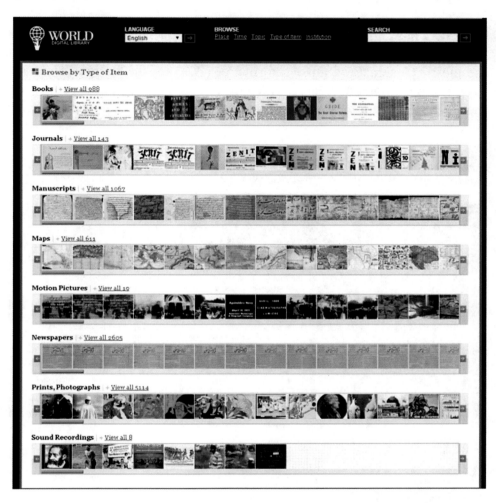

the variables at the moment of listening to the locution. In other words, it is an interactive system which boosts information for all. In the Appendix 1 can be seen other interfaces that make up the structure of the system.

UNESCO: FROM PGI TO THE PROGRAM INFORMATION FOR ALL

UNESCO has carried out in the past a great number of activities aimed at defining its role in the society of information, especially in the framework of the ancient General Program of Information (PGI) and the Intergovernmental Program of Computer Science. With the diffusion of the personal computers, the UNESCO set in motion a project tending to achieve a multilingual free

Figure 6. Functioning of the locution system of the text or karaoke
(Approximate Translation: Title: Description of Egypt. Second Edition. Antiques, Volume II. (plates). In the description, the words take a green hue as the locution progresses.)

Figure 7. Pictures, photos, maps, etc. with high resolution

system, which facilitates the interchange of information and the cooperation at an international level.

In 1980 UNESCO within the activities of the General Program of Information (www.unesco.org –from PGI to IFAP), decided to start a plan of support to the computerizing of libraries, especially aimed at those that were located in developing countries. However, UNESCO in 1980 had a computer system available designed for mainframe with high costs from the point of view of hardware and its maintenance, but which adjusted to plans designed to compile the information of the libraries, thus starting a digitalization process

Figure 8. High resolution zoom

of said libraries for decades. With this purpose, are proposed new projects to cheapen the costs and adapt the software and the hardware so that they were within the reach of the libraries.

A first antecedent of such a program appears in the late 60s, with the development on the International Labour Office (ILO) of a set of computer programs called ISIS (Integrated Set for Information System), designed for a mainframe computer in an IBM 360-30 which worked under the operative system DOS (Gates, Myhrvold, & Rinearson, 1995). With said program was managed the complex file of the ILO, aside from its extensive documentary

Figure 9. Horizontal and/or vertical shifting of the image

Figure 10. Division into three parts of a wide image from the horizontal point of view to preserve the quality of the fruition

funds. The ILO ceded said software to the institutions related to its activity that requested it. Simultaneously, UNESCO developed another system of documental management called CDS (Computerized Documentation System) that it installed in its mainframe, an ICL of the 1900 series. Obviously, there was an incompatibility between both systems, which were used by both organizations in an independent way, until the early IBM-PC appeared.

From 1985 onwards the software began to be distributed more widely in the worldwide geography. The number of official users at the end of 1997 was estimated at 24,000 approximately, concentrating in developing

Figure 11. One of the three parts which make up a big size image

countries, as well as in an important group in Europe: Italy (2,400 users), France 81,800), United Kingdom (1,200), the Eastern European countries: 18,000 is the number of licences formally registered in the offices of the UNESCO in Paris and naturally it does not match the total number of copies of the program in circulation that according to the estimations of UNESCO itself can be figured at about 25,000.

The revolution of the information has given rise to an overlapping of both programs, which have been focusing their activities more and more in two main spheres: on the one hand, the content of a society of information, and on the other the necessary activities to create the info-structure of that society which is taking shape through training, the formulation of information policies the fostering of the constitution of networks. Starting from January 2001, the Program Information for All replaced the General Information Program and the Intergovernmental Computer Program. In the WDL (World Digital Library) which has the collaboration of the UNESCO, reproduces what the libraries of the world have and not only books, but also documents, texts, movies and maps (even ancient). The World Digital Library (WDL) makes available on the Internet, free of charge and in multilingual format, significant primary materials from countries and cultures around the world. This is the first mission.

RESULTS OF THE HEURISTIC EVALUATION AND TOWARDS A FIRST GUIDELINES OF THE IMPENDING ERA FOR COMMUNICABILITY

The users for the evaluation of the communicability of the current interactive system are adults, whose ages oscillate between 30-40 years, experts in the use of computers. They are five women and five men, who have been selected through a random draw of a total of 50. The experiment consisted in locating documents in images format (a total of 20) and finding the first sentence of the texts they had to locate previously in their native language (a total of 20), and later on transcribe that sentence in French and English. The average of the obtained results is presented by categories of design (layout, content and navigation) and where the following attributes of quality: Control of the fruition (CF), Isomorphism (IS), Transparence of Meaning (TM), Naturalness of Metaphor (NM), and divided into two users groups, feminine and masculine. The technique of direct observation, consistency inspections, videotaped sessions and think aloud (Nielsen & Mack, 1994) for the eidomix category. In the scale of values, the minimal value is 0 and the maximum 100.

These first results obtained where there is an interaction of all the categories of design and especially eidomix allows us to establish a first set of components which serve as guideline for the interactive design of the future systems.

Figure 12. Results obtained for the design category of the heuristic evaluation carried out in the World Digital Library website

Results of the Communicability Evaluation with Ediomix

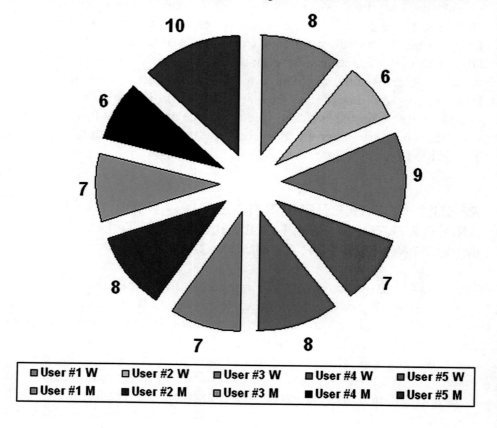

▢ User #1 W	▢ User #2 W	▣ User #3 W	■ User #4 W	■ User #5 W
▢ User #1 M	■ User #2 M	▢ User #3 M	■ User #4 M	■ User #5 M

- **Simplicity in the Navigation:** The unidirectional structures where the linked nodes allow at any moment to go back to home are positive. The guided links to widen the information of the initial contents are also positive.
- **Universality of the Contents:** The use of more than five languages represents the secret of the online and offline interactive systems, aimed at tourism, for instance. A greater number of languages in the touristic portal of a city, region, country, etc., means potential visitors coming from the countries where those languages are spoken. Consequently,

with the passing of time it is easy to verify the equation at greater quantity and quality of the languages in the portals, the more the potential tourists and vice versa.

- **Naturalness:** Minimalism and wealth in the layout. Condensation of the key components in a natural interface but which simultaneously allows the wealth of the information which can be accessed from it. That is, the wealth in the dimension of the set of information units, as well as the paths to access them. Wealth in the multimedia systems traditionally consists in a variety of styles of navigation, variety of paths to access a same information, multiple taxonomies with their matching collections to group the components of the information, a great amount of information for every subject, variety in static and dynamic means, control over the active/dynamic means (video, animations, locutions, etc.)
- **Empathy Towards the Potential Users:** Dividing them always into three great groups: totally unacquainted with the use of the computers, knowledgeable and super experts. It is necessary to seek the common denominator between the three groups. In this sense, the offline multimedia systems of the 90s may be a great help, since they constitute the link between the analogical experts and the neo digital experts, especially in the sector of the graphic arts.
- **Spheronization:** Using the greatest possible number of circular, curve shapes, etc, belonging to nature, and therefore to the world population.

LESSONS LEARNED

The World Digital Library (www.wdl.org) portal is an excellent example of the projects promoted at a worldwide scale through the UNESCO. In it can be seen how all those developing countries are those that have brought more information to the system (in the Figure 3 can be compared the total number of documents among the north, centre and south of the American continent, for instance). This is due to the fact that much of the information stored in their libraries is free to be consulted in situ and that custom has transferred to the digital systems. In contrast, in many economically developed countries, since the appearance of the early supports of offline multimedia information a kind of race took place to acquire the reproduction copyrights of works which in theory are UNESCO patrimony. In the old world, getting the reproduction rights of a monument can definitively paralyze a multimedia project (Cipolla-Ficarra, 2011). However, aside from the legal issues for the free access to the multimedia information, the portal World Digital Library, directly and indirectly, constitutes a kind of style guideline for the designers of similar systems.

In the momentum of the new technologies of the information and the communications, we can find that in the UNESCO, in the preamble of the program Information for All, can be read what follows:

Any individual has the right to the freedom of opinion and expression; this right includes not being molested because of his/her opinions, the right to research and receive information and opinions, and spread them, without limitation of borders, by any means of expression. (Universal Declaration of the Human Rights: www.un.org/en/universal-declaration-human-rights)

Besides, in the article 19, are to be found the following definitions, which are directly related to the lessons learned when carrying out the current research: Information and knowledge are essential for the progress of education, science, culture and communication, for the acquisition of autonomy and responsibility, for the promotion of cultural diversity and to foster good open governance. The mandate of UNESCO is *"facilitating the free circulation of ideas through word and image"* (UNESCO, Universal Declaration on Cultural Diversity –Appendix 2), which indicates clearly the function that devolves upon UNESCO so that all have free access to information and knowledge, with the ultimate goal of bridging the gaps between those who have much information and those who lack it.

In few words, gradually eliminate the digital divide among the world population. In this sense, the interactive design must evolve in view of the new hardware which will mean a new computer revolution when the quanta computers are within reach of every one, among other advances which are still prototypes in the R&D labs. In the current work, it has been presented a new category of design for the new era of communicability that is nearing, and we will perfect it in future investigations.

CONCLUSION

Generating a new category for interactive design has its advantages if the technology to which it is applied already exists in the commercial market, which allows us to carry out experiments with it. In the current work, have been established the first theoretical bases of a category which implicitly exists in the online products design, and which are related with the technology to safeguard and promote cultural heritage. In our case, we have worked with quality attributes and categories in which the interactive designed has divided itself in almost two decades. The positive results in the development of online and offline multimedia systems, always keeping the low costs and high quality equation, allows us to advance new proposals for the immediate future to keep and increase the existing communicability in the traditional multimedia systems as well as in the multimedia mobile phone systems. Finally, we want to stress the importance that a wide cultural wealth still has (a 360 degrees vision), local and global, for those designers and evaluators to boost the human/computer and interactive technological devices communicability in the next decade.

ACKNOWLEDGMENT

The authors would like a special thank you very much to Maria Ficarra. Besides, thanks to Jacqueline Alma, Mary Brie, Luisa Varela, Amélie Bordeaux, Pamela Fulton, Doris Edison, Sonia Flores, Donald Nilson, and Carlos for the important remarks.

REFERENCES

Barnes, J. (1984). *Complete Works of Aristotle*. Princeton, NJ: Princeton University Press.

Bederson, B., & Shneiderman, B. (2003). *The Craft of Information Visualization: Readings and Reflections (Interactive Technologies)*. San Francisco: Morgan Kaufmann Publishers.

Bosch, A., Erp, M., & Sporleder, C. (2009). Making a Clean Sweep of Cultural Heritage. *IEEE Intelligent Systems*, *24*(2), 54–63. doi:10.1109/MIS.2009.33

Bunge, M. (1981). *The science: your method and your philosophy*. Buenos Aires: Siglo XXI.

Cipolla-Ficarra, F. (1996). *Evaluation and communication techniques in multimedia product design for on the net university education. In Multimedia on the Net* (pp. 151–165). Vienna: Springer-Verlag. doi:10.1007/978-3-7091-9472-0_14

Cipolla-Ficarra, F. (1997). Evaluation of Multimedia Components. In *Proceedings International Conference on Multimedia Computing and Systems*. Ottawa: IEEE Computer.

Cipolla-Ficarra, F. (1999). MEHEM: A Methodology for Heuristic Evaluation in Multimedia. In Proceedings Distributed Multimedia Systems. Aizu: KSI.

Cipolla-Ficarra, F. (2010a). *Quality and Communicability for Interactive Hypermedia Systems: Concepts and Practices for Design*. Hershey, PA: IGI Global. doi:10.4018/978-1-61520-763-3

Cipolla-Ficarra, F. (2010b). *Persuasion On-Line and Communicability: The Destruction of Credibility in the Virtual Community and Cognitive Models*. New York: Nova Science Publishers.

Cipolla-Ficarra, F. (2011). Local Tourism and Cultural Heritage Internalization: Myths and Realities from Software. In *Proceedings Second International Workshop on Human Computer Interaction, Tourism and Cultural Heritage*. Heidelberg, Germany: Springer.

Cipolla-Ficarra, F., & Kratky, A. (2011) Security of the Automatic Information On-line: A Study of the Controls Forbid. In *Proceedings Second International Conference on Advances in New Technologies, Interactive Interfaces and Communicability*. Heidelberg, Germany: Springer.

Cooper, J., & Hutchinson, D. S. (1997). *Plato: The Complete Works*. Indianapolis, IN: Hackett Publishing.

Kit, E. (1995). *Software Testing in the Real World*. New York: ACM Press.

Maiden, , Seyff, N., Grunbacher, P., Otojare, O., & Mitteregger, K. (2007). Determining Stakeholder Needs in the Workplace: How Mobile Technologies Can Help. *IEEE Software*, *24*(2), 46–52. doi:10.1109/MS.2007.40

Nielsen, J., & Mack, R. (1994). *Usability Inspection Methods*. New York: Wiley. doi:10.1145/259963.260531

Norman, D. (2009). *The Design of Future Things*. New York: Basic Books.

Quizon, N. (2010). Social Change: Women, Networks, and Technology. *Interaction*, *17*(1), 36–39. doi:10.1145/1649475.1649484

Shiomi, M., Kanda, T., Ishiguro, H., & Hagita, N. (2007). Interactive Humanoid Robots for a Science Museum. *IEEE Intelligent Systems*, *22*(2), 25–32. doi:10.1109/MIS.2007.37

Witte, R. (2010). Converting a Historical Architecture Encyclopedia into a Semantic Knowledge Base. *IEEE Computer*, *25*(1), 58–66.

ADDITIONAL READING

Ander-egg, E. (1986). *Techniques of Social Investigation*. Buenos Aires: Hvmanitas.

Basili, V., & Musa, J. (1991). The Future Engineering of Software: A Management Perspective. *IEEE Computer*, *24*(9), 90–96. doi:10.1109/2.84903

Çetin, G., & Göktürk, M. (2007). Usability in Open Source: Community. *Interaction*, *14*(6), 38–40. doi:10.1145/1300655.1300679

Cipolla-Ficarra, F. (2001). *Communication Evaluation in Multimedia: Metrics and Methodology. Universal Access in HCI* (pp. 567–571). London: LEA.

Cipolla-Ficarra, F. (2003). Table of Heuristic Evaluation for Communication of the Multimedia Systems. In Proceedings HCI International. Crete: LEA, 940-944.

Cipolla-Ficarra, F., Ficarra, V., & Cipolla-Ficarra, M. (2011). New Technologies of the Information and Communication: Analysis of the Constructors and Destructors of the European Educational System. In Proceedings *Second International Conference on Advances in New Technologies, Interactive Interfaces and Communicability*. Heidelberg: Springer, 71-84

Eco, U. (1979). *A Theory of Semiotics*. Indiana: Indiana University Press.

Gates, B., Myhrvold, N., & Rinearson, P. (1995). *The Road Ahead*. New York: Viking Press.

Goesele, M., Ackermann, J., Fuhrmann, S., Klowsky, R., Langguth, F., Mücke, P., & Ritz, M. (2010). Scene Reconstruction from Community Photo Collections. *IEEE Computer*, *43*(6), 48–53. doi:10.1109/MC.2010.176

Maulsby, D., & Witten, I. (1997). Teaching Agents to Learn: From User Study to Implementation. *IEEE Computer*, *30*(11), 36–44. doi:10.1109/2.634839

Mcnamara, N., & Kirakowski, J. (2006). Functionality, Usability, and User Experience: Three Areas of Concern. *Interaction*, *11*(6), 26–28. doi:10.1145/1167948.1167972

Nielsen, J. (1990). *Hypertext and Hypermedia. San Diego*. San Diego: Academic Press.

Nielsen, J. (1996). Usability Metrics: Tracking Interface Improvements. *IEEE Software*, *13*(6), 12–13.

Nöth, W. (1995). *Handbook of Semiotics*. Indianapolis: Indiana University Press.

OLeary, D. (2008). Wikis: From Each According to His Knowledge. *IEEE Computer*, *41*(2), 34–41. doi:10.1109/MC.2008.68

Ould, M., & Unwin, C. (1992). *Testing in Software Development*. Cambridge: Cambridge University Press.

Reeves, B., & Nass, C. (1996). *The Media Equation: How People Treat Computers, Television, and New Media Like Real People and Places*. Cambridge: Cambridge University Press.

Sean, P. (2007). A New Era of Performance Evaluation. IEEE. *Computer*, *40*(9), 23–30. doi:10.1109/MC.2007.296

Vossen, G. (2007). *Unleashing Web 2.0: From Concepts to Creativity*. San Francisco: Morgan Kayfmann Publishers.

KEY TERMS AND DEFINITIONS

Communicability: A qualitative communication between the user and the interactive system, such as mobile phones, augmented reality, immersion multimedia, hypermedia, among others. The extent to which an interactive system successfully conveys its functionality to the user.

Control of the Fruition: The degree of autonomy in navegation that the structure of the interactive system gives the user.

Cultural Heritage or Tangible Cultural Heritage: "It is the legacy of physical artefacts and intangible attributes of a group or society that are inherited from past generations, maintained in the present and bestowed for the benefit of future generations." (UNESCO definition).

Ediomix: A mixture of bidirectional interaction among the categories of the design of the communicability and the mental idea of the designer towards the potential users of the interactive system.

Interactive System: A computer device made up by a CPU and peripherals, whose functioning requires a constant interaction with the user. Currently these systems tend to their miniaturization and/or invisibility, the mobility and wireless connectability among them.

Isomorphism: Sets down a range of constant formal features among the different components and categories design. The isomorphism seeks "regularity in irregularity."

Naturalness of Metaphor: The user's ability to understand the set of images that make up the structure of the interface.

Transparency of Meaning: The usage of terms, (also, images, sounds related to words) of the interface that do not cause ambiguities between contents and expression.

APPENDIX 1: EXAMPLES

*Figure 13. Options of the read speaker which allow to change the configuration/
modality of the karaoke system at the moment that the user wants to listen to the text
(Approximate Translation: Title: Description of Egypt. Second Edition. Antiques, volume II (plates).
In the description is the text (right side), and below are the creator, sponsor, the date of the content,
language, title in the original language, the period, and the topic. On the left side are the links to the
social networks such as Facebook, Twitter, etc., and a list of the related articles.)*

Figure 14. Options of the read speaker which allow to change the configuration/ modality of the karaoke system at the moment that the user wants to listen to the text

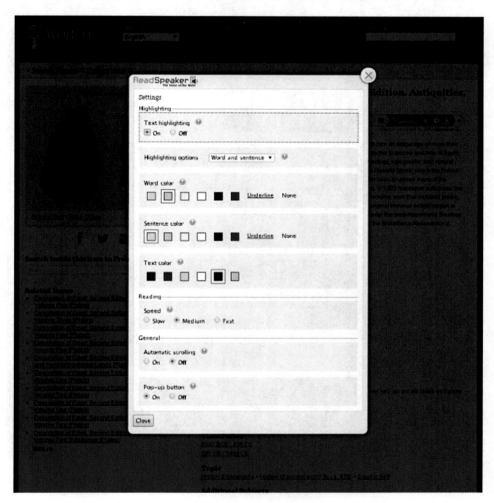

Figure 15. The browse option shows us all the figures it has stored

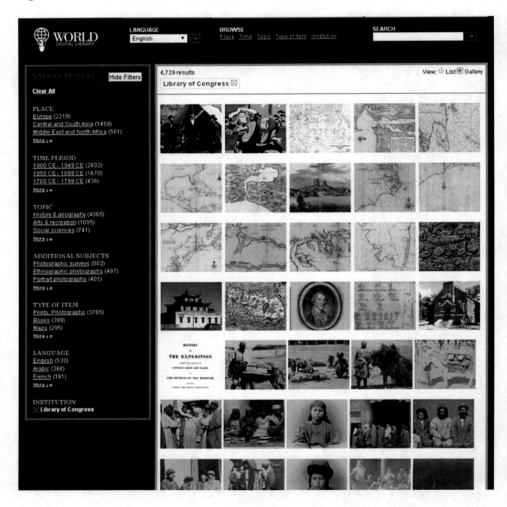

APPENDIX 2: UNESCO UNIVERSAL DECLARATION ON CULTURAL DIVERSITY

Identity, Diversity, and Pluralism

Article 1: Cultural Diversity: The Common Heritage of Humanity

Culture takes diverse forms across time and space. This diversity is embodied in the uniqueness and plurality of the identities of the groups and societies making up humankind. As a source of exchange, innovation and creativity, cultural diversity is as necessary for humankind as biodiversity is for nature. In this sense, it is the common heritage of humanity and should be recognized and affirmed for the benefit of present and future generations.

Article 2: From Cultural Diversity to Cultural Pluralism

In our increasingly diverse societies, it is essential to ensure harmonious interaction among people and groups with plural, varied and dynamic cultural identities as well as their willingness to live together. Policies for the inclusion and participation of all citizens are guarantees of social cohesion, the vitality of civil society and peace. Thus defined, cultural pluralism gives policy expression to the reality of cultural diversity. Indissociable from a democratic framework, cultural pluralism is conducive to cultural exchange and to the flourishing of creative capacities that sustain public life.

Article 3: Cultural Diversity as a Factor in Development

Cultural diversity widens the range of options open to everyone; it is one of the roots of development, understood not simply in terms of economic growth, but also as a means to achieve a more satisfactory intellectual, emotional, moral and spiritual existence.

Cultural Diversity and Human Rights

Article 4: Human Rights as Guarantees of Cultural Diversity

The defence of cultural diversity is an ethical imperative, inseparable from respect for human dignity. It implies a commitment to human rights and fundamental freedoms, in particular the rights of persons belonging to minorities and those of indigenous peoples. No one may invoke cultural diversity to infringe upon human rights guaranteed by international law, nor to limit their scope.

Article 5: Cultural Rights as an Enabling Environment for Cultural Diversity

Cultural rights are an integral part of human rights, which are universal, indivisible and interdependent. The flourishing of creative diversity requires the full implementation of cultural rights as defined in Article 27 of the Universal Declaration of Human Rights and in Articles 13 and 15 of the International Covenant on Economic, Social and Cultural Rights. All persons have therefore the right to express themselves and to create and disseminate their work in the language of their choice, and particularly in their mother tongue; all persons are entitled to quality education and training that fully respect their cultural identity; and all persons have the right to participate in the cultural life of their choice and conduct their own cultural practices, subject to respect for human rights and fundamental freedoms.

Article 6: Towards Access for All to Cultural Diversity

While ensuring the free flow of ideas by word and image care should be exercised so that all cultures can express themselves and make themselves known. Freedom of expression, media pluralism, multilingualism, equal access to art and to scientific and technological knowledge, including in digital form, and the possibility for all cultures to have access to the means of expression and dissemination are the guarantees of cultural diversity.

Cultural Diversity and Creativity

Article 7: Cultural Heritage as the Wellspring of Creativity

Creation draws on the roots of cultural tradition, but flourishes in contact with other cultures. For this reason, heritage in all its forms must be preserved, enhanced and handed on to future generations as a record of human experience and aspirations, so as to foster creativity in all its diversity and to inspire genuine dialogue among cultures.

Article 8: Cultural Goods and Services: Commodities of a Unique Kind

In the face of present-day economic and technological change, opening up vast prospects for creation and innovation, particular attention must be paid to the diversity of the supply of creative work, to due recognition of the rights of authors and artists and to the specificity of cultural goods and services which, as vectors of identity, values and meaning, must not be treated as mere commodities or consumer goods.

Article 9: Cultural Policies as Catalysts of Creativity

While ensuring the free circulation of ideas and works, cultural policies must create conditions conducive to the production and dissemination of diversified cultural goods and services through cultural industries that have the means to assert themselves at the local and global level. It is for each State, with due regard to its international obligations, to define its cultural policy and to implement it through the means it considers fit, whether by operational support or appropriate regulations.

Cultural Diversity and International Solidarity

Article 10: Strengthening Capacities for Creation and Dissemination Worldwide

In the face of current imbalances in flows and exchanges of cultural goods at the global level, it is necessary to reinforce international cooperation and solidarity aimed at enabling all countries, especially developing countries and countries in transition, to establish cultural industries that are viable and competitive at national and international level.

Article 11: Building Partnerships Between the Public Sector, the Private Sector and Civil Society

Market forces alone cannot guarantee the preservation and promotion of cultural diversity, which is the key to sustainable human development. From this perspective, the pre-eminence of public policy, in partnership with the private sector and civil society, must be reaffirmed.

Article 12: The Role of UNESCO

UNESCO, by virtue of its mandate and functions, has the responsibility to:

1. Promote the incorporation of the principles set out in the present Declaration into the development strategies drawn up within the various intergovernmental bodies;
2. Serve as a reference point and a forum where States, international governmental and nongovernmental organizations, civil society and the private sector may join together in elaborating concepts, objectives and policies in favour of cultural diversity;
3. Pursue its activities in standard-setting, awareness raising and capacity-building in the areas related to the present Declaration within its fields of competence;
4. Facilitate the implementation of the Action Plan, the main lines of which are appended to the present Declaration.
5. Including, in particular, the Florence Agreement of 1950 and its Nairobi Protocol of 1976, the Universal Copyright Convention of 1952, the Declaration of the Principles of International Cultural Cooperation of 1966, the Convention on the Means of Prohibiting and Preventing the Illicit Import, Export and Transfer of Ownership of Cultural Property of 1970, the Convention for the Protection of the World Cultural and Natural Heritage of 1972, the Declaration on Race and Racial Prejudice of 1978, the Recommendation concerning the Status of the Artist of 1980, and the Recommendation on the Safeguarding of Traditional Culture and Folklore of 1989.

6. This definition is in line with the conclusions of the World Conference on Cultural Policies (MONDIACULT, Mexico City, 1982), of the World Commission on Culture and Development Our Creative Diversity, 1995), and of the Intergovernmental Conference on Cultural Policies for Development (Stockholm, 1998)

Annex II Main lines of an action plan for the implementation of the UNESCO Universal Declaration on Cultural Diversity

The Member States commit themselves to taking appropriate steps to disseminate widely the "UNESCO Universal Declaration on Cultural Diversity" and to encourage its effective application, in particular by cooperating with a view to achieving the following objectives:

1. Deepening the international debate on questions relating to cultural diversity, particularly in respect of its links with development and its impact on policy-making, at both national and international level; taking forward notably consideration of the advisability of an international legal instrument on cultural diversity.
2. Advancing in the definition of principles, standards and practices, on both the national and the international levels, as well as of awareness-raising modalities and patterns of cooperation, that are most conducive to the safeguarding and promotion of cultural diversity.
3. Fostering the exchange of knowledge and best practices in regard to cultural pluralism with a view to facilitating, in diversified societies, the inclusion and participation of persons and groups from varied cultural backgrounds.
4. Making further headway in understanding and clarifying the content of cultural rights as an integral part of human rights.
5. Safeguarding the linguistic heritage of humanity and giving support to expression, creation and dissemination in the greatest possible number of languages.
6. Encouraging linguistic diversity – while respecting the mother tongue – at all levels of education, wherever possible, and fostering the learning of several languages from the earliest age.
7. Promoting through education an awareness of the positive value of cultural diversity and improving to this end both curriculum design and teacher education.

8. Incorporating, where appropriate, traditional pedagogies into the education process with a view to preserving and making full use of culturally appropriate methods of communication and transmission of knowledge.

9. Encouraging "digital literacy" and ensuring greater mastery of the new information and communication technologies, which should be seen both as educational disciplines and as pedagogical tools capable of enhancing the effectiveness of educational services.

10. Promoting linguistic diversity in cyberspace and encouraging universal access through the global network to all information in the public domain.

11. Countering the digital divide, in close cooperation in relevant United Nations system organizations, by fostering access by the developing countries to the new technologies, by helping them to master information technologies and by facilitating the digital dissemination of endogenous cultural products and access by those countries to the educational, cultural and scientific digital resources available worldwide.

12. Encouraging the production, safeguarding and dissemination of diversified contents in the media and global information networks and, to that end, promoting the role of public radio and television services in the development of audiovisual productions of good quality, in particular by fostering the establishment of cooperative mechanisms to facilitate their distribution.

13. Formulating policies and strategies for the preservation and enhancement of the cultural and natural heritage, notably the oral and intangible cultural heritage, and combating illicit traffic in cultural goods and services.

14. Respecting and protecting traditional knowledge, in particular that of indigenous peoples; recognizing the contribution of traditional knowledge, particularly with regard to environmental protection and the management of natural resources, and fostering synergies between modern science and local knowledge.

15. Fostering the mobility of creators, artists, researchers, scientists and intellectuals and the development of international research programmes and partnerships, while striving to preserve and enhance the creative capacity of developing countries and countries in transition.

16. Ensuring protection of copyright and related rights in the interest of the development of contemporary creativity and fair remuneration for creative work, while at the same time upholding a public right of access to culture, in accordance with Article 27 of the Universal Declaration of Human Rights.

17. Assisting in the emergence or consolidation of cultural industries in the developing countries and countries in transition and, to this end, cooperating in the development of the necessary infrastructures and skills, fostering the emergence of viable local markets, and facilitating access for the cultural products of those countries to the global market and international distribution networks.

18. Developing cultural policies, including operational support arrangements and/or appropriate regulatory frameworks, designed to promote the principles enshrined in this Declaration, in accordance with the international obligations incumbent upon each State.

19. Involving the various sections of civil society closely in the framing of public policies aimed at safeguarding and promoting cultural diversity.

20. Recognizing and encouraging the contribution that the private sector can make to enhancing cultural diversity and facilitating, to that end, the establishment of forums for dialogue between the public sector and the private sector.

For a complete information about "UNESCO Universal Declaration on Cultural Diversity" visit this link:

http://portal.unesco.org/en/ev.php-URL_ID=13179&URL_DO=DO_
    TOPIC&URL_SECTION=201.html

Chapter 2
Biomedical Test Instruments:
Usability, Ergonomics, and Communicability Assessment

Francisco V. Cipolla-Ficarra
Latin Association of Human-Computer Interaction, Spain & International Association of Interactive Communication, Italy

Jim Carré
University of the Netherlands Antilles, Curaçao

ABSTRACT

In the chapter is analyzed the evolution of the ergonomic and interactive design of an instrument of generalized use among people suffering from diabetes, such as is Melitus II. The results obtained in the usability and usefulness of the instrument belong to third age users who in an autonomous way should carry out the examination of their level of sugar in blood. The positive and negative elements are both presented, in the triad ergonomics, usability and communicability.

INTRODUCTION

With the passing of time, the number of people who suffer from diabetes in the world is growing in an exponential way, due to the stress of the daily life, the negative habits in the ingestion of junk food (usually, the term "junk2 refers to the place where the food items whose shelf life is finished end up, but in our case we refer to their composition, such as can be the high level of

DOI: 10.4018/978-1-5225-3437-2.ch002

carbonic hydrates, for instance), the consequences of the chemotherapy and radiotherapy processes, which entail the appearance of the diabetes of the type Melitus II, etc. Once its presence has been detected, the doctors, will advise the use of the blood glucose meter for its daily control (Brown & Brown, 2013; El-Gayar, et al. 2013). In relation to the obtained results in the measurement of sugar, the patient will have to take the pertinent drugs. Traditionally, it is an area multidisciplinary transdisciplinary and interdisciplinary for the global research (e.g., Fischer, 1991; Parker, Doyle, & Peppas, 2001; Preuveneers, & Berbers, 2008; Tatara, et al., 2010) and today, it is special for telemedicine using Internet and new devices, hardware, software, etc., for example (Woodward, Istepanian, & Richards, 2001; Mamykina, Mynatt, & Kaufman, 2006; Jurik, & Weaver, 2008; Das, & Alsos, 2008).

Now the tools for the measurement of glucose, that is, the blood glucose meters, have been at the core of two terms at the moment of carrying out the usability and usefulness test (Nielsen, 1993; Barnum, 2002). Two words which we find in the graphic made by Nielsen in the 90s (Nielsen, 1993; Nielsen & Mack, 1994), where inside the system acceptability, we have a bifurcation between social acceptability and practical acceptability (Figure 1). In the former its components are not defined. In our case of study, we would include the publicity factors of the instrument, whether it is with commercial purposes or not, the positive comments of the users of the different types of measurers (specialized websites, blogs, oral communication, etc.) and the interpretation of the statistic data of the manufacturers and of the public, private and hybrid health institutions who control the patients who use these

Figure 1. Usability and the system acceptability

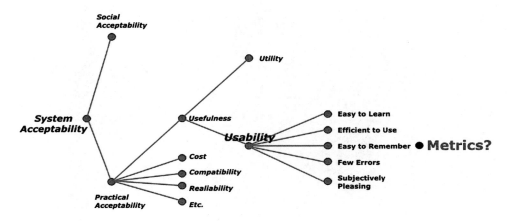

devices. In the second bifurcation, we have two fundamental aspects for the current study; one derives from the word usefulness and the other from usability. The first term includes the cost factor, which in our case is equal to zero, especially in the European public health system, until the second decade of the new millennium. These instruments (Figure 2) are distributed for free among the patients, thanks to the local, regional or state wide health system. The compatibility in our case may refer to the possibility of incorporating the data obtained through the blood glucose meter in the computer, in order to have a clinical record of the evolution of the measurements, or send the information to the specialist physician, for instance.

USABILITY, COMMUNICABILITY, AND ERGONOMICS

In our universe of study, very few users of those instruments carry out the formerly described operations, since they do not have enough skills in the use of the computers in an autonomous way. Consequently, the compatibility option does not occupy a first or second category in the rank of the priorities. In contrast, the usability of the system is present even in the websites that promote other devices (www.niprodiagnostics.com/diabetes_resources), as can be seen in the following listing of ten questions:

Figure 2. (A) Model of the 90s, whose size in mm. Is 125 long, 70 wide and 21 high. (B) Model of the first decade of the new millennium, whose size is 115 long, 51 wide and 22 high. (C) A current model in mobile format, that is, similar to a mobile phone, whose size is 125 long, 57 wide, 26 high.

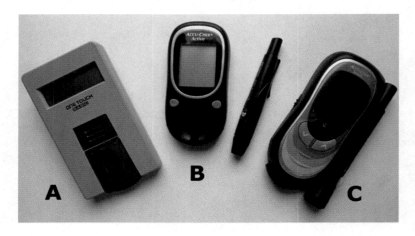

1. Is it easy to use?
2. Can the numbers on the screen be read well?
3. Are the measurer and the reactive strips easy to use?
4. Do the strips come in an easy to open flask?
5. What kind of battery does the meter need?
6. Does the meter have an adequate memory capacity?
7. Can the values be transferred to a computer?
8. Is there a free customer attention number?
9. Is the cost of the reactive strips accessible?
10. Does the meter have a life long guarantee?

Examining each one of them, we can already investigate the presence of the triad: ergonomics, usability, and communicability (Salvendy, 2012; Nielsen, 1993; Cipolla-Ficarra, 2010). Besides, the first social factors related with this disease and the use of the technologies avoiding the digital divide, especially in a population of an elderly age. The ease of use is one of the fundamental aspects enunciated by Nielsen and where the usability engineering uses. It is important to remember that in the late 80s and early 90s was taking place a metamorphosis in the location of the computers, that is, from the work offices to the homes of millions of people, thanks to the apogee of the PCs that were spreading all around our planet. It was the moment in which millions of users learned the use of the operative systems and office automation applications in private academies of the great Latin American cities, for instance, with the goal of getting a better job. That ease of use of the commercial software had to encompass each one of the categories of interactive design (Rubin, 1994; Lidwell, Holden, & Butler, 2003; Cipolla-Ficarra, & Cipolla-Ficarra, 2008). Perhaps this was the reason why to the term usability was enclosed engineering. In the late 90s enclosing engineering to several terms related to interactive communication became a mercantilist fad, especially in certain environments of the private colleges, such as is the case of semiotics engineering in Brazil (Cipolla-Ficarra, 2012). Ease is a term which is repeated several times in the listing of the rhetorical questions. This ease is referred to ergonomic issues, such as can be the container of the strips that are used to introduce the blood sample in the meter, for instance. The communicability of the result after the measurement must apparently only be summed up in the dimension of the numbers on the screen of the device, when in fact there are other components of the category of the interactive design, such as compatibility. A compatibility that is reflected in question seven. Another question that involves the interactive design is the access to the database, that is, the category of the structure of the information and the access to these or other data in relation to the model of the meter. That is, the navigation of the stored information.

Inserting a call number for user's attention in the event of problems is positive in the countries where those devices are made or distributed in the EU (European Union), since out of linguistic reasons, other users won't be able to access the service, even if the phone call were free. Now the same as the printers that have a low cost and are even given as a present in some commercial promotions, it is in the replacement of the ink the toner, etc, where the cost of those consumables or accessories may make a user plump for a model or another (Rogers, 2003). In the blood glucose meter it will be the reactive strips which in principle may have an influence on the use of the different models. Besides, it is necessary to remember that in the measurement process of the glucose lancets are used that are introduced in a punching machine (to take the blood sample). Depending on the health system to which the patient belongs he/she can get those materials for free, since they depend on the public health system of the place of residence. However, the problem may appear when they do not meet the daily needs of those patients. For instance, in the Lombardy region, since the middle of the of the second decade of the 2000s, the patients who do not take insulin injections have only the right to request 30 strips and 30 lancets every 90 days. Consequently, those patients can't control periodically their disease on a free basis, since they have to buy the missing strips. For instance, if they daily need to take two or three tests, when they have stable sugar values in their blood and in the lapse of 1/2 days, that means 90/180 strips, whereas in the Lombardy health system, geographically and theoretically included in one of the four economic engines of Europe: Baden-Württemberg (Germany), Rhône-Alpes (France), Catalonia (Spain), and Lombardy (Italy). Evidently, this is a violation of the "European Charter of Patients' Rights" (see Appendix).

THE MANUAL DEVICES IN THE HANDS OF THE SENIOR USERS

One of the main problems with elderly people is the loss of sensitivity in the hands, especially from 65–70 years of age, in the people who suffer from arthritis, rheumatism etc. Although there are medical studies that allow to evaluate that sensitivity in the limbs, such as an Electromyography (EMG) exam, whose results from a technical-healthcare point of view may yield success, that is, with values within the rules, the truth is that the patients can't even use correctly the utensils to eat. The ergonomics aspect of the glucose measurer should be considered for these users. However, with the passing of time and in the same way as in the mobile phones, their size has been decreasing, which seriously damages their correct use in an autonomous way, as can be seen in the following figure, which denote the passing of time in European Union:

We have worked with these three models in our universe of study. The first model, although it has larger dimensions and a rectangular format, the triad ergonomics, usability and communicability of the device is the ideal for the senior users, as can be appreciated in the section of the obtained results in the experiments carried out. With a simple button the user can make his/her measurement of sugar in blood. Evidently this differs from those general managers who decide to change their whole management system, including textile industrial production, because theoretically by pressing a key of the computer they would have under their view the entrepreneurial reality of a centennial industry in the Lombardy. In fact, the change of that information system prompted an anti-model in the design and implementation of textile computer systems (Cipolla-Ficara & Ficarra, 2010). The reader interested in these anti-model systems may look up the following reference (Cipolla-Ficarra, 2014).

MAKING UP OF THE UNIVERSE OF STUDY, EVALUATION, AND RESULTS

The universe of study is made up by four user groups, randomly chosen. Each one of those groups was made up by five people. The three first groups are Melito Diabetes type II (MD), whose ages oscillate between 65–70 years. The fourth group was made up by non-diabetes (No MD) people and for the first time used the sugar measurers in the blood (models A, B, and C – Figure 2). The ages also oscillated between 65 and 70 years. The latter have been instructed on how to make the measurements with the different devices. The purpose of this group is to make up a group of results which we have called "witness group". That is, to see the behaviour towards interaction of those users and the devices with which they interacted for the first time. All the measurements have been made in a human-computer interaction lab and the heuristic techniques used have been direct observation and the recorded sections (Nielsen & Mack, 1994; Cipolla-Ficarra, 1998; Cipolla-Ficarra, 2008; Bateman et al. 2009; Dumas & Redish, 1994). The experiments consisted in watching the eventual dysfunctions, in the process of the autonomous analysis of the diabetes, including the total number of times necessary to carry out said operation on the same section. Each member of the group had to interact with the different models. All those operations were repeated in six sections, one in the morning and another in the afternoon, for three days in a row. The results obtained within the group constitute the average of the figures that are presented next, related to usability, communicability and ergonomics, (the highest value is 10 and the minimal is 0).

The results obtained make apparent that the model of the 20th century is that which obtained a higher score in the triad usability, communicability, and ergonomics in each one of the user groups, with or without diabetes, whose ages oscillate between 65-70 years. The total number of dysfunctions grows as the models decrease their size and increase the number of functions. In this sense there is a parallelism between these devices and the mobile phones, especially for third age users, where the models with greatest diffusion are those which have the basic functions, without horizontal shifting keys in the menu, for instance. In this regard the interested reader may look up the following reference to go deeper into this functional parallelism between ergonomics and usability of the mobile phones (Woodward, Istepanian, & Richards, 2001).

Figure 3. Total of dysfunctions by groups and measurer models A, B, and C (MD = Melito Diabetis)

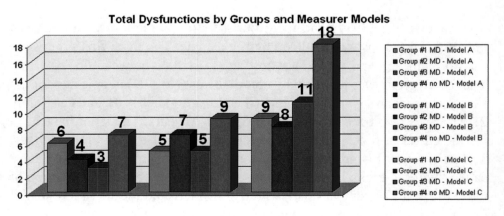

Figure 4. Average of quality in regard to the usability, communicability, and ergonomics

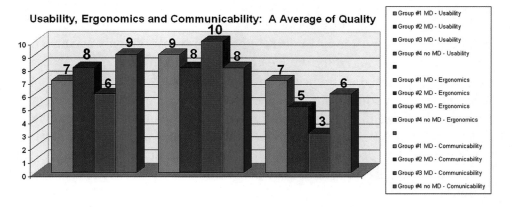

LESSONS LEARNED

Mobile microcomputing applied to the personal usage healthcare instruments or home appliances does not allow their autonomous use, as has been seen in the current work. Although the screens of the latest models of the 21st century have a greater size, facilitating the communicability of the results obtained in the measurements, for instance, that advantage disappears from the point of view of usability. These are instruments that emulate the mobile phones, but from the design point of view and ergonomics apparently they have forgotten that a great share of the adult population usually have problems in their limbs. That is, they present certain disabilities for devices whose mechanisms for

Figure 5. Detail of the screen zone and the keys of the different models

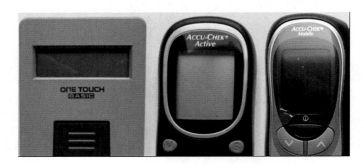

functioning (keys, lids, etc.), are of small size. Unbelievably, the medical examinations of that population of users, such as EMG, may indicate that all their manual functions are 1005 active, the reality detected in the experiments carried out among healthy people and those afflicted with diabetes is that they have serious problems in carrying out the measurements because they entail several steps and if the device has incorporated a timer, sometimes it is necessary to reinitialize the whole process. Obviously we are not in front of a computer, but people from whom a blood sample must be extracted again. Besides, the current study has highlighted that these users are not interested in the compatibility category, between these devices and the computers. In other words, they do not download the stored data in the computer device. In the future works we will focus on widening the models of those devices comparing the first and the second decade of the current millennium, and also the devices that do not need to extract the blood samples. These latter devices use the light to revise the sugar in blood in around 20 seconds. That is, a non-invasive technology for the first time in the sugar measurers in blood and with a diagnose accuracy. A prototype of this device in the Figure 6.

The optical bridge technology uses spectroscopy close to the infrared to measure a person in real time in the sugar in the blood in less than 20 seconds. It is a measurer of personal glucose used in the fingertips or the lobe of the ear.

Figure 6. Sugar measurer in the blood without need to use a punching device

CONCLUSION

In the health devices are concentrated a high number of ISO (International Organization for Standardization) guidelines, related to the quality, reliability of the results, etc. Like guideline ISO 15197 according to which the devices analyzed in the current work must meet with regard to the accuracy standard. These devices entail a myriad aspects which are subjects of study for usability engineering, such as the instruction brochures of multilingual use, for instance. However, there is no internationally homologated style guideline in the industrial design of these measurers, where the potential users of these devices are considered, especially among elderly people so that they can carry out in an independent way the sugar exams in their blood. A diachronic vision of the triad ergonomics, usability and communicability makes apparent the loss of autonomy. An autonomy which it is vital to keep from the industrial and interactive design for the elderly users, who are self-sufficient in their daily life and who make up one-person family units in the great cities or the rural areas. Having to go to the pharmacies, medical practices, etc., or asking help from relatives, friends, etc., are not ideal solutions for a diabetic, in the second decade of the new millennium. All the components of the Information and Communication Technology of the 21st century should adapt to these users and not the other way around, even if they keep all the ISO guidelines.

ACKNOWLEDGMENT

The authors would like to thanks a lot to Maria Ficarra. A very special thanks to Sonia Flores, Donald Nilson, and Carlos for the assistance and collaboration.

REFERENCES

Barnum, C. (2002). *Usability Testing and Research*. New York: Longman.

Bateman, S. (2009). Interactive Usability Instrumentation. In *Proceedings of the 1st ACM SIGCHI Symposium on Engineering Interactive Computing Systems*. New York: ACM Press. doi:10.1145/1570433.1570443

Brown, S., & Brown, T. X. (2013). Value of Mobile Monitoring for Diabetes in Developing Countries. In *Proceedings of the Sixth International Conference on Information and Communication Technologies and Development*. New York: ACM. doi:10.1145/2516604.2516614

Cipolla-Ficarra, F. (1998). Method for evaluation of hypermedia usability. In *Proc. 7th IFAC/IFIP/IFORS/IEA Symposium on Analysis, Design and Evaluation of Man Machine Systems and Human Interface*. Kyoto: Elsevier.

Cipolla-Ficarra, F. (2008). Communicability design and evaluation in cultural and ecological multimedia systems. In *Proceedings MSCommunicability '08*. New York: ACM Press. doi:10.1145/1462039.1462041

Cipolla-Ficarra, F. (2010). *Quality and Communicability for Interactive Hypermedia Systems: Concepts and Practices for Design*. Hershey, PA: IGI Global. doi:10.4018/978-1-61520-763-3

Cipolla-Ficarra, F. (2012). *Emerging Software for Interactive Interfaces, Database, Computer Graphics and Animation: Pixels and the New Excellence in Communicability, Cloud Computing and Augmented Reality*. Bergamo: Blue Herons Editions.

Cipolla-Ficarra, F. (2014). *Advanced Research and Trends in New Technologies, Software, Human-Computer Interaction and Communicability*. Hershey, PA: IGI Global. doi:10.4018/978-1-4666-4490-8

Cipolla-Ficarra, F., & Cipolla-Ficarra, M. (2008). Interactive Systems, Design and Heuristic Evaluation: The Importance of the Diachronic Vision. In *Proceedings International Symposium on Intelligent Interactive Multimedia Systems and Services, KES IIMSS*. Berlin: Springer-Verlag. doi:10.1007/978-3-540-68127-4_64

Cipolla-Ficarra, F., & Ficarra, V. (2010). Software Managment Applications, Textile CAD and Human Factors: A Dreadful Industrial Example for Information and Communication Technology. In *Proceedings International Conference on Advances in New Technologies, Interactive Interfaces and Communicability*. Berlin: Springer-Verlag.

Das, S., & Alsos, A. (2008). The Contextual Nature of Usability and Its Relevance to Medical Informatics. *Journal of Studies in Health Technology and Informatics*, *136*, 541–546. PMID:18487787

Dumas, J., & Redish, J. (1994). *A Practical Guide to Usability Testing*. Norwood, NJ: Ablex Publishing.

El-Gayar, O., Timsina, P., Nawar, N., & Eid, W. (2013). A Systematic Review of IT For Diabetes Self-Management: Are We There Yet? *International Journal of Medical Informatics*, *82*(8), 637–652. doi:10.1016/j.ijmedinf.2013.05.006 PMID:23792137

Fischer, M. E. (1991). A Semiclosed-Loop Algorithm for the Control of Blood Glucose Levels in Diabetics. *IEEE Transactions on Bio-Medical Engineering*, *38*(1), 57–61. doi:10.1109/10.68209 PMID:2026432

Jurik, A., & Weaver, A. (2008). Remote Medical Monitoring. *IEEE Computer*, *41*(4), 96–99. doi:10.1109/MC.2008.133

Lidwell, W., Holden, K., & Butler, J. (2003). *Universal Principles of Design*. Gloucester, UK: Rockport Publishers.

Mamykina, L., Mynatt, E. D., & Kaufman, D. R. (2006). Investigating Health Management Practices of Individuals with Diabetes. *Proceedings of the SIGCHI Conference on Human Factors in Computing Systems*, 45-54 doi:10.1145/1124772.1124910

Nielsen, J. (1993). *Usability Engineering*. Boston: Academic Press.

Nielsen, J., & Mack, R. (1994). *Usability Inspection Methods*. New York: Wiley. doi:10.1145/259963.260531

Parker, R. S., Doyle, F. J., & Peppas, N. A. (2001). The Intravenous Route to Blood Glucose Control. *IEEE Engineering in Medicine and Biology Magazine*, *20*(1), 65–73. doi:10.1109/51.897829 PMID:11211662

Preuveneers, D., & Berbers, Y. (2008). Mobile Phones Assisting with Health Self-care: A Diabetes Case Study. In *Proceedings of the 10th International Conference on Human computer interaction with mobile devices and services*. New York: ACM Press. doi:10.1145/1409240.1409260

Rogers, E. (2003). *Diffusion of Innovations*. New York: Free Press.

Rubin, J. (1994). *Handbook of Usability Testing: How to Plan, Design, and Conduct Effective Tests*. New York: Wiley.

Salvendy, G. (2012). *Handbook of Human Factors and Ergonomics*. New York: John Wiley. doi:10.1002/9781118131350

Tatara, A. E. (2010). Mobile Phone-Based Self-Management Tools for Type 2 Diabetes: The Few Touch Application. *Journal of Diabetes Science and Technology*, 4(2), 328–336. doi:10.1177/193229681000400213 PMID:20307393

Woodward, B., Istepanian, R. S. H., & Richards, C. I. (2001). Advances in Telemedicine Using Mobile Communications. *IEEE Transactions on Information Technology in Biomedicine*, 5(1), 13–15. doi:10.1109/4233.908361 PMID:11300210

ADDITIONAL READING

Axisa, F., Schmitt, P. M., Gehin, C., Delhomme, G., McAdams, E., & Dittmar, A. (2005). Flexible Technologies and Smart Clothing for Citizen Medicine, Home Healthcare, and Disease Prevention. *IEEE Transactions on Information Technology in Biomedicine*, 9(3), 325–336. doi:10.1109/TITB.2005.854505 PMID:16167686

Ballegaard, S. A., Hansen, T. R., & Kyng, M. (2008). Healthcare in everyday life: designing healthcare services for daily life. In *Proceedings of the SIGCHI Conference on Human Factors in Computing Systems*. New York: ACM Press, 1807-1816 doi:10.1145/1357054.1357336

Carey, J. (1989). *Communication as Culture: Essays on Media and Society*. Boston: Unwin Hyman.

Cipolla-Ficarra, F., & Cipolla-Ficarra, M. (2009). Attention and Motivation in Hypermedia Systems. In *Proceedings HCI International 2009, LNCS.* Berlin: Springer-Verlag, 78-87

Colborne, G. (2010). *Simple and Usable Web, Mobile, and Interaction Design.* Berkeley: New Riders Publishing.

Coursaris, C. K., & Kim, D. J. (2011). A meta-analytical review of empirical mobile usability studies. *Journal of Usability Studies, 6*(3), 117–171.

Fogg, B. (2003). *Persuasive Technology: Using Computers to Change What We Think and Do.* San Francisco: Morgan Kaufmann Publishers.

Frokjaer, E., Hertzum, M., & Hornbaek, K. (2000). Measuring Usability: Are Effectiveness, Efficiency, and Satisfaction Really Correlated? In *Proceedings of the SIGCHI conference on Human factors in computing systems.* The Hague: ACM Press, 345-352 doi:10.1145/332040.332455

Halperin, D., Heydt-Benjamin, T. S., Fu, K., Kohno, T., & Maisel, W. H. (2008). Security and Privacy for Implantable Medical Device. *IEEE Pervasive Computing / IEEE Computer Society [and] IEEE Communications Society, 7*(1), 30–39. doi:10.1109/MPRV.2008.16

Jones, C. (2000). *Software Assessments, Benchmarks, and Best Practices.* Boston: Addison-Wesley.

Klenk, S., Dippon, J., Fritz, P., & Heidemann, G. (2011). A personalized medical information system. In *Proceedings of the 3rd Workshop on Software Engineering in Health Care.* New York: ACM Press doi:10.1145/1987993.1987997

Lee, T. et al.. (2007). Usability and feasibility of PmEB: A Mobile Phone Application for Monitoring Real Time Caloric balance. *Mobile Networks and Applications, 12*(2-3), 173–184. doi:10.1007/s11036-007-0014-4

Li, M., Lou, W., & Ren, K. (2010). Data Security and Privacy in Wireless Body Area Networks. *IEEE Wireless Communications, 17*(1), 51–58. doi:10.1109/MWC.2010.5416350

Liljegren, E. (2006). Usability in a medical technology context assessment of methods for usability evaluation of medical equipment. *International Journal of Industrial Ergonomics, 36*(4), 345–352. doi:10.1016/j.ergon.2005.10.004

Maldonado, T. (1997). *Critica della ragione informatica*. Milano: Feltrinelli. in Italian

Mougiakakou, K. et al.. (2010). Mobile Phone Technologies and Advanced Data Analysis Towards the Enhancement of Diabetes Self-Management. *International Journal of Electronic Healthcare*, *5*(4), 386–402. doi:10.1504/IJEH.2010.036209 PMID:21041177

Neuvirth, H., ... (2011). Toward Personalized Care Management of Patients at Risk: The Diabetes Case Study. In *Proceedings of the 17th ACM SIGKDD International Conference on Knowledge Discovery and Data Mining*, ACM Press, 395-403 doi:10.1145/2020408.2020472

Nielsen, J., & Loranger, H. (2006). *Prioritizing Web Usability*. Indianapolis: New Riders.

Norman, D. (2009). *The Design of Future Things*. New York: Basic Books.

Parker, R. S., Doyle, F. J., & Peppas, N. A. (1999). A Model-Based Algorithm for Blood Glucose Control in Type I Diabetic Patients. *IEEE Transactions on Bio-Medical Engineering*, *46*(2), 148–157. doi:10.1109/10.740877 PMID:9932336

Quinn, C. C., Shardell, M. D., Terrin, M. L., Barr, E. A., Ballew, S. H., & Gruber-Baldini, A. L. (2011). Cluster-randomized trial of a mobile phone personalized behavioral intervention for blood glucose control. *Diabetes Care*, *34*(9), 1934–1942. doi:10.2337/dc11-0366 PMID:21788632

Rosson, M. B., & Carroll, J. M. (2002). *Usability engineering: Scenario-based Development of Human-Computer Interaction*. San Francisco: Morgan Kaufmann Publishers.

Virzi, R. A. (1992). Refining the Test Phase of Usability Evaluation: How Many Subjects Is Enough? *Human Factors Journal*, *34*(4), 457–468.

Warschauer, M. (2003). *Technology and Social Inclusion: Rethinking the Digital Divide*. Cambridge: MIT Press.

KEY TERMS AND DEFINITIONS

Communicability: A qualitative communication between the user and the interactive system, such as mobile phones, augmented reality, immersion multimedia, hypermedia, among others. The extent to which an interactive system successfully conveys its functionality to the user.

Ergonomics: An applied science concerned with designing and arranging things (electronic, informatics, medical, etc. instruments) people use so that the people and things interact most efficiently and safely.

Human-Computer Interaction (HCI): The study and plannned design of human and computer activities.

Interactive Design: A user-oriented field of study that focuses on communicability through cyclical and collaborative processes (schematically: input, process, output and feed-back) between people and technology.

Interactive System: A computer device made up by a CPU (central processing unit) and peripherals, whose functioning requires a constant interaction with the user. Currently these systems tend to their miniaturization and/or invisibility, the mobility and wireless connectability among them.

Usability: A quality attribute that assesses how easy user personal computers (traditionally, PCs). Today, mobile phones, tablets PC, smartwatches, etc.

APPENDIX: FOURTEEN RIGHTS OF THE PATIENT IN EUROPEAN UNION

1.   Right to Preventive Measures

Every individual has the right to a proper service in order to prevent illness.

The health services have the duty to pursue this end by raising people's awareness, guaranteeing health procedures at regular intervals free of charge for various groups of the population at risk, and making the results of scientific research and technological innovation available to all.

2.   Right of Access

Every individual has the right of access to the health services that his or her health needs require. The health services must guarantee equal access to everyone, without discriminating on the basis of financial resources, place of residence, kind of illness or time of access to services.

An individual requiring treatment, but unable to sustain the costs, has the right to be served free of charge. Each individual has the right to adequate services, independently of whether he or she has been admitted to a small or large hospital or clinic. Each individual, even without a required residence permit, has the right to urgent or essential outpatient and inpatient care.

An individual suffering from a rare disease has the same right to the necessary treatments and medication as someone with a more common disease.

3.   Right to Information

Every individual has the right to access to all kind of information regarding their state of health, the health services and how to use them, and all that scientific research and technological innovation makes available.

Health care services, providers and professionals have to provide patient-tailored information, particularly taking into account the religious, ethnic or linguistic specificities of the patient.

The health services have the duty to make all information easily accessible, removing bureaucratic obstacles, educating health care providers, preparing and distributing informational materials.

A patient has the right of direct access to his or her clinical file and medical records, to photocopy them, to ask questions about their contents and to obtain the correction of any errors they might contain.

A hospital patient has the right to information which is continuous and thorough; this might be guaranteed by a "tutor".

Every individual has the right of direct access to information on scientific research, pharmaceutical care and technological innovations. This information can come from either public or private sources, provided that it meets the criteria of accuracy, reliability and transparency.

4. Right to Consent

Every individual has the right of access to all information that might enable him or her to actively participate in the decisions regarding his or her health; this information is a prerequisite for any procedure and treatment, including the participation in scientific research.

Health care providers and professionals must give the patient all information relative to a treatment or an operation to be undergone, including the associated risks and discomforts, side-effects and alternatives. This information must be given with enough advance time (at least 24 hours notice) to enable the patient to actively participate in the therapeutic choices regarding his or her state of health.

Health care providers and professionals must use a language known to the patient and communicate in a way that is comprehensible to persons without a technical background.

In all circumstances which provide for a legal representative to give the informed consent, the patient, whether a minor or an adult unable to understand or to will, must still be as involved as possible in the decisions regarding him or her. The informed consent of a patient must be procured on this basis.

A patient has the right to refuse a treatment or a medical intervention and to change his or her mind during the treatment, refusing its continuation.

A patient has the right to refuse information about his or her health status.

5.   Right to Free Choice

Each individual has the right to freely choose from among different treatment procedures and providers on the basis of adequate information.

The patient has the right to decide which diagnostic exams and therapies to undergo, and which primary care doctor, specialist or hospital to use. The health services have the duty to guarantee this right, providing patients with information on the various centres and doctors able to provide a certain treatment, and on the results of their activity. They must remove any kind of obstacle limiting exercise of this right.

A patient who does not have trust in his or her doctor has the right to designate another one.

6.   Right to Privacy and Confidentiality

Every individual has the right to the confidentiality of personal information, including information regarding his or her state of health and potential diagnostic or therapeutic procedures, as well as the protection of his or her privacy during the performance of diagnostic exams, specialist visits, and medical/surgical treatments in general.

All the data and information relative to an individual's state of health, and to the medical/surgical treatments to which he or she is subjected, must be considered private, and as such, adequately protected.

Personal privacy must be respected, even in the course of medical/surgical treatments (diagnostic exams, specialist visits, medications, etc.), which must take place in an appropriate environment and in the presence of only those who absolutely need to be there (unless the patient has explicitly given consent or made a request).

7. Right to Respect of Patients' Time

Each individual has the right to receive necessary treatment within a swift and predetermined period of time. This right applies at each phase of the treatment.

The health services have the duty to fix waiting times within which certain services must be provided, on the basis of specific standards and depending on the degree of urgency of the case. The health services must guarantee each individual access to services, ensuring immediate sign-up in the case of waiting lists.

Every individual that so requests has the right to consult the waiting lists, within the bounds of respect for privacy norms.

Whenever the health services are unable to provide services within the predetermined maximum times, the possibility to seek alternative services of comparable quality must be guaranteed, and any costs borne by the patient must be reimbursed within a reasonable time.

Doctors must devote adequate time to their patients, including the time dedicated to providing information.

8. Right to the Observance of Quality Standards

Each individual has the right of access to high quality health services on the basis of the specification and observance of precise standards.

The right to quality health services requires that health care institutions and professionals provide satisfactory levels of technical performance, comfort and human relations. This implies the specification, and the observance, of precise quality standards, fixed by means of a public and consultative procedure and periodically reviewed and assessed.

9. Right to Safety

Each individual has the right to be free from harm caused by the poor functioning of health services, medical malpractice and errors, and the right of access to health services and treatments that meet high safety standards.

To guarantee this right, hospitals and health services must continuously monitor risk factors and ensure that electronic medical devices are properly maintained and operators are properly trained. All health professionals must be fully responsible for the safety of all phases and elements of a medical treatment.

Medical doctors must be able to prevent the risk of errors by monitoring precedents and receiving continuous training. Health care staff that report existing risks to their superiors and/or peers must be protected from possible adverse consequences.

10. **Right to Innovation**

Each individual has the right of access to innovative procedures, including diagnostic procedures, according to international standards and independently of economic or financial considerations.

The health services have the duty to promote and sustain research in the biomedical field, paying particular attention to rare diseases. Research results must be adequately disseminated.

11. **Right to Avoid Unnecessary Suffering and Pain**

Each individual has the right to avoid as much suffering and pain as possible, in each phase of his or her illness.

The health services must commit themselves to taking all measures useful to this end, like providing palliative treatments and simplifying patients' access to them.

12. **Right to Personalized Treatment**

Each individual has the right to diagnostic or therapeutic programmes tailored as much as possible to his or her personal needs.

The health services must guarantee, to this end, flexible programmes, oriented as much as possible to the individual, making sure that the criteria of economic sustainability does not prevail over the right to health care.

13. **Right to Complain**

Each individual has the right to complain whenever he or she has suffered a harm and the right to receive a response or other feedback.

The health services ought to guarantee the exercise of this right, providing (with the help of third parties) patients with information about their rights, enabling them to recognise violations and to formalise their complaint.

A complaint must be followed up by an exhaustive written response by the health service authorities within a fixed period of time.

The complaints must be made through standard procedures and facilitated by independent bodies and/or citizens' organizations and cannot prejudice the patients' right to take legal action or pursue alternative dispute resolution.

14. **Right to Compensation**

Each individual has the right to receive sufficient compensation within a reasonably short time whenever he or she has suffered physical or moral and psychological harm caused by a health service treatment.

The health services must guarantee compensation, whatever the gravity of the harm and its cause (from an excessive wait to a case of malpractice), even when the ultimate responsibility cannot be absolutely determined.

Finally, the reader interested in the "European Charter of Patients' Rights" may look up the following link, for a complete information:

http://ec.europa.eu/health/ph_overview/co_operation/mobility/docs/health_
    services_co108_en.pdf

Chapter 3
Multimedia, Scientific Information, and Visualization for Information Systems and Metrics

Francisco V. Cipolla-Ficarra
Latin Association of Human-Computer Interaction, Spain & International Association of Interactive Communication, Italy

ABSTRACT

We present the main aspects of the importance of carrying out quality measurements in multimedia/interactive systems in the current era of expansion of communicability. Besides we disclose the first key elements to carry out techniques and/or methodologies to discover the quality attributes of an interactive system, such as the realization of quality metrics and the process of a heuristic evaluation. A set of examples online and off-line complete the current research work. In this set is stressed the economic importance of the process of evaluation in services and products related to the software, as well as some of the human factors to gain the hegemony of quality control.

INTRODUCTION

In the process of communication among people, the 20th century has boosted audiovisual and interactive communication: a communication where new technologies have generated a continuous and uninterrupted process of

DOI: 10.4018/978-1-5225-3437-2.ch003

feedback between users and digital contents. However, instead of speaking of new technologies, it is better to define them as "latest" technologies from a temporal point of view in view of the changes that take place at every passing second in the R&D (research and development) international sector aimed at ICT (information and communication technology).

Now with the latest technologies, in the 90s., there was a process of greater democratization of those digital contents, easier and more extensive, towards the base of the population pyramid, than in the current era of expansion of communicability (Cipolla-Ficarra, 2014). The digital divide has been boosted from the end of the first decade of the new millennium because the potential enjoyers of those digital contents cannot afford the new technologies. Consequently, there are now three groups in relation to potential users of such technologies and the interactive systems for those digital contents. In the former, are those who stay with the traditional systems, that is, they take years to update the hardware and/or software, for instance. In the latter, there are a few users who purchase vertiginously the latest technological breakthroughs (they keep up with the fashion of the latest novelties). Finally, there is the third group that situates itself between both, they are users of the new technologies (they wait for the drop of costs to interact with the new devices, after a few months have passed since the presentation of the new hardware and/or software. In other words: the cost factor and services purchase and/or products in the ICT have split access to digital contents into three areas.

In the 90s, there was a bipolarization between users and non-users of the interactive systems of the off-line multimedia, for instance. The PCs of most users in the south of Europe were adapted for interactive multimedia, through the internal or external connection of CD-ROM readers in the first place and later DVDs. It was also the time in which the massive digitalization process of the information in paper support was started. Those were excellent contents whose fruition was limited by the hardware, the software to create interactive multimedia systems, the lack of training of the of multimedia sector professionals, etc. An example are the first interactive multimedia commercial systems for the works of art, such as the off-line multimedia system CD-ROM Art Gallery by Microsoft in the mid 90s (Microsoft, 1993; Cipolla-Ficarra & Cipolla-Ficarra, 2008). Those were excellent contents, but in the interactive design failings in the programming of the contents could be seen deriving from the lack of control in their productive process. For instance, in the Art Gallery multimedia system (Microsoft, 1993) there are screens with two keys, one to activate the animation through a key called analysis or animation and another which restarts the animation through a key called painting. The rebooting consists in leaving to the animation the first frame of the sequence that makes it up. However, these two keys aren't present in all the nodes of a guided link that contains animations.

These failings signalled the lack of methods and/or evaluation techniques of the interactive design. Failings that in the 90s made many programmers of those systems blame those responsible for the interactive design, and vice versa. However, those failings were not related to the quality of the content, since the software, the hardware or even the digitalization techniques in the late 20th century allowed high level contents when paper was the initial support. An excellent example from the point of view of content is the off-line multimedia system called "Orquidáceas de Mexico y Guatemala –The Orchidaccae of Mexico & Guatemala" (Bateman, James) with illustrations from the 19th century (SEG, 1997).

Other failings started to become more frequent in the combination of the dynamic and the static means of the commercial multimedia systems in the south of Europe and with international distribution. In principle, the use of those multimedia systems with didactical purposes, for instance, and the rest of interactive systems, were analyzed from the perspective of usability engineering (Nielsen, 1993). However, in the usability principles were missing the possibility of measurement of the quality of the design, from the different categories that make up the interactive design, that is, content, presentation, navigation, structuring of the information, etc. (Cipolla-Ficarra, 1996; Cipolla-Ficarra, 2014).

TOWARDS THE FIRST METRICS OF THE QUALITY OF USE AND COMMUNICABILITY OF AN OFF-LINE INTERACTIVE SYSTEM

In the new millennium, striking is the trivial aspect that is made of the metrics, from an academic point of view by those organizations or institutions that subsist thanks to the European funds for the financing of research projects. Once again this shows the lack of knowledge that derives from the training and/or experience, like the presence of the Garduña factor, parochialism, the dynamic persuader, etc. (Cipolla-Ficarra, 2010a; Cipolla-Ficarra, 2014). In few words, a set of chaotic elements and in contraposition, direct or indirect,

Figure 1. The animation key replaces the analysis and painting key which are present in other interfaces

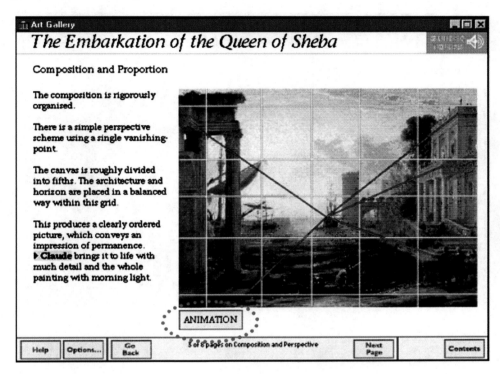

where an expert in communicability stands, for instance. That expert hails from the intersection of the factual and formal sciences. The formative and professional profile was presented in 1999 (Cipolla-Ficarra, 1999; Cipolla-Ficarra & Quiroga, 2013).

The evaluation work of this professional can be carried out either in an isolated way or in a team. The team work allows you to verify the results obtained in previous evaluations with other experts of the evaluation sector. The advantage of the method consists in that every expert can work on a common portion of the systems but also on different aspects.

Human and Social Factors

One of the main characteristics of factual science is that scientific knowledge is clear and precise. Now clarity and precision can be achieved in several ways. One of them is measurement and registration of phenomena. Besides,

Figure 2. At the end of the animation you do not go back to the start. The lines of the perspectives can be observed

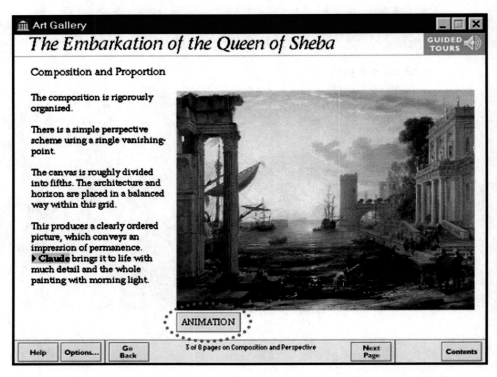

what characterizes scientific knowledge is the accuracy in a general sense rather than numeric or metric exactness, which is useless if conceptual vagueness stands in the way. This conceptual vagueness can be found in the environments of the software engineering in cities of the south of Europe, like Barcelona in the decade of the 90s in view of the proposal of carrying out quality metrics for multimedia systems (Figure 4). Normally, in that "sui generis" context for foreign students (European and American, for example), they needed ten or more years for a PhD (commonly were three or four years for local citiziens). Besides, the foreing PhD students needed change two, three, etc., universities, for a doctoral research about interfaces, design, usability, evaluation, multimedia/hypermedia, and HCI, for instance, in a Language and Computer Systems Department (L.S.i.I. –www.cs.upc.edu), Politechnic University of Catalunya (UPC). We can see a first change, from Barcelona (UPC) to University of Zaragoza, in the Figure 5.

Figure 3. High level of realism of the digital images which can be reached with the drawing of the 19th century in paper support, without need of resorting to digital photography
(Approximate Translation: In the text is the botanic name of the orchid, as well as a brief description of the plant.)

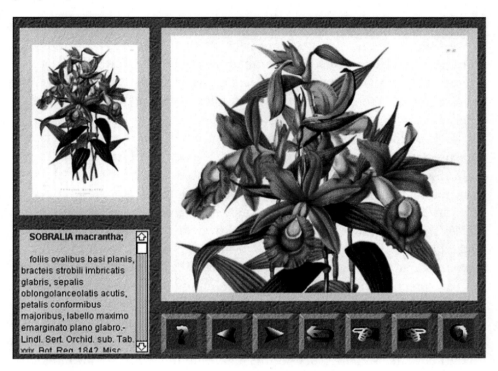

A way of eradicating the problem of avant-garde proposals in the field of ICT consists in declaring the lack of interest inside the language and computer systems department (L.S.I., UPC), for instance (Figure 4 –a document signed for dean, director of the software engineering PhD program, PhD tutor, etc.). That is, by removing the academic support to the student who had demonstrated and overcome the autonomous capacity to carry out research (research sufficiency in Spain). Besides, that mockery, sadism and criminal behaviour is awarded in the Royal Academy of Engineering (www.raing. es), Scientific and IT Society (www.scie.es), etc. A university department that may even belong to the teaching public sector but which apparently is not interested in the issues of research aimed at the multimedia systems, interfaces, human-computer interaction, usability engineering, etc., because it was regarded as a "phenomenon" or "fleeting fashion" in the 90s. Really nobody can be surprised by the consequences in the current Figures 6 and 7 of unemployment in Spain or other places of the south of Europe, seeing the serious mistakes made in predicting the future lines of research in the Mediterranean academic context, which is perennial and immutable to the passing of time.

A myriad of professionals trained in those centres do not have any prospects of working in the new millennium because they have not been trained in relation to the needs of the local communities but to the tune of the personal interests of the managers or group leaders inside the universities. The only valid option for them is migration. Examples of this reality are the Figures 6 and 7.

Some of the methods and techniques used in usability engineering to measure the five attributes mentioned by Nielsen (efficient to use, easy to learn, few errors, easy to remember, and subjectively pleasing) stemmed from the factual sciences (Nielsen, 1993), such as observation, interview, user surveys, questionnaires, think-aloud, focus group, etc. (Nielsen & Mack, 1994). These techniques and methods followed the epistemological methods of the factual sciences, enunciated by Mario Bunge such as (Bunge, 1981): science is analytic, scientific research is specialized, scientific knowledge is clear and precise, scientific knowledge is communicable, scientific knowledge is verifiable, scientific research is methodical, science is explicative, scientific knowledge is predictive, science is open, science is useful, etc. Starting from these epistemological principles, methods and techniques can be generated for the heuristic evaluation of usability and communicability of the interactive multimedia systems, for instance. Now why was it not done immediately? This is related to other rhetorical questions: How can it be that a new area of scientific knowledge generated in computer science of the 90s, such as usability engineering and the metrics of quality have not established what the interactive systems must have? How can it be that inside the PhD programs of software engineering, computer systems, etc., in Spanish universities of the mid 90s measurement of the quality of the interactive design was regarded as something "trivial" or a "fleeting fashion"? The listing of questions can be extended but the answers are to be found in the set of human and social factors of university training.

A way to approach the solution to the lack of metrics consists in breaking down in detail the interactive system that is going to be analyzed (Cipolla-Ficarra, 2010a). In this sense, it is necessary to count with some strategy such as can be the design models aimed at the hypertext, multimedia, hypermedia

Figure 4. Rejection by unanimity of the research "Methods and Techniques for Design Oriented Multmedia Evaluation"

(Approximate Translation: Official document of the obtainment and approval of research proficiency of the doctórate, in Software program of the Polytecnich University of Catalonia – UPC (theoritically, three years). The tutor of the doctorate (Pere Brunet i Crossa), the director of the doctor program (Fernando Orejas Valdés), the dean of the faculty (Pere Botella i López) and other members of the panel declare by unanimity and writing in hand the nullity of interest of the group of researchers-professors in the department to accompany the doctorate to keep on researching until reaching the title of doctor.)

Figure 5. The first university and city change (from Barcelona to Zaragoza, Spain)
(Approximate Translation: Official document of transfer of doctoral study from the Polytecnich University of Catalonia – UPC (Barcelona, Spain) to the University of Zaragoza (Zaragoza, Spain))

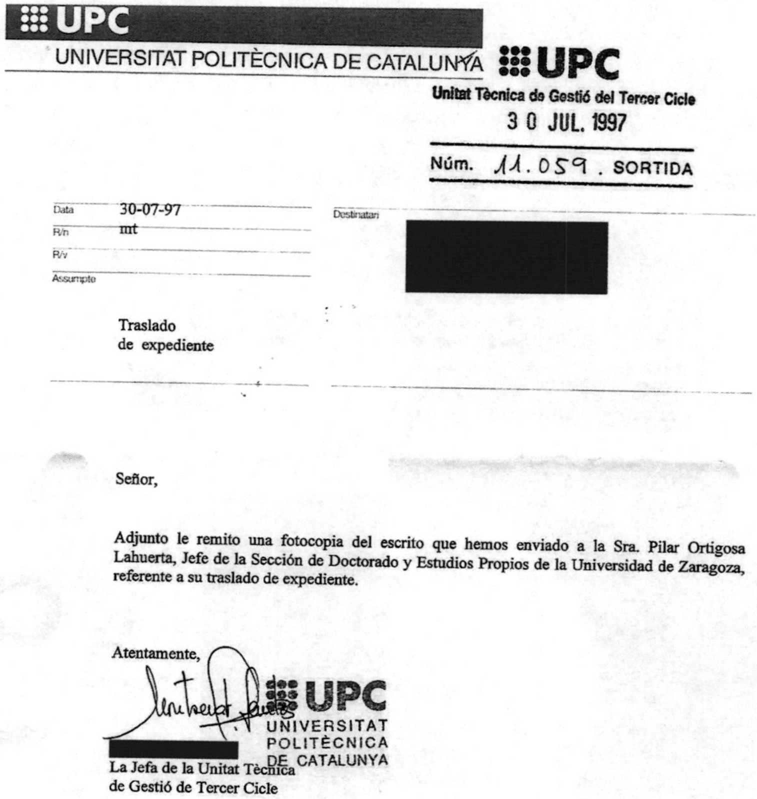

systems, etc, or to semiotics as has been our case, without a need of turning it, commercially and mistakenly, into an engineering problem (de Souza, 2004).

STRATEGY LOW-COST AND HIGH QUALITY

A strategy that has yielded excellent results across two decades can be summed up in the following way.

- Establishing the theoretical framework about the topic of the research. The continuous compiling of information and bibliographical research of articles published in specialized magazines, books, handbooks, etc.

Figure 6. Increase Spanish migration
(Approximate Translation: "How many Spaniards have been expelled by the crisis?") www.elpais.es

in international conferences, symposiums, workshops, etc., including the online articles of organizations such as ACM (Association for Computing Machinery –www.acm.org) and IEEE (Institute of Electrical and Electronics Engineers –www.ieee.org) which are simple rehashes of commercial publicity, press notes, etc., where plagiarism is the common denominator. The goal is to obtain a wide knowledge of the studied topic. In these publications basically use the methods deriving from the human computer interface/interaction, software engineering, the design models for multimedia/hypermedia systems,

Figure 7. Increase of migration among countries of the south of Europe and destination countries of the migratory masses
(Approximate Translation: Article of the Spanish paper El País with the information from National Institute of Statistic from Spain where the graphic information refers to the migration movements, growth of the number of Spaniards in other countries, migrants with an intent to work in the United Kingdom and the Spanish migration abroad.) www.elpais.es

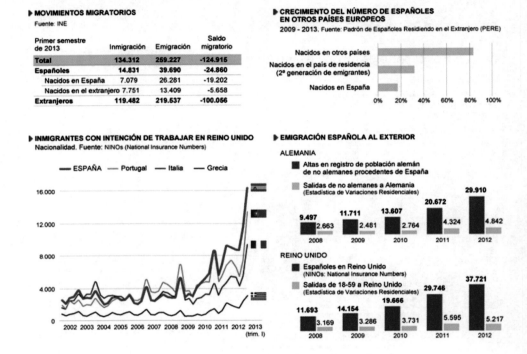

semiotics and the fundamental notions of the multimedia systems, such as node, link, frame, etc.

- Adapting and generating a set of heuristic attributes which affect the quality of the multimedia systems applied to the main design categories which are interrelated among themselves in a bidirectional way. These attributes which during research have been constantly modified to reach a better definition and relation among them. The relationship of these attributes among themselves is of an orthogonal type. In our first set of heuristic attributes they had been related with the usability attributes defined by Nielsen (Nielsen, 1993).

- Breaking down the heuristic attributes of quality into metrics. These metrics apply descriptive statistics to quantify several aspects of the heuristic evaluation such as the total of components of the system or

Figure 8. Growth on migration of the young towards other countries
(Approximate Translation: "Youth unemployment of 40,1%. It is a historic record, figures that go back to 1977") www.unita.it

the total of detected failings. The results of descriptive statistics have allowed to depict graphically components and failings detected in the system to make easier the understanding of those interested in the evaluation such as can be the designers, manufacturers of multimedia systems, final users, etc. Graphics have also been inserted for the components of the system to evaluate thus speeding up not only the task of evaluating but also knowing the scope of the component to be examined inside the system, that is, if it is the whole structure of the interactive system or a part of it.

- Generating a metrics called of binary presence. This set of metrics has been carried out through a table for the heuristic evaluation aimed at the design of a multimedia/hypermedia system. The table has allowed to detect the first failings and has helped to set up an approximate dimension of the system to be analyzed through the totals registered in some components. Therefore, with the table it is possible the early realization of a previous estimate about the cost of the evaluation. This table has been modified constantly until encompassing the largest part of components of a multimedia system. Besides, the components in the table have been classified by design categories. With the classification, more detailed results were obtained. This kind of results in the design stage have delimited the responsibilities of failings among the participants of the elaboration of the multimedia system.

- Establishing with the method a procedure in two stages to combine with other evaluation techniques. In the first, the heuristic evaluator detects the errors of the system. With the mistakes a series of tasks or actions is drawn up by a group of users. In the second stage a new evaluation of the system is made where the users participate and the existence of the errors detected in the first stage is checked. The purpose of the utilization of the users is to control the results reached in the first stage.

- Dividing the modalities of evaluation. For instance, representative and total. The representative modality is based on the concepts deriving from descriptive statistics such as the average and the frequency. With this modality, the costs of the evaluation to the client have been cut down and the level of reliability of the obtained results has been maintained. The other modality allows one to verify the results obtained in the representative modality and consists in evaluating each one of the components of the system.

Starting from this set of strategies, the basis has been set so that the new multimedia systems count with indispensable quality criteria for their usability and communicability. These quality criteria have demonstrated that they improve the interaction of the users with the multimedia systems. Besides, a professional in heuristic evaluation for the communicability in the interactive multimedia systems can guarantee that these quality criteria are fulfilled before an assembly line production of the systems starts. Therefore, with the current methodology, the production costs are reduced by eradicating the possible failings from the design stage, and it is an economical methodology, since in order to carry it out there is no need to have a lab or auxiliary staff available. The interested reader may look up the following references (Cipolla-Ficarra, 1996; Cipolla-Ficarra & Cipolla-Ficarra, 2008; Cipolla-Ficarra, 2010a).

TRIVIALIZATION AND PAROCHIALISM

A way to remedy the apparent lack of interest towards the quality metrics in the origins of the democratization of the off-line and online multimedia contents consists in passing on the topics of university research to local associations or organizations, where the interrelations among their members make up a network of destructive parochialism. For instance, in Spain there are human-computer interaction (HCI = IPO –in Spanish: *Interacción Persona-Ordenador*) associations which are allegedly non-profit, but they cash an annual fee to their members which is higher to what is paid for associations of great international prestige such as ACM or IEEE in 2000 to 2006, for instance.

Besides, they are set up inside the university faculties of Computer Science and ICT with purposes of economic expansion. They use the university structure to be updated with the latest technological novelties. Besides, they resort to other external organizations, to develop R&D projects such as the exercise of territorial control through power concentration in issues related to the HCI, inside and outside the state territory. The issues that were trivial in a university department are trivialized temporally by these pressure groups until they can generate a whole network of training and technology transfer and sell those services to firms and industries (Cipolla-Ficarra, Nicol & Cipolla-Ficarra, 2011), not as quality evaluators any longer, but as auditors. The use of the terms evaluator and auditor could already be detected in the presence of the mercantilist factor on the members of parochialism. The first hailed from the educational context and the latter from the commercial. Slowing down the advance of the metrics for the multimedia systems or trivializing that field of study through the organizations and associations akin to those academic fields, denoted the presence of pressure groups "Garduña factor" (Cipolla-Ficarra, 2014) with the purpose of achieving an absolute control on the quality parameters which the interactive multimedia systems must follow, oriented at the production of goods and services.

LESSONS LEARNED

The current work has made apparent the importance of the metrics (Fenton, 1994; Fenton & Pfleeger, 1998), not only from the point of view of keeping and/or increasing the quality of the interactive multimedia systems of the past, present and future, but also the human and/or social factors of those groups who try to control everything related to the quality in the goods and services of computer science and all its derivations (Cipolla-Ficarra, 2014), inside a territory and even beyond its borders. Some examples in email format where cone can see the presence of the Garduña factor can be located in the following reference (Cipolla-Ficarra, 2010b; Cipolla-Ficarra, 2014). Obviously, a field where this quality is demanded to the utmost, is computer graphics, especially in the images deriving from scientific visualization (Thalman, 1990; Earnshaw, 1992; Rhyne, 2002; Keefe & Isenberg, 2013). Even in some static images of computer graphics that the human eye cannot make out whether they are real or not. For instance, Figures 11, 12, 13, and 14:

- Antonella[1],
- Tintin[2].

Figure 9. Computational tomography of the spine, stored in a DVD, where the user still depends on other people for its interpretation

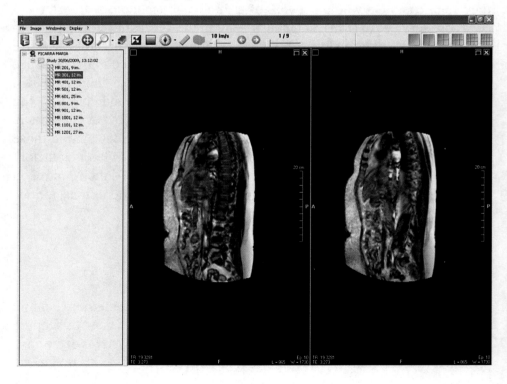

Figure 10. Computational tomography in a DVD, with a special tools, for example, zoom in and zoom out

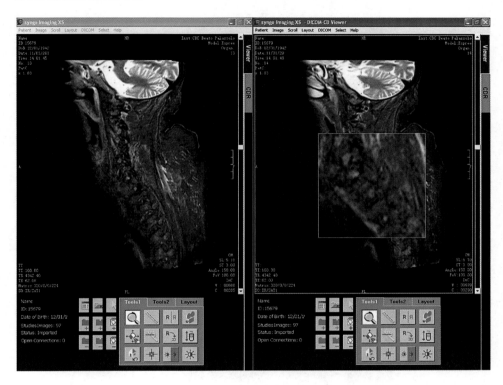

Figure 11. A virtual character created by Ford designers: Antonella
Combination of the photography and 3D.

Figure 12. An excellent example of the virtual character (3D): Tintin

Figure 13. The realism is very high for adult and old people

Figure 14. The human eye cannot make out whether they are real or virtual images

"The Adventures of Tintin", known as, "The Adventures of Tintin: The Secret of the Unicorn", generally, the adult and/or old people cannot distinguish whether it is real or not.the first scenes and others frames of the 3D film, for instance, Figures 12, 13 and 14.

This denotes the importance that the virtual image has in the communication process, where some author claim that as a result of the death of the real image it is necessary to go back to the text (Debray, 1992), that is, to the origin of the evolution of the hypertext to the hypermedia. Something similar has happened with the mobile phones, which went from the SMS (Short Message Service) until becoming an interactive multimedia device, with online access, in almost the whole planet, transforming positively the current era of expansion of communicability among human beings.

That is, we are in the face of phenomena which can be cyclical to implement new multimedia devices where the nanotechnologies and preventive medicine can revolutionize the prevention of chronic diseases, for instance (Sharver, et al., 2004).

In this sense, it is necessary to continue with the improvement of the quality metrics in those services and products and also make scientific and/or medical information more legible or of easier interpretation for potentially millions of users of new devices where the quality multimedia metrics, scientific visualization and information make up areas of continuous interaction and bidirectional among each one of the human and technological components.

CONCLUSION

Getting a correct interrelation between human-technological in the quartet of presented components (scientific visualization, scientific information, multimedia and metrics) is one of the main challenges, not only for 2020, but also along the whole 21st century. Quality is one of the key elements that allows technological progress, the end user, sooner or later, will have access to these technological breakthroughs, and even technological jumps may take place in spots where the economies are not developed, but the multimedia communications are, through multimedia mobile phones. Perhaps they do not have the latest technological advances, but they have enough time available to use over 90% of the potential of the hardware and the software that they have in their hands. A percentage which is lower than the 50% in many users, residing in the south of Europe. Finally, in the mid 90s, a transversal researcher of many disciplines such as software engineering, usability engineering, design models of interactive systems, etc., was rejected in the Barcelona (Spain) computer context for reasons of scientific nullity. The passing of time has verified that theory. The Garduña factor makes them become the epicentre of a radial power structure for quality metrics in the multimedia systems, but contradicting the epistemological principles of scientific knowledge and the democratization of scientific information. In short, in the era of the expansion of communicability these university centres are antimodels for the universality of the formal and factual sciences.

ACKNOWLEDGMENT

I would like to thank all the people who contributed in some way to the research work described in this chapter, for instance, Maria Ficarra (25 years). Besides, special thanks to Alejandra Quiroga, Jacqueline Alma, Mary Brie, Luisa Varela, Amélie Bordeaux, Pamela Fulton, Doris Edison, Sonia Flores, Julia Ruiz, Giselda Verdone, Jim Carré, Donald Nilson, and Carlos for the assistence and collaboration.

REFERENCES

Bunge, M. (1981). *The science: your method and your philosophy*. Buenos Aires: Siglo XXI.

Cipolla-Ficarra, F. (1996). A User Evaluation of Hypermedia Iconography. In *Proceedings Computergraphics* (pp. 182–191). Paris: GRASP.

Cipolla-Ficarra, F. (1999). Evaluation Heuristic of the Richness. In *Proceedings International Conference on Information Systems Analysis and Synthesis*. Orlando, FL: ISAS.

Cipolla-Ficarra, F. (2010a). *Quality and Communicability for Interactive Hypermedia Systems: Concepts and Practices for Design*. Hershey, PA: IGI Global. doi:10.4018/978-1-61520-763-3

Cipolla-Ficarra, F. (2010b). *Persuasion On-Line and Communicability: The Destruction of Credibility in the Virtual Community and Cognitive Models*. New York: Nova Science Publishers.

Cipolla-Ficarra, F. (2014). *Advanced Research and Trends in New Technologies, Software, Human-Computer Interaction and Communicability*. Hershey, PA: IGI Global. doi:10.4018/978-1-4666-4490-8

Cipolla-Ficarra, F., & Cipolla-Ficarra, M. (2008). Interactive Systems, Design and Heuristic Evaluation: The Importance of the Diachronic Vision. In *Proceedings New Directions in Intelligent Interactive Multimedia 2008* (pp. 625–634). Heidelberg, Germany: Springer. doi:10.1007/978-3-540-68127-4_64

Cipolla-Ficarra, F., Nicol, E., & Cipolla-Ficarra, M. (2011). Research and Development: Business into Transfer Information and Communication Technology. In *Proceedings First International Conference on Advances in New Technologies, Interactive Interfaces and Communicability*. Heidelberg, Germany: Springer. doi:10.1007/978-3-642-20810-2_6

Cipolla-Ficarra, F., & Quiroga, A. (2013). Creativity, Mobile Multimedia Systems, Human and Social Factors in Software: Communicability Excellence for All. In *Proceedings HCI International 2013*. Heidelberg, Germany: Springer.

de Souza, C. (2004). *The Semiotic Engineering of Human-Computer Interaction*. Cambridge, MA: MIT.

Debray, R. (1992). *Vie et mort de l'image*. Paris: Gallimard. (in French)

Earnshaw, R. (1992). *An Introductory Guide to Scientific Visualization*. Berlin: Springer. doi:10.1007/978-3-642-58101-4

Fenton, N. (1994). Software Measurement: A Necessary Scientific Basis. *IEEE Transactions on Software Engineering*, *20*(3), 199–206. doi:10.1109/32.268921

Fenton, N., & Pfleeger, S. (1998). *Software Metrics: A Rigorous and Practical Approach*. Cambridge, UK: Chapman & Hall.

Keefe, D., & Isenberg, T. (2013). Reimagining the Scientific Visualization Interaction Paradigm. *IEEE Computer*, *46*(5), 51–57. doi:10.1109/MC.2013.178

Microsoft. (1993). *Art Gallery* [CD-ROM]. Author.

Nielsen, J. (1993). *Usability Engineering*. London: Academic Press.

Nielsen, J., & Mack, R. (1994). *Usability Inspections Methods*. New York: John Wiley & Sons. doi:10.1145/259963.260531

Rhyne, T. M. (2002). Computer Games and Scientific Visualization. *Communications of the ACM, 45*(7), 40–44. doi:10.1145/514236.514261

SEG. (1997). *Orquidáceas de México y Guatemala*. Puebla: Benemérita Universidad Autónoma de Puebla. (in Spanish)

Sharver, C. (2004). Designing Cranial Implants in a Haptic Augmented Reality Environment. *Communications of the ACM, 47*(8), 32–38. doi:10.1145/1012037.1012059

Thalman, D. (1990). *Scientific Visualization and Graphics Simulation*. Chichester, UK: Whiley.

ADDITIONAL READING

Bull, C., & Whittle, J. (2014). Supporting Reflective Practice in Software Engineering Education through a Studio-Based Approach. *IEEE Software, 31*(4), 44–50. doi:10.1109/MS.2014.52

Cipolla, R., & Pentland, A. (1998). *Computer Vision for Human-Machine Interaction*. Cambridge: Cambridge University Press. doi:10.1017/CBO9780511569937

Cipolla-Ficarra, F. (1999). MEHEM: A Methodology for Heuristic Evaluation in Multimedia. In *Proceedigns Distributed Multimedia Systems (DMS'99)* (pp. 89–96). Aizu: KSI.

Cipolla-Ficarra, F. (2001). *Communication Evaluation in Multimedia: Metrics and Methodology. Universal Access in HCI* (pp. 567–571). London: LEA.

De Saussure, F. (2002). *Écrits de linguistique générale*. Paris: Gallimard. In French

Debray, R. (1992). *Vie et mort de l'image*. Paris: Gallimard. In French

Fuchs, H., State, A., & Bazin, J. (2014). Immersive 3D Telepresence. *IEEE Computer, 47*(7), 46–52. doi:10.1109/MC.2014.185

Holzinger, A. (2005). Usability Engineering Methods for Software Developers. *Communications of the ACM, 48*(1), 71–74. doi:10.1145/1039539.1039541

Horn, R. (1989). *Mapping Hypertext: The Analysis, Organization, and Display of Knowledge for the Next Generation of On-Line Text and Graphics*. Massachusetts: The Lexington Institute.

Kellog, W., & Thomas, J. (1993). Cross-Cultural Perspective on Human-Computer Interaction. *SIGCHI, 25*(2), 40–45. doi:10.1145/155804.155816

Marcus, A. (2003). Icons, Symbols, and Signs: Visible Languages to Facilitate Communication. *Interactions of ACM, 10*(3), 37–43. doi:10.1145/769759.769774

Nielsen, J., & del Galdo, E. (1996). *International User Interfaces*. New York: Wiley.

Preece, J. (1998). Empathic Communities. *Interactions of ACM, 5*(2), 32–43. doi:10.1145/274430.274435

Schraefel, M. C. (2009). Building Knowledge: Whats Beyond Keyword Search? *IEEE Computer, 42*(3), 52–59. doi:10.1109/MC.2009.69

Sterne, J. (2002). *Web Metrics*. New York: Wiley.

Trappl, R., & Petta, P. (1997). *Creating Personalities for Synthetic Actors*. Berlin: Springer-Verlag. doi:10.1007/BFb0030565

Vaz, M., & Duignan, P. (1996). *Industrial Light+Magic into the Digital Realm*. Hong Kong: Ballantine Books.

Welbergen, H., Nijholt, A., Reidsma, D., & Zwiers, J. (2006). Presenting in Virtual Workds: An Architecture for a 3D Anthropomorphic Presenter. *IEEE Intelligent Systems, 21*(5), 47–53. doi:10.1109/MIS.2006.101

Zeki, S. (1993). *A Vision of the Brain. Color vision and brain* (pp. 227–240). Oxford: Blackwell Scientific Publications.

KEY TERMS AND DEFINITIONS

Communicability: A qualitative communication between the user and the interactive system, such as mobile phones, augmented reality, immersion multimedia, hypermedia, among others. The extent to which an interactive system successfully conveys its functionality to the user.

Interactive System: A computer device made up by a CPU and peripherals, whose functioning requires a constant interaction with the user. Currently these systems tend to their miniaturization and/or invisibility, the mobility and wireless connectability among them.

Scientific Visualization: An interdisciplinary branch of science. For example, today, it is consideraed a subset of computer graphics. In other words, a branch of computer science. The main action is to graphically ilustrate scientific date, with 2D/3D rendering, illumination sources, special effects, animation, etc.

Usability: In software engineering is a crtierion consisting of several factors such as: easy to use, utility, orientation, etc. Nielsen consideres the following usability attributes: ease to learn, efficient to use, ease to remember, few errors, and subjectively pleasing. These factors must be taken into account, especially at the system design stage, in order to avoid failings in human-computer interaction.

User Interface: The "component" that mediates between the user and the application program, translating the user's demands into an acceptable size for application and the answers of the progrma into a language which the user can understand.

ENDNOTES

[1]   (a Ford advertising: www.nytimes.com/2009/07/19/automobiles/19design.html).

[2]   (film: web.archive.org/web/20110520233828/http://www.us.movie.tintin.com)

Chapter 4
An Exemplary Interface for All

Francisco V. Cipolla-Ficarra
Latin Association of Human-Computer Interaction, Spain & International Association of Interactive Communication, Italy

Alejandra Quiroga
Universidad Nacional de La Pampa, Argentina

Jim Carré
University of the Netherlands Antilles, Curaçao

Jacqueline Alma
Electronic Arts, Canada

ABSTRACT

In the current chapter is analyzed the latest interface of the video game that has been capable of adapting to the evolution of the software and the hardware for almost a quarter of a century: SimCity. By using notions of semiotics and interactive design the isotopies have been detected that boost the interaction of the users. Besides, the elements of the layout of the Web 2.0 are studied which have been incorporated into the latest version of the video game.

INTRODUCTION

Since the first official and commercial version of SimCity (www.simcity.com) the design of its interface (1988) has followed the design of the icons of the programming languages of the interactive system of the computers (Wilson, 1990; Rabin, 2009; Tavinor, 2009), as the whole evolution of Windows has been (Appendix). That is, square buttons and/or in a rectangular shape, like

DOI: 10.4018/978-1-5225-3437-2.ch004

the unfolding menus of the first commercial version, which worked with the MS-DOS (Microsoft –Disk Operating System).

The original version was developed in Commodore 64 in 1985. It was also adapted to the hardware of each period, for instance, the cathodic rays screens, whether it was the television that was connected to the Commodores 64 when they were developed or the early screens of personal computers (Figure 1).

The continuous interaction for several hours by the users required not only the visual protection of the users through special glasses or filters on the screens of the computers, but also being placed at a certain distance in front of the computer. Currently the new plasma technology has eliminated this problem. This is one of the reasons for the expansion of the oriented contents in new interactive devices: video consoles, multimedia phones, Tablet PC, etc. do not require special protections for the user-computer interaction.

In the interface can still be seen the design of the unfolding menus of MS-DOS which went to Windows 3.1, Windows '98, Windows 2000, Windows XP, etc. These interactive systems have had an influence on the interaction habits of the users (who were born non-digital) and the distribution of the commands on the computer screen. The freedom to move the bars of the

Figure 1. Picture of the interface of SimCity 2000 (year of marketing 1993) on a computer screen of cathodic rays, where the curving effect of the image can be appreciated

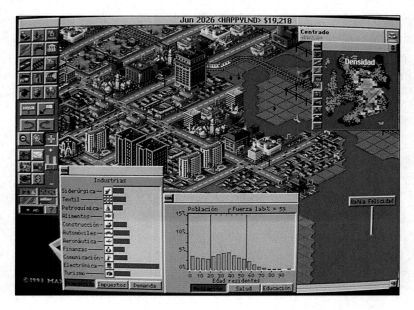

unfolding menus on the margins of the computer screen was an important factor within the set of users who are currently called "non-digital generation" (Maybury, Stock, & Wahister, 2006; Cipolla-Ficarra, 2015). However, they were a generation who knew how to program the Commodore 64 in BASIC, manage the databases with dBase III, write texts with the WordStar or the WordPerfect, etc. That is, they turned the automatic office (analogical) into a computer office (digital).

CLASSICAL GUIDELINES FOR INTERNATIONAL USERS

The use of commercial applications of office automation such as Excel (spreadsheet application), Adobe Photoshop (graphics editing program), CorelDraw (vector graphics editor), etc., gave a greater freedom to the tool boxes of those programs for the different kinds of users who were vertiginously joining the digital office. If a parallelism is drawn of the lay out of these applications with the SimCity it is easy to detect a first set of common denominators which make up the style guidelines for the interfaces in applications which work in PCs under the Windows operative system, like those of Macintosh (Apple, 1992; Clarke, & Mitchell, 2007). The presence of these latest rules or style guidelines in the interfaces design for offline and online multimedia systems of Macintosh can still be detected in the latest version of SimCity, for instance.

Next a listing of the same (alphabetical order). For more details, are found in (Apple, 1992):

1. Accessibility,
2. Aesthetic Integrity,
3. Consistency,
4. Direct Manipulation,
5. Feedback and Dialog,
6. Forgiveness,
7. Knowledge of Your Audience,
8. Metaphors,
9. Modelessness,
10. Perceived Stability,
11. See-and-Point,
12. User Control, and
13. WYSIWYG (What You See Is What You Get).

Although with the passing of time, some of those human interface design principles have become quality attributes such as is accessibility in all the online interactive systems, for instance. Others of those principles, such as the knowledge of the audience, have entailed long years of studies from the point of view of communicability, usability and international design, due to the globalization of information, as a positive consequence of the democratization of the online multimedia contents (Cipolla-Ficarra, 2015). These contents had their origins in the off-line multimedia systems.

ISOTOPIES AND ISOMORPHISM

Greimas borrowed the term isotopy (Colapietro, 1993). In structural semantics, isotopy describes the coherence and homogeneity of texts. Greimas develops the theory of textual coherence on the basis of this concept of contextual semes. The isotopies are sense lines that act upon the structures. That is to say, from a semantic point of view lines are drawn which unite several components of the multimedia in order to help comprehension of the rest of the multimedia system.

The sense lines are independent of our location inside a multimedia, since they draw a unity in relation to the four basic categories used in the heuristic analysis of the system. For example, if we are inside a guided tour or on the first frame of a certain entity type, we can detect that there is a set of elements belonging to the presentation of the content which do not change (typography, the background to the frames, the positioning of the navigation keys, the icons that represent the navigation keys, the kind of transitions between different frames or animations, etc.).

The lines link those elements which remain identical among themselves and which belong to the different categories of design: presentation, content, dynamism, panchronism, structure, etc. (Cipolla-Ficarra, 2010). For example, the organisation of the textual content as is the inverted pyramid, the activation and deactivation of the dynamic media, and the way to reach the hyperbase and structure of the whole of the nodes, etc. (Cipolla-Ficarra, 1996a).

By means of the isomorphism notion it can easily be detected whether the system is easy to use, easy to learn and whether it avoids mistakes in interaction with a user. These invisible lines which link the design categories also have an influence on the quality of the system.

Isomorphism determines the same form of presentation (topology in the distribution of elements in the frame), the behaviour of dynamic mediums, and different ways of structuring the organisation of the content (passive media such as texts, photos, maps, graphics, etc. and active media such as animation, video sound) and the synchronization between passive and dynamic media (Cipolla-Ficarra, F. et al., 2012). For instance, that of the same place being maintained inside the frame in the set of navigation keyboards, be it in frames that belong to a manual or automatic guided link, a sequential collection or a perspective. These formal features act as common denominators for some of the constituents of an entity, thereby establishing a global and distinctive wholeness in the application.

Isomorphism seeks regularity within irregularity. This is the main difference between it and consistency. Consistency means verifying that those elements which are conceptually equal have similar behaviours, while those which are different, have different behaviour patterns. There is a direct underlying relationship which can be shown by two the relationships: an equality relationship and an inequality relationship. For example, if A = B, and B = C, then A = C (an equality relationship between A, B, C); if A is not equal to B, then A is not equal to C (an inequality relationship between the components).

Isomorphism goes beyond this regularity or direct relationship because it seeks in the inequality relationship (in the example, the variable factor C as related to A and to B) those elements that remain equal and that somehow make it possible to maintain homogeneity and coherence between the constituents of the categories of the multimedia/hypermedia system. These common denominators are called isotopies (Nöth, 1995).

TOPOLOGY AND FORM

Now among those principles from the category of the layout design must be included the topology and the shape. The topology is the place that the components occupy (icons, texts, pictures, etc.) inside the interface. If these elements stay constant in each one of the menus that make up the structure of the interactive system, we are in view of a topological isotopy.

This isotopy is very positive for the users since it can be anticipated to the place the icons occupy by defect in the interface, in those sections of the structure of the system with which they haven't interacted. That is, it boosts several quality attributes, such as the isomorphism (it is a set of constant formal features among the different components and design categories), the control of fruition (it is the degree of freedom in navigation that gives to the user the structure of the interactive system), the naturalness of the metaphor (it is the ability of understanding by the user of the set of images that make up the structure of the interface, an image is natural when by itself it tends to transmit a single meaning), etc.

Shape has to do with those elements that are present in the interface of the interactive system: circles, points, lines, rectangles, etc. About the circles some assert the form is to be found everywhere in nature –in the shape of the sun and moon, in randrops, bubbles, and flowers— and it is our desidere to mirror its natural beauty that drives creative interpretations of the circle.

Others maintain that the circle does not occur naturally, but is a man-made conceit that reflects the worlds of physics and mathematics-engineering tools that perpetuate the desive to create order from a chaotic world, awards and medals that commemorate human achievements.

Aside from these opinions, from a perspective of the social sciences, the importance of the circle in society can be charted through representations of the sun in primitive art, the building of stone circles, etc. This latter notion makes clear an aspect of the latest version of the video game, the prevalence of the circles in the constructions made with SimCity as can be seen in Figures 2 and 3.

Circles which are made in the tracing of the streets to draw a kind of symbol of peace, the future highways, the selection of an area inside the

Figure 2. The circles in the shapes of the constructions, drawing of roads, etc. prevail in the promotional examples of the analyzed video game

Figure 3. The use of curve lines boosts the acceptance by the users of the Web 2.0 of the interactive system we are analyzing

city, whether to delimit the construction or demolition of a building (Hillis, 2002; Houston, et al., 2004). Circles which also appear on the icons, as can be seen in Figures 2 and 3, for instance.

Some circles which are reproduced in many icons to activate commands in the different menus. Besides, the curved line where are included those icons in the left lower part has been kept from previous versions and boosts the acceptance of the interface. There is a feeling of warmth by obliterating the 90° angles from the squares or rectangles in the dropdown menus.

MULTIPLAYER DESIGN AND WEB 2.0: LAYOUT COHERENCE

The coherence of the graphic aspects is one of the main factors in the isotopies. The modality of multiplayer online that for the first time is incorporated into this video game has influenced the design of the interface (Brown, 2008; Wolf, 2008; Straubhaar, LaRose, & Davenport, 2012). That is, the possibilities that potential users from diverse cultures interact, belonging or not to the digital culture at the moment of its birth, has led to a series of interactive design strategies such as: the use of transparencies in the dropdown menus to increase the information on the screen, the blurring efect (it is more present in the SimCity scenes as a background effect in the horizon), typography, colour, illustration or drawing, etc.

TRANSPARECIES AND BLURRED IMAGES

With the use of menus or transparent boxes it is possible to "duplicate" the information that is presented on a screen. These menus may take the whole screen or part of it. Studies made by Harrison, B. et al. (Harrison, B. et al., 1995) demonstrate the effectiveness of this technique in the interfaces, since the transparencies (slides) focus the attention of the user on the interface by giving more interest to the slide than to its background. For a correct use of the transparencies in video games it is advisable to avoid very transparent backgrounds, since they may cause a visual disorientation in the case of resorting to transparent menus or navigation keys. In the Figure 4 of the dropdown menu of the screen can be seen a correct use of the transparencies in the interface. Another way to "duplicate" the information on a screen is the use of blurred images. A set of graphic elements maintains its colors more neat and the rest that have been blurred acquire a uniform color, in relation to that which prevails on the nearest constructions. For instance, the buildings of

Figure 4. Transparence and menus: An excellent use in SimCity. The sims (residents of the city) communicate through comic balloons and in the lower part can be seen a transparency to carry out an action by the user.

the centre of the image are neat, and as they become smaller by the distance of the horizon, they blur into uniform colors.

The difference between a transparent image and a blurry one in an interface is that the former can be seen in the backdrop of the screen, whereas in the latter not. There is then more information in the interface when transparencies are used when blurring is used. Blurring is a three-dimensional effect that belongs to the lightening environment.

COLOURS

Through the color of the components of the interface can be reached a greater or lesser coherence. The element of the interface where a same color more prevails is the backdrop of the interface, especially if the backdrop is a color and not a texture. The background color or base of the screen can be grouped basically into primary colors and secondary colors. In the current research work are not approached the aspects of the "correct" combination or mixture of the colors, as it happens in the graphic arts, being this a topic for future research. The use of colors must be analyzed previously at the moment of the design of the interface, since it has different connotations. These connotations are related to the meaning and depend on the culture and/or geographical location of the user of the system (Cipolla-Ficarra, 1996a). In the Western countries of the northern hemisphere, the blue color is the preferred by the

Figure 5. Blurring effects in the backdrop of the interface and transparency in the menu of the upper right part

adult users, followed by green, white and red. In Spain the red color prevails over the other three. In Japan, the white color takes the first place of the preferences, followed by black and yellow (Maffei, 1995). In the Web 2.0 we are under the Argentinization phenomenon –two colors of the Argentinian flag: sky blue and white (Cipolla-Ficarra, F., Cipolla-Ficarra, M., & Alma, 2012). On the video game screens, those colors prevail in the bars that hold the different icons on the lower left side of the screen. In some the circle of the left margin has the same colors as the flag, thus generating parallelisms of high similarity with symbols of that nation, such as the national ensigns, in the shape of circles. This phenomenon is widely explained in the following reference (Cipolla-Ficarra, F., Cipolla-Ficarra, M., & Alma, 2012).

TYPOGRAPHY

The kind of print or typography used in the titles, subtitles and texts must be the same in the whole system. The typography can be grouped as classic and artistic. This classification is due to the purpose of the content of a hypermedia system, for instance. If the purpose is to educate and inform, the typography that must be used is the classical one, whereas if the purpose is a pastime the artistic or special typography can be used. The classical typography is that which belongs to the Anglosaxon and Novarese classification, that is, *arial, times, sans-serif, helvetica, courtier,* etc. Those kinds of print which do not belong to the Anglosaxon and Novarese classification are called artistic or special in the current research work. The homogeneity among the words with an artistic typography is in the color and the possible surroundings, since the characters may have irregular shapes among them and be placed on the screen also in an irregular way, that is, without following a straight line. The users waste more time for the understanding and reading of the text, due to these irregularities.

The SimCity texts follow the Anglosaxon and Novarese classification although they occupy small spaces such as can be the elongated menus (upper part of the Figures 6 and 7) or those in the shape of comic balloons, are easy to read. Also in the balloons can be seen with an angle to indicate the components or icons to which refers the person who is talking to the user, as can be seen in the Figure 4. The same happens with the figures which accompany the statistic data. The statistic data are a constant feature along time in the current video game. These data may be accompanied with dates (statistic or animated), or other symbols of road signs, but that in the case of

Figure 6. Distribution of the statistic information with animated arrows to indicate to the users the actions to follow

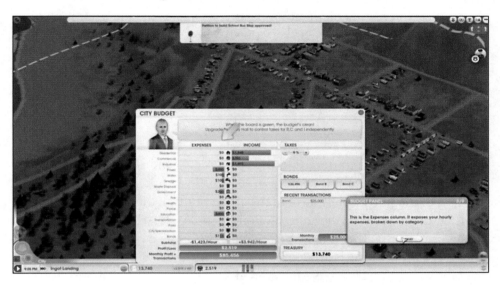

Figure 7. Road traffic signs to indicate the eventual catastrophes. The special effects thereof are depicted with blurring and/or transparencies effects in the explosions, for instance.

the Figure 7 refer to natural and man-made catastrophes of the societies created with this simulator: fires, earthquakes, UFO attacks, tornados, meteorites rains, etc. The use of the comic balloons to include texts is very positive for most interactive users, considering its high value in e-learning, demonstrated along time, for instance (Cipolla-Ficarra, 1996).

Another interesting element for future analysis is the incorporation of the breaking news. This element is very positively valued by the social networks, irrespective that the videogame news are related to unreal situations such as the attack of the aliens, for instance.

ILLUSTRATION

The drawing or illustration, like the typography and other elements which make up the interface may have a greater or lesser degree of abstraction in relation to the purpose of the content of the multimedia system. In SimCity, the illustrations refer to the constructions, people, etc. which give information to the user so that they make a decision. The same as in typography, if the purpose of the drawing is to educate and inform, the drawing must be figurative. In contrast, if the purpose is a pastime, the drawing can be abstract. However, in the present video game can be seen a constant use of figurative drawing, that is, with little abstraction.

One of the elements that have been incorporated into the current version of the video game are the classical emoticons. An emoticon is a pictorial representation of a facial expression marks the degree of satisfaction of the inhabitants in view of the evolution of society as can be seen in the lower

Figure 8. The comic balloons for the human dialogue or indication of information, is a visual design resource of great international acceptance

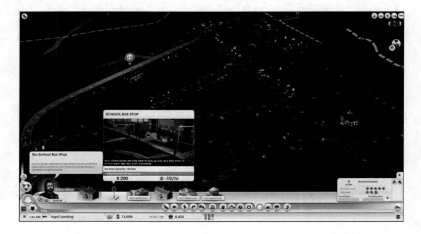

central part of the figures a, b and c. The colors with the gestures of the emoticons oscillate between red, orange, yellow, light green and dark green. Dark green denotes the highest approval of the tasks made, while red is the sign of total disapproval. The colors used in the Figure 9 are the classical which are used in architectural CAD to represent the strong and weak points of a real structure.

ILLUMINATION FOR INTERACTION

The relief effect of the icons is trying to emulate the shadows caused by the environment lightening in the elements of the screen. The purpose is that these bidimensional elements "acquire" a three-dimensional quality. Emulation is obtained by darkening correctly the borders of those elements that are supposed to be highlighted in the interface.

In SimCity we find it in the lower part of the different objects emulating the 3D that the user may pick, as is the case of the different kinds of roads (Figure 10). Among these elements can be mentioned the navigation keys, the typography, the boxes of the images, etc. It is a positive effect in the navigation keys, since these are easier to recognize on an interface, or the different options the user has. The interface of an interactive system has a higher degree of realism with the emulation of the shadows, which boosts its acceptance (Cipolla-Ficarra, 1996b). The effects deriving from the lightening such as are the shadows, the reflection, the diffusion, etc. must also stay constant in the whole interactive system or the video game. The lightening effects stem from the kind of light that is used in scenes with three-dimensional objects. This kind of light can be ambiance light or directional light. In ambiance light the objects that receive the light generate shadows (Figure 10), whereas

Figure 9. Use of icons of great international diffusion such as are the emoticons in classical or 2D format

Figure 10. Emulation of shadows in the lower part of each one of the different modalities of pathways, roads and highways, etc. In the central part an animated light shine serves to draw the attention of the user.

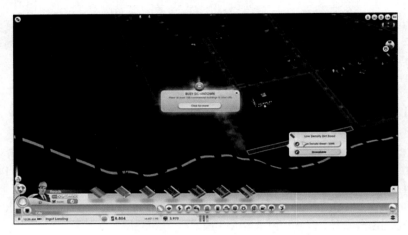

in directional lightening a light beam is sent on a given object in the scene. When there is more than a beam of light, lightening is multidirectional. In the next figure can be seen the correct use of directional lightening, are shown and activated the main options that the interactive system offers to the user, at the moment he/she must choose a road.

The lighting between the icons and the scenes must be very well differentiated to avoid confusions. The new version of SimCity has developed an interesting solution in that relationship, which will be a line of study for future research related to the special effects and lighting, for instance.

The effects of the kind reflection or shine simulate the arrival of the light to a point on an object. This light can be depicted in the shape of a star, sun or any other shape with beams. The shine may be static or dynamic. It is dynamic when it has associated an animation. The animation may consist in a 360° twist on its axis or in an increase and diminution of the shine. The shines mean prestige or superiority of an element with regard to others that make up the interface. They may also serve to call or draw the attention on an element of the screen. In the Figure 10 we have in the centre a lightening effect, which twists 360 degrees on a central axis to draw attention on the information on the box.

LESSONS LEARNED AND FUTURE RESEARCH

The communicability of the elements of the layout in the new version of the video game is excellent. The existence of isotopies and isomorphisms boosts the navigation of the user in the different interfaces which make up the construction of the city with the current simulator. The curved shapes prevail in the icons, dialogue frames between the system and the user, etc., which fosters the navigation of the current interactive system for virtual construction and the management of the simulated city. The topology of the main components of the interface is 100% correct, that is, the location of the main menu and the spot chosen inside the screen to constantly communicate with the user such as the left lower margin. The use of the colors boosts the communicability process in that area belonging to the Web 2.0 phenomenon called Argentinization (Cipolla-Ficarra, Cipolla-Ficarra & Alma, 2012). The combination of primary and secondary colors like the use of the text belonging to the Anglosaxon and Novarese classification, the illustrations resorting static images of SimCity also generate isotopies. The lightening effect and the animated arrows, for instance, allow to attract the attention of the users in the right way. The rest of special effects in 3D will be studied in future research where we will work with users of different ages. We will also analyze the aspects of those animations which are related to ecology, cartography and the natural effects (meteorology, the seasons of the year, etc.).

CONCLUSION

Keeping isotopies in each one of the design categories adapting to the evolution of the software and the hardware has been one of the reasons for the acceptation of the present video game for years. Although the potentiality of the current software allows even to watch and influence the behavior of the residents of the city, that is, the Sims, through the glassbox, the maintenance and adaptation of the interface to the Web 2,0 has been very effective from the point of view of communicability. Consequently, it is a commercial product aimed at multimedia entertainment which has a high degree of acceptance by the global market in the era of the expansion of communicability. The emulations, simulations, special effects, etc., are depicted in a correct way on the interface. An interface where the visual elements for interaction are easy to recognize and interact with them. In each one of those elements there are direct and indirect interrelations with the social communication media, such as the new "dialects" of multimedia communication as can be the signalization of those places where the videogame is working, the use of emoticons, etc. These communicability resources allow to establish a generational bridge among the global users. Finally, the use of curve lines as circles make the present interface a set of entertaining and appealing elements for most of the potential new users of the video game.

ACKNOWLEDGMENT

We would like to give special thanks to Maria Ficarra. Besides, special acknowledgements go to Mary Brie, Luisa Varela, Donald Nilson, and Carlos for their collaboration.

REFERENCES

Apple. (1992). *Macintosh Human Interface Guidelines.* Addison-Wesley.

Brown, H. J. (2008). Videogames and Education. New York: Armonk.

Cipolla-Ficarra, F. (1996a). *Evaluation and Communication Techniques in Multimedia Product Design for On the Net University Education. Multimedia on the Net.* Heidelberg, Germany: Springer-Verlag. doi:10.1007/978-3-7091-9472-0_14

Cipolla-Ficarra, F. (1996b). A User Evaluation of Hypermedia Iconography. In *Proceedings Compugraphics '96* (pp. 182–191). Paris: GRASP.

Cipolla-Ficarra, F. (2010). *Quality and Communicability for Interactive Hypermedia Systems: Concepts and Practices for Design.* Hershey, PA: IGI Global. doi:10.4018/978-1-61520-763-3

Cipolla-Ficarra, F. (2012). *New Horizons in Creative Open Software, Multimedia, Human Factors and Software Engineering.* Bergamo: Blue Herons Editions.

Cipolla-Ficarra, F. (2015). *Handbook of Research Interactive Information Quality in Expanding Social Network Communications*. Hershey, PA: IGI Global. doi:10.4018/978-1-4666-7377-9

Cipolla-Ficarra, F., Cipolla-Ficarra, M., & Alma, J. (2012). The Argentinization of the User Design. In *Proceedings Second International Conference on Advances in New Technologies, Interactive Interfaces and Communicability*. Heidelberg, Germany: Springer.

Clarke, A., & Mitchell, G. (2007). *Videogames and Art*. Chicago: University of Chicago Press.

Colapietro, V. (1993). *Semiotics*. New York: Paragon House.

Harrison, B. (1995). An Experimental Evaluation of Transparent User Interface Tools and Information Content. In *Proceedings Symposium on User Interface Software and Technology*. New York: ACM Press. doi:10.1145/215585.215669

Hillis, D. (2002). The Power to Shape the World. *Communications of the ACM, 45*(7), 32–35. doi:10.1145/514236.514259

Houston, M., Niederauer, C., Agrawala, M., & Humphreys, G. (2004). Visualizing Dynamic Architectural Environments. *Communications of the ACM, 47*(8), 54–59. doi:10.1145/1012037.1012062

Maffei, L. (1995). Paper. In *Proceedings Colours of Life*. Turin: La Stampa.

Maybury, M., Stock, O., & Wahister, W. (2006). Intelligent Interactive Entertainment Grand Challenges. *IEEE Intelligent Systems, 21*(5), 14–18. doi:10.1109/MIS.2006.98

Newman, J. (2004). *Videogames*. London: Routledge.

Nöth, W. (1995). *Handbook of Semiotics*. Bloomington, IN: Indiana University Press.

Rabin, S. (2009). *Introduction to Game Development*. Hingham.

Straubhaar, J., LaRose, R., & Davenport, L. (2012). *Media Now. Understanding Media, Culture, and Technology*. Boston: Wadsworth.

Tavinor, G. (2009). *The Art of Videogames*. John Wiley. doi:10.1002/9781444310177

Wilson, J. L. (1990). *The Simcity Planning Commission Handbook.* Berkeley, CA: Osborne McGraw-Hill.

Wolf, M. (2008). *The Video Game Explosion. A History from Pong to PlayStation and Beyond.* Westwood, CT: Greenwood Press.

ADDITIONAL READING

Andersen, P. B. (1990). *A Theory of Computer Semiotics.* Melbourne: Cambridge University Press.

Apperley, T. H. (2006). Genre and Game Studies: Toward a critical Approcah to Video Game Genres. *Simulation & Gaming, 37*(1), 6–23. doi:10.1177/1046878105282278

Barthes, R. (1973). *Le Plaisir du texte.* Paris: Editions du Seuil. In French

Boal, A. (1992). *Games for Actor and Non-actors.* London: Routledge.

Collins, K. (2008). *Game Sound. An Introduction to the History, Theory and Practice of Video Game Music and Sound Design.* Cambridge: The MIT Press.

Dix, A. et al.. (1993). *Human-Computer Interaction.* Cambridge: Prentice Hall.

Grier, D. A. (2009). Virtual Walls. *IEEE Computer, 42*(3), 8–12. doi:10.1109/MC.2009.98

Kane, S. (2009). Virtual Judgement: Legal Implications of Online Gaming. *IEEE Security and Privacy, 7*(3), 23–28. doi:10.1109/MSP.2009.81

Kushner, D. (2003). *Masters of Doom: How Two Guys Created an Empire and Transformed Pop Culture.* New York: Random House.

Manovich, L. (2001). *The Language of New Media.* Cambridge: MIT Press.

McLuhan, M. (2013). *Understanding Media. The Extensions of man.* Berkeley: Ginko Press.

Mitra, A. (2010). *Digital Games. Computers at Play.* New York: Infobase Publishing.

Ozturk, G. R. (2014). *Handbook of Research on the Impact of Culture and Society on the Entertaiment Industry*. Hershey: IGI Global. doi:10.4018/978-1-4666-6190-5

Schneider, P., & Eberly, D. H. (2002). *Geometric Tools for Computer Graphics*. San Francisco: Morgan Kaufmann.

Weiss, B. (2009). *Classic Home Video Games, 1985–1988. A Complete Reference Guide*. London: McFarland & Company.

Zeigler, B. P. et al.. (2000). *Theory of Modeling and Simulation*. London: Academic Press.

KEY TERMS AND DEFINITIONS

Interface or Graphical User Interface: A visual way of interaction with a interactive system/computer using items such icons, menues, windows, etc.

Isotopies: Sense lines that act upon the structures. From a semantic point of view lines are drawn which unite several components of the interactive system in order to facilite the comprehension of the rest of the system.

Playability: A set of propierties that describe the user/player experience using a specific game system/video game whose main objective is to provide enjoyement, entertainment and learning strategies, for example.

Semiotics: The study or doctrine of signs, sometimes supposed to be a science of signs but not an engineering, for example.

Video Game: An electronic game that involves human interaction with one or more user/s interface/s to generate audio-visual feedback, for example, on a video device.

APPENDIX

Figure 11. SimCity (1989): first commercial interface (operating system: MS-DOS)

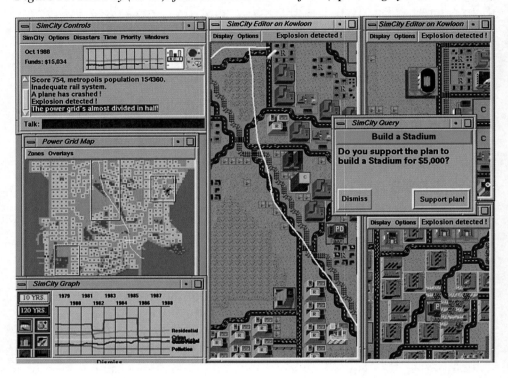

Figure 12. SimCity 2000: second commercial interface (operating sytem: Windows); feedback with illustrations, comic balloons, etc.

Figure 13. SimCity 2000 (1994)

Figure 14. SimCity 3000 (1999)

Figure 15. SimCity 4 (2003)

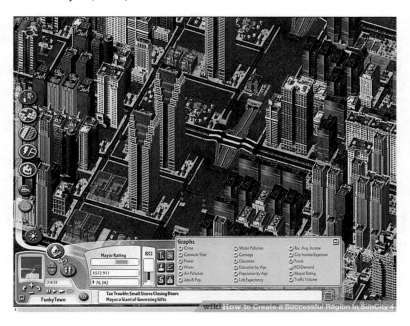

Figure 16. SimCity Societies (2007)

Figure 17. SimCity 5 (2013)

Chapter 5
A Lisibility Assessment for Mobile Phones

Francisco V. Cipolla-Ficarra
Latin Association of Human-Computer Interaction, Spain & International Association of Interactive Communication, Italy

Jacqueline Alma
Electronic Arts, Canada

Jim Carré
University of the Netherlands Antilles, Curaçao

ABSTRACT

In the current chapter the lisibility or readability factor in mobile phones is analyzed, together with other components of usability engineering, communicability and ergonomics. Besides, we present the first results of readability in multimedia mobile phones for adult users, between classical mobile phones and the last generation of multimedia phone devices. In both cases the experiments have been carried out with the low price-range of those devices.

INTRODUCTION

Currently there is a tendency to range the potential users of the new technologies in relation to their date of birth, thus generating pseudosets of potential knowledge for the use of ICT (information and communication technology) devices. The term 'pseudo' refers to the fact that these classifications respond

DOI: 10.4018/978-1-5225-3437-2.ch005

rather to mercantilists factors of the sciences than to the purely scientific aspects. Some examples are given in (Cipolla-Ficarra, 2014). Those mercantilists factors interrelate with the workplace market, where in principle, the people who were not born in the digital era are theoretically not capable of the interaction in the new ICTs devices. That is, the greater the age, the more are the communicability problems. However, these communicability programs belong to the set of lack of heuristic information in the process of design of the interactive systems, whether they are of the latest generation or not. For example, evaluating the size and disposition of the keys in the different phone models on the screen of the device, the wealth of the interactive design of the device, in adapting quickly and automatically vertical or horizontal reading of those keys, etc. Factors of the interactive design must be constantly evaluated in the design process to boost the communicability between the user and those multimedia devices for telecommunications.

Through the lisibility or readability notion of semiotics, it is possible to detect quickly the communicability, for instance. Lisible is a French word meaning legible or readable but often translated "readerly". Roland Barthes (Nöth, 1995) used this term to identify a particular kind of text, one in which the reader is called upon to do nothing more than consume a pregiven meaning.. The reading of the components of the interface brings about that an adult user, in our work, can interact in an intuitive way the first time that he/she gets in touch with the phone device. The notion of readability is superior to the quality attributes within usability engineering, aimed at multimedia systems, such as prediction, self-evidence and the transparency of meaning. Now the readability has a bidirectional relationship with the self-evidence and transparency of meaning quality attributes.

Briefly, the prediction attribute is the skill of the user to anticipate the meaning of a structure or the result of an operation, previously analyzing a structure or a similar operation but in different situations. The transparency of the meaning is the use of terms (mainly), images and sounds within the interface that do not bring up ambiguities between the level of content and the level of expression (these two levels are related to the notion of significant and signification. Both concepts have their origin in linguistics and that later on have been studied in semiotics or semiology). The elements that make up the interface are interrelated: thus accomplishing a function of bolstering of the signification (Saussure, 1983; Cipolla-Ficarra, 1995). Finally, the self-evidence is related to the ability of inference of the user towards the different components of the system. When self-evidence exists, the user has the feeling of gaining time in the navigation, since the signification is anticipated and the purpose of the components are presented to the user the first time (Cipolla-Ficarra, 1997). The anticipation of the knowledge has a positive influence on motivation. Besides, self-evidence is essential to increase the confidence among those users who lack any previous experience in the use of multimedia systems, which generates a greater motivation to keep on using the system.

The readability of the use in both traditional and multimedia mobile phones has been an attribute which has boosted the democratization of those devices in almost the whole planet, irrespective of whether the users belong or not to the biological set of those born in the digital era.

HYPERTEXT, MULTIMEDIA, AND HYPERMEDIA: DESIGN MODELS

The design of interactive systems has entailed a series of models since the late 80s and early 90s, whether they are based on the aspects of the databases, presentation of the information on the computer screen, programming languages, etc. In short, some of those "classical" design models related to use with their main components and/or qualities are:

Garg

The research and the developments of Garg are aimed at multimedia documents (Garg, 1988), especially those systems capable of considering the duration cycles of the contents of electronic documents. Garg develops a model of a mathematical kind in hypermedia where several stages of abstraction are established, which allows for more detailed research. The goal of the system is the elaboration and search of documents made up by several segments: that is, a system capable of detecting if the creation of said systems was independent or joined and indicates besides the several versions of the documents. It regards hypermedia as a whole, which is made up in turn by several subsets: dominion (definition of the types), objects of information (defining the instances of the types, that is, the contents), predicates (that serve for the representation of the relations, that is, the links), and attributes (properties of the objects which may be used to identify the objects from several perspectives). The search of the information is carried out in two ways:

- Through the navigation across the structure of the objects (through the connectors or links).
- With relation to the contents, that is, through the use of key words.

Tompa

Tompa defines a model called "database aimed at the websites" (Tompa, 1989) –in fact it is a multimedia/hypermedia database. The author starts from the hypertextual networks notions and of the limitations of certain graphs models, especially the direct with a label. Some of these limitations are briefly described next. In this model, each node is a unity related to a page of content and moreover the data substructures cannot be correctly depicted. Another limitation is that the structure of the model cannot be separated from the contents. The navigation also presents difficulties given its limitations since in every moment there is only an active node, whose content is visualized. Nevertheless, the user of the system, when starting from the active node, can only be directed at another node, which previously has been selected in the connection.

The Tompa model uses hypergraphs directed and labelles for the design of hypertextual networks (Tompa, 1989). A hypergraph is made up by a finite set of nodes and another of edges. These edges are made up by a finite set of nodes. The set makes feasible the separation between content and structure, and it also signals the composed objects and links n-arios. In this kind of links, the origin or the destination is made up by a set of components. For instance, different nodes can share a same page, for which the nodes are depicted with a circle and the contents with a square in the graphic of Figure 1.

A first node is allocated to a single content as in the case of A. In contrast, the content of B is allocated to two different nodes. In the case of C, the content has links n-arios in several labels C1, C2, since they keep between themselves a relationship (see elipsis).

HB1

The HB1 is a semantic model of data aimed at the connections, developed by Leggett, J. and Schnase, J. (Leggett & Schnase, 1994; Schnase, et al., 1993). The connections are considered by these authors as the key factor of the hypermedia systems. Leggett, J. And Scnase, J. created a system of management for the databases in hypermedia called HB1. The HB1 was

Figure 1. Hypergraph of a document

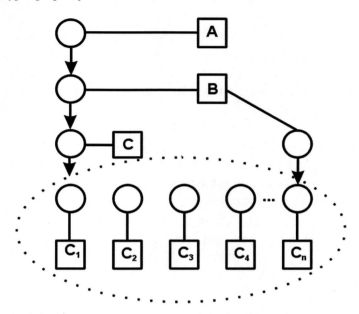

elaborated for a system of management of semantic IBM databases, hence the initials Hyperbase, related to the hyperbase management system .

In the conclusions of the research carried out by both authors they highlight the fact that in the semantic models more structural primitives are obtained than in the traditional models. The relational model is designed basically for the search and the storage of the information, leaving in the background the representation of the links among them. In the HB1, six components are used for the design of the hypermedia systems: associations, connectors, components, continuous selections, anchors and applications. Next a short explanation of each one of these components:

- The applications are the hypermedia programs.
- The components are the contents of the applications.
- The continuous selections are data areas in the components to which the connectors will be joined.
- The anchors and the connectors are calculation processes which define from the perspective of behaviour the presentation of the data and the passing of the connections, the anchors are associated to the continuous selections and the links are joined to the anchors.

The structural relationships existing between continuous selections, anchors and links are depicted by the associations. The semantic model allows the division between objects, connections among objects and their performance (Date, 1990; Peckham & Maryanski, 1988). The structure of the semantic model contains the following primitives: entity (an object), propriety (element of information which distinguished an entity), interrelations (entity which serves to connect between themselves two or more entities) and subtypes (the type of entity Y is a subtype of the type of entity X and only if all Y is an X) (Date, 1990). These primitives can be combined in several ways and without restrictions. Besides, with the semantic models it is possible to define in a structural way the relational integrity links among the data. That is, those criteria which are defined as operations of incorporation, erasing and modification of objects. These operations affect the interrelated objects in such a way which make the data set consistent.

AHM

The AHM model (Amsterdam Hypermedia Model) is an extension of the Dexter model. In the AHM, in contrast to the Dexter model, a stress is made on the temporal aspect and the semantics of the navigation (Hardman et al., 1988). The notion of time in the hypermedia systems is defined through primitives for the synchronization of the active data such as video, animation and sound. The semantic notion of navigation is related to the links. In the definition of the temporal aspect of a hypermedia system, the AHM model considers the presentation of the simple and composed components. In the simple components is taken into account the information of the time of duration of the data contained in the sound, the video and so on while in the composed components the information about the temporal relationships and the synchronization existing among the contents of the components is added.

In the AHM some variables are introduced related to the presentation and which are not related directly to the components, but rather to the general use such as are the channels. A channel is an abstract outlet device for the presentation of data, that is, with a channel for the text, the size and the type of the characters to be used for physical visualization can be defined, with a channel for the audio, wherein the level of volume of the audition can be defined, etc. Each simple component refers to a single channel, which will later on be used at the moment of the activation (runtime), that is, when the data are presented.

Dexter

The Dexter model (Dexter Hypertext Reference Model) starts from the analysis of the hypertext and hypermedia systems (Horn, 1989), such as: Augment, HyperCard (Horn, 1989), Concordia/Document Examiner (Horn, 1989), KMS (Akscyn, 1988), Intermedia (Yankelovich, et al., 1988), NoteCards (Halasz, 1988). The analysis of these systems allows one to detect the most relevant primitives of the systems. The purpose of these primitives is to establish a common language for the description. The Dexter model regards as a hypermedia system that which is constituted by three levels: the activation level (run-time), the storage level and with-component level. Next a summary of the basic characteristics of the levels is made.

One of the most outstanding aspects of the model is the level of storage. The level of storage allows one to describe the structure of a hypermedia system as a set of components which are interrelated by the links. The components are containers of data which may be a text, a graphic, a sound, etc. A component can be simple or composed. A simple component is that which contains only data, whereas a composed component is that which contains both simple and composed data. The links serve to connect two or three components. Within the storage level no description is made of the internal structure of the data, but it is in the level of internal component. The level of internal components has been created for the definition of the content and of the internal structure of the data. From that point of view, the Dexter model admits the use of other models for the modelling of data. In this model, a difference is established between the level of storage and the internal component level. Besides, the concept of anchor is introduced. The anchor is the mechanism with which you may refer to specific environments or portions of information from within a component.

The level of activation describes the dynamic performance of a hypermedia, defining the general mechanisms of presentation of the information. However, there is no reference to the details of the interface (Apple, 1992). In contrast, the interface is taken into account because of the relationship that exists between the storage level and the activation level with the concept of specific presentation. This specific presentation is linked to the components, for which reason it is memorized at the same level of storage. Consequently, the presentation of a component is not only a specific function of the used navigation instrument, but besides it is a propriety of the component itself and/or the pathway of access to the information.

MacWeb

The MacWeb model allows to resolve the disorientation problem in the navigation process. This problem is due to a design issue, since the mental model of the system is scarcely intuitive and predictable. MacWeb is based on the orientation to objects where the types (kinds) are used to understand the hypertext, whereas the instances are used to keep the information (content), of the hypertext. The primitives of MacWeb are: links, link types, chunks, chunk types, anchors and webs. Next a short description is made of these primitives:

- The links are binary relationships between two anchors. Each link is an instance of a type of link (link type). The links are addressable, that is, they have an origin anchor and a destination anchor, and the transit between both at the moment of the navigation can be carried out in both directions.
- The chunks are the information nodes of the hypertext networks. Each chunk is an instance of the chunk types.
- The anchors are logical elements which contain the links among the portions of the information of the nodes or as in this case chunks of the hypertext. Besides, the anchors are active, that is, they can be selected to follow an associated link.
- The webs are a set of nodes and connections which can have any topology of representation with direct graphs. Each hypertext MacWeb is defined by two networks. These networks are those of the types and the instances. One network of the types can be defined as that network which is constituted by the types of chunks, which are united by the types of links. This type of networks are generally used to maintain a description of the hypertext. Whereas a network of instances can be defined as that network which is made up by chunks, links and anchors. These networks are used to maintain the information of the hypertext.

The types within the model can be organized in classes and subclasses and the same as to the orientation of objects. The relationships of sub-types existing between two different classes are depicted through types of links, existing for this a type of specific link called inheritance or inherit (inherits).

MODELS AND INTERACTIVE SYSTEMS

The readability of the information on the screen of the mobile phones started with the SMS (Short Message Service). Messages could be read on monochromatic screens of the early commercial models. With the use of the color of the screens and the icons that reading had to keep on being direct (e.g., Windows 3.1, '95, etc.), thus avoiding ambiguity and vagueness between significant and signification. Currently, for instance, the degree of ambiguity and vagueness of the icons used, prevent the correct use of the devices of last generation multimedia mobile phones. At the moment, where a user has a problem of use of an interactive system, a regress of the conception of the design of the interactive systems automatically takes place, towards the late 80s and early 90s (Chiu, 2013; Kurniawan, 2007). This regression is due to the fact that we are referring to the basic principles of usability engineering, especially that which refers to the ease of use.

Although other models of interactive systems design exist, the ease of use in the multimedia mobile phones is non-existent in some cases, as is described in the section of the obtained results of the evaluations carried out in the current work. Each one of the design models briefly described is focused on access to information, storage of multimedia data, synchronization and so on of the dynamic and/or static means which make up a hypermedia, multimedia system and hypertext. The problem is that those models of design have not been democratized in the context of the designers. That is, generators of interactive systems who resort to commercial software for the realization of the multimedia applications or programming languages. An example is the use of a same technical language among programmers and other participants in the productive process to refer to the different components of a multimedia system. Theoretically, a good model of design should be uniform conceptually re: the different components of the system to speed up the task of finding mistakes in the design stage of a multimedia system.

The faster the mistakes are located, the less will be the costs for the production of the system. This lack of uniformity in the denomination of the components of a multimedia system has its origins in human factors. There is a sort of rejection of the term model, because it entails accepting a set of rules. Traditionally, in the creative or artistic context of the multimedia system, a greater rejection of those rules arises. Besides, in the last decade, there was a tendency to generate models for each one of the aspects which converge on the multimedia systems. Those models were related to the hardware used, the software, etc. In the case of some denominations which coincided with the name of cities, that is due to the place where they had been generated, that is, where the research centre was located. However, the name of a city, for instance, does not mean that said model has an application or universal following by the designers. Today the word "Milano" (capital of the Lombardi region, in Italy) cannot be regarded as synonymous with "universal model", although it has been an industrial focus of clothes in the 20th century, for example. Besides, "fashion" and the "model" are totally different notions from one other. Although in the surroundings of the local educational mercantilism both notions tend to merge, it is a mistake when models are generated in those places, where educational mercantilism prevails over the sciences. These are some of the examples, which lead the designers, evaluators, programmers and so on to use the primitive notions of the hypertext systems enunciated by Ted Nelson (Nelson, 1993). The use of these primitives has been positive for us in the development of off-line and on-line hypermedia systems, methods and evaluation of quality techniques, etc. (Cipolla-Ficarra, 1995; Cipolla-Ficarra, 1997)

HEURISTIC EVALUATION WITH ADULT USERS

In the process of heuristic evaluations carried out inside the lab we have worked with a group of adult users and computer science experts. Our universe of study has been made up by 12 people, whose ages oscillate between the 30–50 years, without disabilities and with over 10 years experience in the use of computers. The universe of study of mobile phone devices is made up by two models: a classical one and another of last generation multimedia or "modern" model, that is, 12 new phones, of each one of the models. Both belong to the low-cost range from the point of view of costs, that is, models which reduce the digital divide. The "classical" model (LG-A170) has been chosen due to the excellent results obtained in a heuristic evaluation for adult and elderly users. The interested reader can look up those results in the following bibliographical references (Cipolla-Ficarra, 1997; Barnes & Meyers, 2011; Cipolla-Ficarra, 2014). The second model has been randomly chosen, through a draw, among the following set of models belonging to offers and special promotions in Portugal, Spain, France and Italy. In short, a quality products at an economical price:

- HTC Desire 500,
- HTC One.
- Huawei Ascend P6,
- LG G2,
- NGM Dynamic STYLO+,
- NGM Forward PRIME,
- Nokia Lumia 625,
- Nokia Lumia 925,
- S4,
- Samsung Galaxy Core,
- Samsung Galaxy S III mini,
- Samsung Galaxy S III,
- Samsung Galaxy S4 mini,
- Samsung Galaxy Young,
- Samsung Galaxy, and
- Sony Xperia Z.

The model that has resulted from that draw is the following (Samsung Galaxy Young):

None of the users taking part in the experiment had previously used those phone models. The experiments carried out in the lab consisted in making a simple call from each one of the mobile phones ("modern" model and "classical" model). The time used has been timed in minutes (mean). An operation has been divided in three stages or tasks. Task #1: preparation of the phone device (opening of the device to insert the chip of the card and the battery); task #2: turning it on for the first time, insertion and modification of the PIN (Personal Identification Number), and finally, task #3: realization of a local call to a nine-figure phone number. Besides, each one of the participants had a computer at hand, with an internet connection. The heuristic evaluation techniques used have been direct observation and videotaped sessions. The results obtained are in the following graphics:

The results obtained show that the adult users, with experience in the use of computers, require a high amount of minutes to carry out a phone call with a last generation multimedia phone. The problems detected in the current study can be divided into two great sets. The first, ergonomic, such as the opening of the back cover of the phone to insert the chip and the battery, and also its closure without damaging it. A total of three phones have ended up with that cover damaged and another four have not been opened to avoid damage. Five users have used internet to find videos about the opening of

Figure 2. Phone device belonging to the economic range or low-cost for the potential users

Figure 3. Mobile phone: a classical LG-A170 model

the phone (YouTube, for instance). The second is understanding of the text and/or icons, that is, readability. Locating the icon and then the option for the change of PIN took more than ten minutes. Once it is locate, then the change of PIN, a task that all the users carried out in less than three minutes.

Figure 4. Results task #1: time used to set the phone into motion for the first time

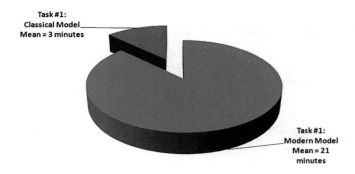

Figure 5. Results task #2: time used for turning it on and change of PIN

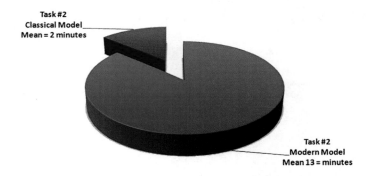

Carrying out the phone call was not intuitive in the second model, since it involved first carrying out some trials by 80% of the users, until they finally contacted the local number. These inconveniences were not detected in the first model, and the average used for the turning on and change of the PIN is two minutes, and to dial the phone number, a minute and a half.

LESSONS LEARNED

Having to resort to the internet to see how a mobile phone is opened, which is used for the first time, denotes a failure in the industrial design of these devices. The breaking of the components of the phone, in the attempt to open it, was confirmed by data gathered in the current study. Although there is a tendency to the diminution of the sequential reading with the momentum of the hypertext systems, the handbooks which accompany the new technologies

Figure 6. Results task #3: time used for dialling the local phone number

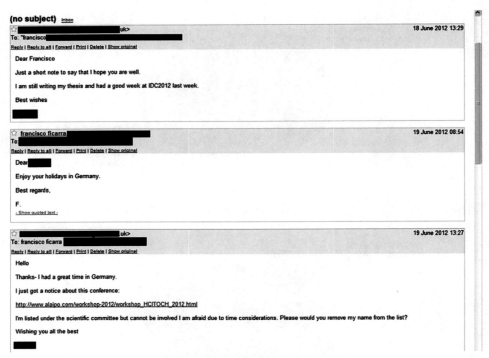

devices have considerably reduced the total of pages, due to the possibility of storing that information in the Internet. However, that access is not universal, nor free for millions of users. Consequently, there is a readability problem in the scarce information in paper or analogical support, and also in the textual and iconographic options which the operative system of the mobile phone offers, when it is used for the first time. Although the minimalism of the interactive design is positive in the interfaces of computers, tablet PC, and so on, in the current study it has been demonstrated that the use of reduced textual messages in the operative systems of the multimedia mobile phones in the era of the expansion of communicability may be negative for adult users, with experience in computers, since they do not have enough textual information, denotative and comprehensible, neither in the analogical nor in the digital support. The use problems of the current mobile phones models show that many notions of the design models of hypermedia, multimedia and hypermedia systems, related to the quality of the software, the human computer interaction, the style guides for interfaces, etc., have not been applied since the late 80s. Besides, the analogical information, that is, in paper support, is so scarce that the readability problem reactivates the old issues of the usability of the interactive systems, which had been theoretically left behind in the new millennium. In other words, the usability and ergonomics, derived from the industrial design of these new devices, are generating a temporal regression of almost a quarter of a century in the interaction user and new technologies. In future investigations, the results obtained will be verified through the study of other devices for mobile phones such as the Tablet PC and the medium range (cost) of the multimedia mobile phones.

CONCLUSION

At the start of the new millennium there was a tendency in the south of Europe to own two or more cell phones simultaneously (one for the workplace and another for the family, friends, etc.). However, that multiple possession is not synonymous with a greater social communication, as it happened with the fruition of the traditional means, that is, movie houses or the family gatherings to listen to a radio drama in the last century. The problems of usability, ergonomics, linked to a negative lisibility, can lead the user of a new multimedia mobile phone to participate unwittingly in the phenomenon of autism in the current era of global communications. In the current work, we have seen how the advantages of freedom and socialization of the individual which the new means of interactive communication implicitly entail, not only for vocal, audiovisual, social communication (web 2.0) are lacking because of the complexity of access to the contents and degree of complexity or functionalities of said means among certain potential users. In our case of study, a universe of adults had experience in the computer environment of 10 years or more. It is necessary that the textual information, with an excellent lisibility, is present in the analogical and digital supports of the new devices to quickly overcome the eventual problems, in the first contact between users of multimedia systems with multimedia mobile phones: which belong to the set of the last technological generation within the context of the ICTs.

ACKNOWLEDGMENT

We should like to express special appreciation to Maria Ficarra. A special acknowledgment to Alejandra Quiroga, Donald Nilson, and Carlos for the valuable help and remarks.

REFERENCES

Akscyn, R., McCracken, D. L., & Yoder, E. A. (1988). KMS: A Distributed Hypermedia System for Managing Knowledge in Organizations. *Communications of the ACM*, *31*(7), 820–835. doi:10.1145/48511.48513

Apple. (1992). *Macintosh Human Interface Guidelines*. New York: Addison-Wesley.

Barnes, M., & Meyers, N. (2011). *Mobile Phones: Technology, Networks and User Issues*. Nova Publishers.

Chiu, D. K. W. (2013). *Mobile and Web Innovations in Systems and Service-Oriented Engineering*. Hershey, PA: IGI Global. doi:10.4018/978-1-4666-2470-2

Cipolla-Ficarra, F. (1995). A Method that Improves the Design of Hypermedia: Semiotics. In *Proceedings International Workshop Hypermedia Design*. Montpellier: Springer-Verlag.

Cipolla-Ficarra, F. (1997). Evaluation of Multimedia Components. In *Proceedings International Conference on Multimedia Computing and Systems*. New York: IEEE Computer Society. doi:10.1109/MMCS.1997.609769

Cipolla-Ficarra, F. (2014). *Advanced Research and Trends in New Technologies, Software, Human-Computer Interaction, and Communicability*. Hershey, PA: IGI Global. doi:10.4018/978-1-4666-4490-8

Date, C. (1990). *An Introduction to Database Systems*. Addison-Wesley.

Garg, P. (1988). Abstraction Mechanisms in Hypertext. *Communications of the ACM*, *31*(7), 862–870. doi:10.1145/48511.48516

Halasz, F. (1988). Reflections on Notecards: Seven Issues for the Next Generation of Hypermedia Systems. *Communications of the ACM*, *31*(7), 836–852. doi:10.1145/48511.48514

Halasz, F., & Schwartz, M. (1990). The Dexter reference model. *Proceedings of the First Hypertext NIST Standardization Workshop*, 95-133.

Hardman, L., Bulterman, D. C. A., & van Rossum, G. (1994). The Amsterdam Hypermedia Model: Adding Time and Context to the Dexter Model. *Communications of the ACM*, *37*(2), 50–62. doi:10.1145/175235.175239

Horn, R. (1989). *Mapping Hypertext*. Waltham, MA: Lexington Press.

Kurniawan, S. (2007). Mobile Phone Design for Older Persons. *Interaction, 14*(4), 24–25. doi:10.1145/1273961.1273979

Leggett, J., & Schnase, J. (1994). Viewing Dexter with Open Eyes. *Communications of the ACM, 37*(2), 76–86. doi:10.1145/175235.175241

Nelson, T. (1993). *Literary Machines*. Sausalito: Mindful Press.

Nöth, W. (1995). *Handbook of Semiotics*. Bloomington, IN: Indiana University Press.

Peckham, J., & Maryanski, F. (1988). Semantic Data Models. *ACM Computing Surveys, 20*(3), 153–189. doi:10.1145/62061.62062

Saussure, F. (1983). *Course in General Lingistics*. New York: McGraw-Hill.

Schnase, J. (1993). Semantic Database Modeling: Survey, Applications, and Research Issues. *ACM Transactions on Information Systems, 11*(1), 27–50. doi:10.1145/151480.151521

Tompa, F. (1989). A Data Model for Flexible Hypertext Database Systems. *ACM Transactions on Information Systems, 7*(1), 85–100. doi:10.1145/64789.64993

Yankelovich, N., Haan, B. J., Meyrowitz, N. K., & Drucker, S. M. (1988). Intermedia: The Concept and the Construction of a Seamless Information Environment. *IEEE Computer, 21*(1), 81–96. doi:10.1109/2.222120

ADDITIONAL READING

Brusilovsky, P., & Maybury, M. (2002). From Adaptive Hypermedia to Adaptive Web. *Communications of the ACM, 45*(5), 30–33. doi:10.1145/506218.506239

Carey, D. (1996). Is Software Quality Intrinsic, Subjective, or Relational? *Software Engineering Notes, 21*(1), 74–75. doi:10.1145/381790.565678

Chilamkurti, N. (2013). *Security, Design and Architecture for Broadband and Wireless Network Technologies*. Hershey: IGI Global. doi:10.4018/978-1-4666-3902-7

Dieter, R. (1990). Design Measurement: Some Lessons Learned. *IEEE Software*, *7*(2), 17–25. doi:10.1109/52.50770

Dunn, R. (1990). *Software Quality: Concepts and Plans*. New Jersey: Prentice Hall.

Fenton, N. (1991). *Software Metrics: A Rigorous Approach*. New York: Chapman & Hall.

Fernandes, T. (1995). *Global Interface Design: A guide to Designing International User Interfaces*. Boston: Academic Press.

Garrand, T. (1997). *Writing for Multimedia*. Boston: Focal Press.

Grimes, J., & Potel, M. (1991). What is Multimedia? *IEEE Computer Graphics*, *11*(1), 49–52. doi:10.1109/38.67700

Henderson, R., Smith, M. C., Podd, J., & Varela-Alvarez, H. (1995). A Comparison of the Four Prominent User-based Methods for Evaluation the Usability of Computer Software. *Ergonomics*, *38*(10), 2030–2044. doi:10.1080/00140139508925248

Mitchell, W., & McCullough, M. (1995). *Digital Design Media*. New York: Van Nostrand Reinhold.

Nielsen, J. (1992). The Usability Engineering Life Cycle. *IEEE Software*, *25*(3), 12–22.

Reisman, S. (1991). Developing Multimedia Applications. *IEEE Computer Graphics and Applications*, *11*(4), 52–57. doi:10.1109/38.126881

Virzi, R. (1997). Usability Inspection Methods. In *Handbook of Human Computer Interaction* (pp. 705–716). Amsterdam: Elsevier. doi:10.1016/B978-044481862-1.50095-9

Wiklund, M. (1994). *Usability in Practice*. London: Academic Press.

Yi, J. Ch. (2010). User-Research-Driven Mobile User Interface Innovation: A Success Story from Seul. *Interaction*, *17*(1), 58–61. doi:10.1145/1649475.1649487

KEY TERMS AND DEFINITIONS

Communicability: A qualitative communication between the user and the interactive system, such as mobile phones, augmented reality, immersion multimedia, hypermedia, among others. The extent to which an interactive system successfully conveys its functionality to the user.

Hypermedia: A nonlinear medium of information which includes graphics, audio, video, animation, text, hyperlinks, etc., in other words, it is a system in which various forms of information, as data, text, graphics, video, and audio (dynamics and static media), are linked together by a hypertext program.

Hypertext: Non-linear text in which block of linear text are cross-referenced by links.

Lisible: A French word meaning legible or readable but often translated "readerly". The reading of the components of the interface brings about that an user, can interact in an intuitive way the first time that he/she gets in touch with the mobile multimedia system, for example, a phone device. The notion of readability is superior to the quality attributes within usability engineering, aimed at multimedia systems, such as prediction, self-evidence and the transparency of meaning.

Multimedia: The combined use (intersection) of several media, as sound and/or video/animation in computer applications. Traditionally, is content that uses a combination of different content forms such as text, audio, images (photography, maps, etc.), animations (2D, 3D, 2D and 3D, etc.), video and interactive content.

Chapter 6
Kernel of the Labyrinths Hypertextuals

Francisco V. Cipolla-Ficarra
Latin Association of Human-Computer Interaction, Spain & International Association of Interactive Communication, Italy

Alejandra Quiroga
Universidad Nacional de La Pampa, Argentina

Valeria M. Ficarra
Latin Association of Human-Computer Interaction, Spain & International Association of Interactive Communication, Italy

ABSTRACT

In the chapter, the semantemes are amalyzed which serve as dychotomic links in the core of the online links with the negative goal of online interactive communication. We present the importance of literary recourses to describe or locate the way to be followed until reaching the origin of a node or set of them, which have been intertwined among themselves in the shape of a labyrinth with the purpose of disguising illicit deeds in the network, such as can be online attacks. In the analysis is presented a practical case and the strategy followed to detect in a reliable and safe way the kernel of those hypertextual labyrinths.

INTRODUCTION

The same as happens with the notion of bit (binary digit), the minimal unit of information used in computer science in any digital device or in information theory, we have the notion of semantemes in linguistics (Eco, 1996; Nöth,

DOI: 10.4018/978-1-5225-3437-2.ch006

1995). A semanteme is a unit of meaning. In other words, a linguistic element that itself expresses as concept and, in turn, is combinable with other such elements. With the bit we can depict two values whatever (0 and 1, for instance), as true or false, open or closed, black or white, north or south, etc. On the face of it, we have the possibility of bifurcating the ways, in the logical diagram of a program, for instance (Farrell, 2013). That is, we are in the face of a decision to be made which leads us to one place or another, in order to achieve the goals of the computer program.

A good computer program is that which uses the least possible number of instructions to reach 100% reliable results in the shortest way possible. As a rule, the shortest way entails gaining time in the information process and besides cut down production costs, if we are inside a factory, for instance. Now through those bifurcations or decision making that the computer carries out, a writer may interrupt the sequential narration of a story and generate a labyrinth which leads us to the core of the plot that he is telling. An excellent example is the work of Jorge Luis Borges (Borges, 1941) *"El jardín de senderos que se bifurcan"* (The Garden of Forking Paths). In this sense, a communicability expert may detect the key elements of the written texts to determine the source of the online attacks. The authors of the messages, their content, the moment and place in which they were sent, the channels of diffusion used, the measure of the consequences beforehand, etc., are sematemes which analyzed as a unit draw ways that fork out, making up a virtual maze in the net, with the purpose of masking the main and secondary goals that have been preordained by the cyberdestroyers before carrying out the attacks. That is, linguistics may serve as a compass in the links of the different nodes of a cyber attack (Cipolla-Ficarra, 2014). Cyber attacks or attacks online are used as synonymous in the current work.

We will examine some of the semantemes in the digital contents that circulate in the Internet. The analysis of a practical case with international ramifications, and across time, allows us to know the kernel of those cyberattacks, and the place where some of those cyberdestroyers are located. In this sense, the notions of hypertext from both the computer science point of view and the literary allows us to collect a series of analysis tools to make up a study technique. Finally, the issue of the psychological or psychiatric aspects of the cyberattackers is not approached in the current work.

BIFURCATION IN HYPERTEXT: A SHORT HISTORIC REVIEW

Although from the computer science point of view in 1945 Vannevar Bush publishes the article "As We May Think" (Kaprow, 1991; Gray, 1996; Nielsen, 1990), we find that in 1941, in the literature of that period, a fantasy, short story called "Ficciones" (Borges, 1941) was published. In both cases the bifurcations in a linearity and the decision making that they involve, would boil down to reading of the analogical or digital information under the form of going from one place to the other (nodes and links), without the need of following a single path (labyrinths).

The problem that was posed by Vannevar Bush was the difficulty of access by the information management media of that time (printed paper and physical files where these were stored, occupying huge spaces), therefore a media is needed that fits better to the way in which the mind works (Bush, 1946): that is, it highlights the associative character of ideas. Said notion breaks away from the sequence of the classification of ideas that was the paradigm of that time. In this way, it presents the two main notions of the hypertext such as the nodes and the links. The need also arises for a system or device which serves as a support to intellectual work. Both aspects of a personal file and of a library had to be combined, that is, a system with a capacity to store large volumes of information in a relational way added to a fast and flexible consultation of all the information (in Figure 2, there is an analogical representation of that consultation). That system was called "memex" (memory extender). The structuring of the information in the memex was characterized by:

- Addition of information to the same document, through notes,
- Association of correlated concepts,
- Direct access to the information through indexes,
- Elaboration of a listing of the links (traits of links), and
- Transfer of the information through links.

Said characteristics generate a change in the concept of the reading in the hypertext reading is an active process which entails writing. The need arises to think of the text as being more "virtual" than physical. When several articles have been assembled to shape a trajectory it is exactly as if physical articles had been gathered from very different sources and they had been bound together to make up a new book. Within that virtuality, the movement through the nodes of the different texts was of a bidirectional character, and besides, a text might have more than a node (see Figure 1). The ideas proposed by Bush remained a theory until in the 60s Douglas C. Engelbart and Theodor H. Nelson developed independently the first hypertextual systems (Gray, 1996; Berners-Lee, 1996).

In that original intersection between computer science and literature it can be said that hypertext is "an electronic text made up of nodes (blocks of texts), which are linked among themselves in a non-sequential way" (The Electronic Labyrinth). Frequently the definition is also intended to incorporate the experience of readers and authors. One of the distinctive characteristics of hypertext is that it provides the reader with many reading itineraries. The freedom of the reader is frequently invoked when non-sequential literature is described, the hypertext would present a network of nodes through which

Figure 1. Cover book: "Literary Machines"

THIS BOOK DESCRIBES THE LEGENDARY AND DARING
PROJECT XANADU, AN INITIATIVE TOWARD
AN INSTANTANEOUS ELECTRONIC LITERATURE:
the most audacious and specific plan for knowledge, freedom and a better world
yet to come out of computerdom; the original (perhaps the ultimate)
HYPERTEXT SYSTEM.

Figure 2. Cover book: "The Garden of Forking Paths"

the readers might travel in all directions. Now the hypertext can also be defined as a system to join screens with diverse information, using for that associative links: that is, it can be characterized as a knowledge purchase system, or of storage and availability of information, or as a structure of data ordination which allows transversal travels, such as those provided by a particularly comprehensive and improved analytical index which collected all kinds of information, not only textual. In this way, the hypertext would not be comparable to a book (and not even to an e-book), but rather to a library or an archive, that is, to complex and potentially infinite systems to guard, have available and get information.

The title of the short story "The Garden of Forking Paths", refers to a labyrinth and to a text that end up being the same thing. The peculiar thing about the book is what follows: whereas in the conventional storytelling a fact is followed by only a consequence and at every single moment only a choice is possible, in this all possibilities are accomplished. In the story, time forks out perpetually towards a myriad of futures.

The scientific community mentions Borges as a forerunner among other authors of hypertextual literature (Landow, 1991; Bolter & Joyce, 1987). The

Figure 3. Representation of the search and/or reading of information in a set of books. The arrows indicate the links and the numbers of the books, their nodes.

Borgian links represent a multilineal advance in literature, but "organized around the traditional philosophical forms of the lineal plot" (Borges, 33). Borges claimed that a good writer creates his predecessors, the new hypertextual writing has also created or reconstructed its tradition and its precedents. The hypertextual literary theory has revised literary history in the search of cases of non-sequential writing in the printed books, and in particular, the narrative. The list of the proto-hypertexts is variegated. "Rayuela" by Julio Cortázar, are "many books", but essentially they are two books: the one that can be read in a conventional way, which the author indicates at the head of the page, and at the end of every chapter (Cortazar, 2006). Other examples are: Il castello

Figure 4. Representation of the search and/or reading of information in an electronic book

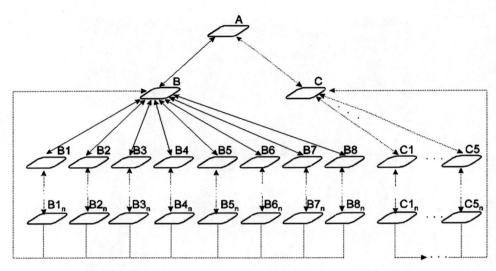

dei destini incrocciati, by Italo Calvino (Calvino, 1999), Dans le labyrinth by Alain Robbe-Grillet (Robbe-Grillet, 1950), Pale Fire by Vladimir Nabokov (Nabokov, 1989), etc.

Although the invention of the term hypertext is attributed to Theodor Holm Nelson (Nelson, 1993) to refer to "the non-sequential writing", it would not materialize until the end of the 80s, with the conformation of the World Wide Web: that is, the international system that allows the publication of systems related among themselves by electronic means. The definition of hypertext by Theodor Nelson (in Literary Machines, Figure 1). Is the most simple and most quoted in the theory of writing. He defined that as a "non-sequential writing, to a text that forks out, which allows the reader to choose and to be able to read better on an interactive screen. In keeping with the popular notion, it is a series of text blocks connected among themselves by nexuses which make up different itineraries for the user". George W. Landow defines the hypertext as the use of the computer to overcome the characteristics of linearity, limitation and static of the traditional written text (Landow, 1991). In contrast to the static book, a hypertext can be made up and read in a non-sequential way, that is, it is a series of electronic nexuses which assemble text fragments internal or external to the work, creating a text which the reader experiences as non-linear, or rather, as multilineal or multisequential (Landow, 1991).

Automatically, these new definitions were expanded in the late 20th century and start of the 21st by the multimedia notions of Negroponte (Negroponte, 1995; Cipolla-Ficarra, F. et al., 2011). Negroponte contended in the 90s the merger of television, print and computer led towards a computer-based multimedia technology. However, there are not only several technologies referring to multimedia and related to the computer, that it is necessary to differentiate to avoid linguistic ambiguities, such as: sequential multimedia, partially interactive multimedia and totally interactive multimedia (Cipolla-Ficarra, 2014), but its project One Laptop per Child (OLPC) intends to generate a global unification of the elemental education of children [19], while at the same time a parochialism of the Garduña Factor (Cipolla-Ficarra, 2014) is building up: i.e. there is a contraposition to the freedom derived from the traditional notion of the hypertext, from the computer science and literary point of view, in the current era of the expansion of communicability, which theoretically allows a wealth of contents and qualitative methods of teaching. Methods and contents which should take into account the aspects of enculturation and transculturation of the users, regardless of their age and the place where they are to be found.

ANALYSIS OF THE DIGITAL SEMANTEMES: THE TROJANS' CASE

Our case study starts with the analysis of the semantemes in the conformation of the "scientific committee", to evaluate the works presented in international events. In it, and through the study of the semantemes, some member will

Figure 5. Unification of education of children for the use of the personal computer and global alienation process of the educational human-computer interaction

fulfill a double negative function, such as the inclusion in the ensemble and later destruction of the group. In other words, a similar behaviour to a Trojan virus (Stanger, 2000). We will call these members "Trojans". The goal was to open a gap in the structure of the international event to demolish it through discredit.

The same as a Trojan, they have opened a door through a recurring sentence: "we didn't know that we belonged to a committee", or "who authorized them to include us in that group", or "every time that you want us to participate you have to ask our authorization", or "you have to erase us urgently because we belong to other committees", etc. However, they had all given a previous writing consent – in a formal or informal way that they would be included in those committees. Besides, by being included in the database of exclusive messages, they got constant information of the international events that took place, the deadlines to submit the works, etc, and undoubtedly they could see their names and surnames in the online listing of the websites where those events were advertised. Then our first task was to retrieve the digital information stored in e-mail format.

In second place, it was observed that the Trojan members of the committee were included in other committees of similar events in Portugal and Spain, mainly, who devoted themselves to contacting one by one the members of the original committee, inviting them to take part in their committees (an example of those messages are in Appendix 1. That is, to become a mirror of the event, through the members (Figure 9). Whereas in the original listing those people appeared in the honorary committee, in the other listing of the plagiarizers, they were simply one more of the bunch of students, professors, employees of the commercial firms related to computer science, etc. That is, mixed with members who didn't even have a PhD, for instance. This is another of the Trojan strategies to discredit the organizers of the international events without the need to resort to illegal practices or ethically null, such as go looking for Trojans in the scientific committee.

Third, we detected that the Trojans, by attending international events related to childhood, interactive design, human-computer interaction, pedagogy, computer art, etc. activate each other and activate the attack. The attack consists in sending simultaneously deterring messages requesting the immediate cancellation from the websites of their names in the "scientific committee". Logs of the universities to which they belong, etc. as it can be seen in the Figures 6, 7, 8, 9, 10, 11 and 12 whose surnames have been hidden because of privacy reasons. Evidently, changing the websites requires time and it is not a task that can be carried out in the fraction of a minute. This

Figure 6. Sending of a message requesting the immediate dropout from the international event from the German city of Bremen, on day June, 19th 2012 at 13:27 time

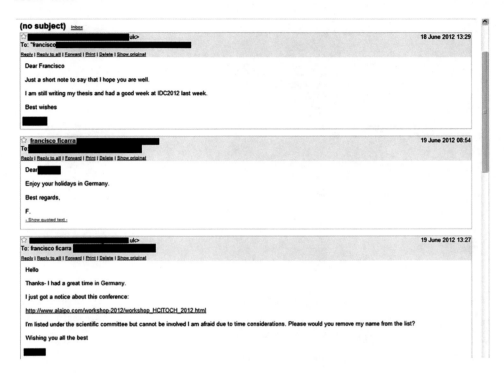

is the attack of the Trojans which most harms the international image of an event, because the potential attendees see how the logos and the members of those universities disappear from the websites.

In the Figures 6 and 7 can be seen the destructive synchronism of two Trojans who participate in the same international conference in Germany –Bremen (June 12 - 15, 2012).

Fourth, a diachronic examination makes apparent that the Trojan groups belonging to Dutch, American universities etc., behave in the same way as the Trojans from Finnish and Scottish universities. In the Figures 6 and 7 can be seen how the Trojans were already present in the "scientific committees" and that they have activated themselves quickly for the attack, to the request of the leaders of the parochialism (Cipolla-Ficarra, 2014) to which they belong. It is striking how these latter Trojans have also attacked on the same dates in which the same German international conference of 2012 took place, in the previous edition from the city of Barcelona (Spain).

Figure 7. Message received where is requested the discharge from the same event of the Figure 6, sent from the German of Bremen, on day June, 19th 2012 at 13:37 time

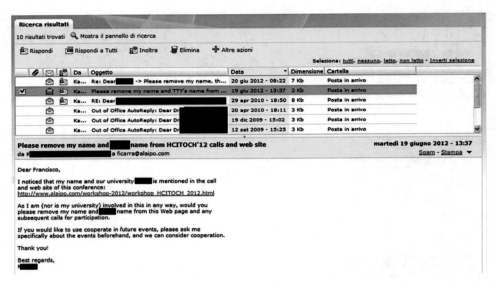

Finally, the University of Twente from which the Trojan requested his/her immediate discharge from the committee (Figure 12 –Appendix 1) is that which together with the Universidade Aberta (Portuguese Open University), they devote themselves to generate mirrors of international events to destroy them, through the trivialization of the contents such as the doubling of the members of the "scientific committee".

These are the first four points that we have been able to detect through a diachronic analysis of the somatemes by communicability specialists. All the examples are true, and they are presented in partial obscurity in some of their parts in the figures to keep the anonymity of the authors.

LESSONS LEARNED

The case study makes apparent the dichotomous nexuses which exist in the structure of the attacks which a priori may appear as isolated cases. However, the diachronic analysis through the sementemes makes apparent the presence of the Garduña Factor, in the parochialism of the Trojans. Evidently these attacks are human factors and social factors which destroy the democratization of the information society, slow down the advance of the ICTs and discourage the neutrality of R&D. Those attacks are very well planned from the start and there is no computer system which may detect the presence of these Trojans because even the written text they send is false 100%, as can be the messages celebrating the incorporation in a "scientific committee", and with the passing of time another message insulting to those who have inserted him in that scientific committee. These Trojan patterns of behaviour can only be detected through the main notions of the hypertext, logical programming, linguistics, semiotics, the categories of interactive design and diachronic analysis of the text as well as the analysis of speech. Currently there is no computer system which can foresee them. However, it is feasible starting from the collected data to establish the first psychological profiles of the behaviour of the Trojans. Although they work in a single core or kernel, to destroy whatever their leaders ask them to destroy, and protected by the labyrinths of the network, it will be possible to set up heuristic prevention techniques to those attacks, excluding beforehand the Trojans from the scientific, local, national, regional and international context. Finally and fortunately, Borges and your book "The Garden of Forking Paths" (Borges, 1941; Borges, 1970) were thus a source of inspiration for a real, beatiful and very big labyrinths project (Mariotti, Biondetti & Ricci, 2013) in Fontanellato, near to Parma, Italy (Appendix 2).

CONCLUSION

Once again can be verified the validity of the static written text as a valuable means for a reliable and economic analysis in the interactive systems. In this case, to establish links in the great labyrinth which is the network, allowing it to detect the places and who have a destructive behaviour and who profit temporally from the apparent anonymity offered by the net. In this occasion, we have not resorted to any special software related to computer safety to detect the attacks, but to the minimal element of meaning, such as sementemes. Evidently, it is a study which has focused on the examination of actions already carried out, which can go back in time to days, months or years. Now it is a matter of generating mechanisms or techniques to prevent them. For this purpose, we intend to establish the common denominator of harmful behaviour. The damage that those attacks cause from the economic and social point of view are incalculable, because they spoil the future of future generations, that is to say, the potential users of interactive systems. Currently it has been detected that the Trojan kernel is related to the technological future for the potential users of the new technologies (children and teenagers) starting from the end of the current decade (2020). In short, users and key interactive contents (entertainment and education) related to the ICTs sector in the short run.

ACKNOWLEDGMENT

We should also like to extend a word of thanks to Maria Ficarra. Besides, a special acknowledgment to Sonia Flores, Jim Carré, Donald Nilson, and Carlos for the valuable collaboration.

REFERENCES

Berman, F. (2008). Got Data? A Guide to Data Preservation in the Information Age. *Communications of the ACM, 51*(12), 50–56. doi:10.1145/1409360.1409376

Berners-Lee, T. (1996). WWW: Past, Present, and Future. *IEEE Computer, 29*(10), 79–85. doi:10.1109/2.539724

Bolter, D., & Joyce, M. (1987). Hypertext and Creative Writing. In *Proceedings Hypertext '87* (pp. 41–50). New York: ACM Press. doi:10.1145/317426.317431

Borges, J. (1941). *El Jardín de senderos que se bifurcan. In Ficciones*. Buenos Aires: Editorial Sur. (in Spanish)

Borges, J. (1970). *Labyrinths*. Harmondsworth, UK: Penguin.

Bush, V. (1946). *As We May Think*. Washington, DC: Endless Horizons – Public Affairs Press.

Calvino, I. (1999). *Il castello dei destini incrocciati*. Milano: Mondadori. (in Italian)

Cipolla-Ficarra, F. (2011). *Advances in Dynamic and Static Media for Interactive Systems: Communicability, Computer Science and Design*. Bergamo: Blue Herons Editions.

Cipolla-Ficarra, F. (2014). *Advanced Research and Trends in New Technologies, Software, Human-Computer Interaction, and Communicability*. Hershey, PA: IGI Global. doi:10.4018/978-1-4666-4490-8

Cortazar, J. (2006). *La Rayuela*. Madrid: Santillana Ediciones. (in Spanish)

Eco, U. (1996). *A Theory of Semiotics*. Bloomington, IN: Indiana University Press.

Farrell, J. (2013). *Programming Logic and Design*. Boston: Course Technology - Cenage Learning.

Gray, J. (1996). Evolution of Data Management. *IEEE Computer, 29*(10), 47–58. doi:10.1109/2.539719

Kaprow, A. (1991). *New Media Applications in Art and Design*. New York: ACM Siggraph.

Landow, G. (1991). *Hypermedia and Literary Studies*. Cambridge, MA: The MIT Press.

Mariotti, G., Biondetti, L., & Ricci, F. M. (2013). *Labyrinths: The Art of the Maze*. New York: Rizzoli.

Nabokov, V. (1989). *Pale Fire*. New York: Vintage International.

Negroponte, N. (1995). *Being Digital*. New York: Knopf.

Nelson, T. (1993). *Literary Machines*. Sausalito: Mindful Press.

Nielsen, J. (1990). *Hypertext and Hypermedia*. San Diego, CA: Academic Press.

Nöth, W. (1995). *Handbook of Semiotics*. Bloomington, IN: Indiana University Press.

Robbe-Grillet, A. (1960). *In the Labyrinth*. New York: Grove Press.

Stanger, J. (2000). *E-mail Virus Protection Handbook: Protect your E-mail from Viruses, Tojan Horses, and Mobile Code Attacks*. Rockland: Syngress.

ADDITIONAL READING

Chilamkurti, N. (2013). *Security, Design and Architecture for Broadband and Wireless Network Technologies*. Hershey: IGI Global. doi:10.4018/978-1-4666-3902-7

Cipolla-Ficarra, F. (2015). *Web Attacks, Security Computer Science and Prochialism of the Cyber Destructors*. Bergamo: Blue Herons Editions.

Cipolla-Ficarra, F., Ficarra, V. M., & Cipolla-Ficarra, M. (2012). New Technologies of the Information and Communication: Analysis of the Constructors and Destructors of the European Educational System. In *Proceedings Advances in New Technologies, Interactive Interfaces and Communicability* (pp. 71–84). Heidelberg: Springer. doi:10.1007/978-3-642-34010-9_7

Conklin, J. (1987). Hypertext: An Introduction and Survey. *IEEE Computer*, *20*(9), 17–41. doi:10.1109/MC.1987.1663693

Fagan, M. (1986). Advances in Software Inspections. *IEEE Transactions on Software Engineering*, *12*(7), 744–751. doi:10.1109/TSE.1986.6312976

Gray, J. (1996). Evolution of Data Management. *IEEE Computer*, *29*(10), 47–58. doi:10.1109/2.539719

Guesgen, H., & Marsland, S. (2013). *Human Behavior Recognition Technologies: Intelligent Applications for Monitoring and Security*. Hershey: IGI Global. doi:10.4018/978-1-4666-3682-8

Hanna, L., Risden, K., & Alexander, K. (1997). Guidelines for Usability Testing with Children. *Interaction*, *4*(5), 9–14. doi:10.1145/264044.264045

Horn, R. (1989). *Mapping Hypertext*. Waltham: Lexington Press.

Johnson, J. (2000). Textual Bloopers. *Interaction*, *7*(5), 28–48. doi:10.1145/345242.345255

Laurel, B. (1990). *The Art of Human-Computer Interface Design*. Massachusetts: Addison-Wesley.

Lim, W. (1994). Effects of Reuse on Quality, Productivity, and Economics. *IEEE Software*, *11*(5), 23–30. doi:10.1109/52.311048

Mallon, B., & Webb, B. (1997). Evaluating Narrative in Multimedia. In *Proceedings Design, Specification and Verification of Interactive System '97* (pp. 83–98). Vienna: Springer-Verlag.

Preece, J. (1998). Empathic Communities. *Interaction*, *5*(2), 32–43. doi:10.1145/274430.274435

Reynolds, L., & Derose, S. (1992). Electronics Books. *Byte*, *17*(6), 263–268.

Walker, J. (1998). Supporting Document Development with Concordia. *IEEE Computer*, *21*(1), 48–59. doi:10.1109/2.222116

Wiklund, M. (1994). *Usability in Practice*. London: Academic Press.

KEY TERMS AND DEFINITIONS

Communicability: A qualitative communication between the user and the interactive system, such as mobile phones, augmented reality, immersion multimedia, hypermedia, among others. The extent to which an interactive system successfully conveys its functionality to the user.

Cyber Attack: An attempt by hackers to damage or destroy a computer net. It is deliberate exploitation of computer systems, technology-dependent enterprises and networks.

Hypertext: Non-linear text in which block of linear text are cross-referenced by links.

Interactive System: A computer device made up by a CPU and peripherals, whose functioning requires a constant interaction with the user. Currently these systems tend to their miniaturization and/or invisibility, the mobility and wireless connectability among them.

Kernel: A central or essential part. It has complete control over everything that occurs in the system. For example, is a program that constitutes the central core of a computer operating system.

Semanteme: A unit of meaning. In other words, a linguistic element that itself expresses as concept and, in turn, is combinable with other such elements.

APPENDIX 1

Figure 8. Message received where is requested the discharge from the same event of the Figures 6 and 7
(Approximate Translation: Message in Spanish from a bipolar member for the destruction of the sciences inside the ACM – HCI area. Regrettably I can't be a member of this program committee ... From now on, if you want you can offer me to participate. Thanks a lot and Happy new year! (no comment).)

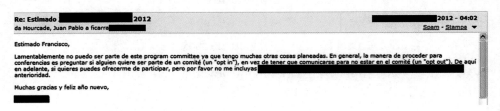

Figure 9. International association or organization, which from Universidade Aberta (Portuguese Open University) and University of Twente devote themselves to the stalking of other analogue international associations. Unbelievably, the manager of said organization requests the integration to the scientific committee, to the person they constantly attacks in a manifest or hidden way.

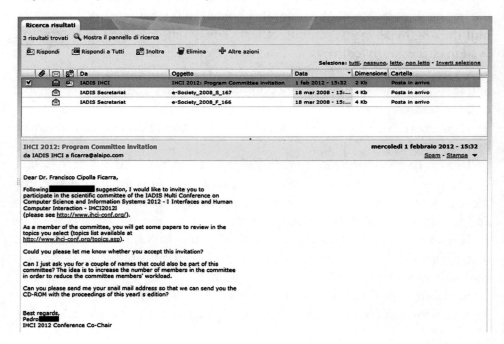

Figure 10. We sent information about international events with an OK request for an eventual inclusion into the scientific committee, on day January, 10 2011

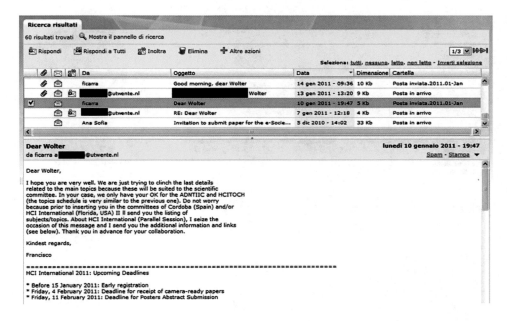

Figure 11. Message received from the Netherlands where he accepts the participation in the scientific committee, on day January, 13 2011

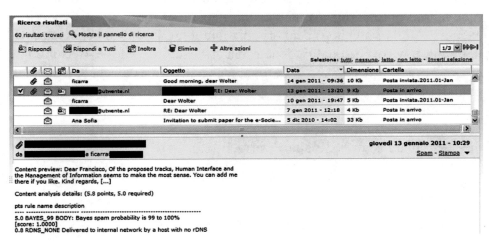

Figure 12. Message received from University of Twente where shows the dropout request, on day February, 15 2011. He requests to be erased from the listing of scientific committee and he/she does not understand why he/she has been included.

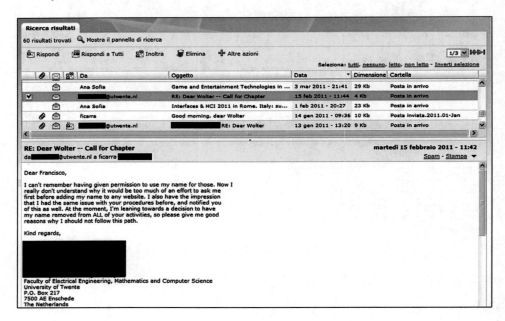

None of those persons has made any comment about the real or authentic motivations of their requests and all the allegations received are hypocritical excuses. All those dichotimical or schizophrenic patterns of behaviour, with doubling down of personality, denote that in the future of the new technologies does not enjoy a good health in Europe, especially if the daily behaviour of the main responsible who organize or participate constantly in the international events related to childhood and in the ICTs in the Old World is like this. For instance, in the case of the Figures 8, 9 and 12 can be seen the influence of the "Garduña Factor" (Cipolla-Ficarra, 2015).

APPENDIX 2

More information about this garden project: http://www.grandigiardini.it/
lang_EN/giardini-scheda.php?id=211

Figure 13. Cover book: "Labyrinths: The Art of the Maze"

Figure 14. Real Labyrinths in Fontanellato –a small town in the province of Parma, in Italy

Figure 15. Map of the Labyrinths in Fontenellato (in Italian –Il labrinto di Franco Maria Ricci)

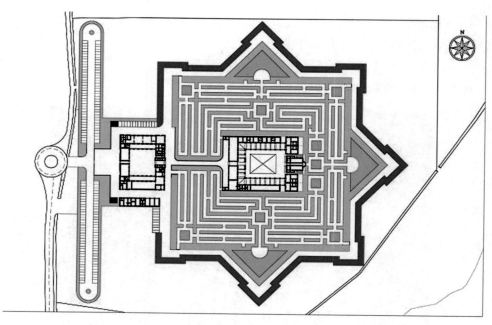

Figure 16. Combination of the real and virtual image (photography and 3D computer graphics)

Chapter 7
Digital Television and Senior Users:
Design Evolution or Involution?

Francisco V. Cipolla-Ficarra
Latin Association of Human-Computer Interaction, Spain & International Association of Interactive Communication, Italy

Jacqueline Alma
Electronic Arts, Canada

Miguel Cipolla-Ficarra
International Association of Interactive Communication, Italy

ABSTRACT

In this chapter the increase of the digital divide among the third age users and the digital television is studied. From an ergonomic point of view of the remote command keys the technological impact is analyzed of the introduction of the digital television, in a sample of the senior population in the south of Europe, at the moment of interacting with television. We also present the results of the experiments in a communicability and usability lab such as the changes of habits to get information about the latest local, national and international news.

INTRODUCTION

Currently, there are several syllogisms to divide the population of the users of interactive systems, in relation to the age they have, the time they spend connected to the internet, etc. For instance, Digital Sapiens or Homo Sapiens

DOI: 10.4018/978-1-5225-3437-2.ch007

Digital, Digital Immigrants, Digitally Illiterate, Generation Z, etc. (Palfrey, 2008). Native Digital or digital Homo Sapiens are all those people born in the decades of the 80s, 90s or later, when a quite developed digital technology already existed within the reach of many. It is the group of people who have had contact with the with the ICT since they were very small and have developed use capabilities together with the development of their personality (Livingston, 2007).

In the subgroup of digital immigrants are included all those users born between the years 1940 and 1980, since they have been spectators and actors generally privileged of the evolutional process of technology (Moragas-Spa, 1985; Reeves & Nass, 1996; Veltman, 2006). In other words, they are those people who must learn to use the ICT to do other things that in the past they were used to do with analogical supports, especially paper, for instance, to send a congratulation card through the mail. Although inside these two groups there are socioeconomic differences, at a same socioeconomic level there is a relative gap, of cognitive character in the handling of the ICTs, between the digital natives and the digital immigrants. There is a third category, which would be the digitally illiterate, who because of their advanced age should be digital immigrants, but who have not had any experience in the use of computers or another digital technology. From a sociological perspective, this users group can be included in the set of digital immigrants. The Z generation does not have a precise starting data in the new millennium, but it is a group of very young users who are constantly connected to the Internet, to communicate with other users or interacting with digital contents online. It is a generation where the common denominator is the World Wide Web, instant messaging, text messaging, MP3 players, mobile phones, etc. Biologically, in the current study, we carry out the division of the potential users of the ICT in the following way: child (4/11), junior (12/17), adult (18/64), and senior (over 65 years). In our universe of study, we focus on this latter group of people or users.

Now in the current syllogisms to divide the population of users of interactive systems, it is necessary to consider what is the purpose of the interaction, because apparently it is as if the whole process of interaction user-new technologies were oriented at the pastime of the digital native or Z generation. Traditionally, the potential users of the interactive multimedia systems have been divided in relation to the type, profile, time for the use of the system and the previous experience with the multimedia interactive system used.

Although there are some senior users who interact with the digital television from their personal computer, tablet PC, multimedia mobile

Table 1. As a rule, the users of multimedia systems in the 20th century were classified in the following way at the moment of interacting with the digital contents

Type	Profile	Time for the Use of the System	Previous Experience in Interactive Systems
Eventual	They check the system a single time, such as can be the timetable of trains, buses, etc.	Very short (less than an hour)	No
Intentional	Interested in the issue and want to go deeper into it	Short (between 1 and three hours)	Yes
Experts	Researchers about one or several issues, related to the content of the system.	Unlimited	Yes
Experts and intentional	They are those users who do not count with previous experience in the handling of interactive systems, but they show a great interest in learning.	Unlimited	No

phone, etc. (Brown, 2004). Our universe of study is focused on those senior users who had an analogue television and whom the European guidelines of the start of the second decade of the new millennium have switched to the Digital Terrestrial Television (DTT–DTTi, i = interactive). The binary codification, and through a network of terrestrial repeaters (Benoit, 2008). Besides, the DDT provides a better quality picture, and lower operating costs for broadcast and transmission evidently, after the initial upgrade costs). The digital coding of the information brings several advantages. In the first place, the possibility of compressing the signal. A more effective use can be made of the radioelectronical spectrum. After proceeding to its multiplexaton, more channels can be broadcast.(in the digital system they change their name to "digital programs") in the space previously used by one, called "digital multiple channel" or simply "multiplex". The number of programs broadcast in each multiple channel depending on the ratio of understanding used. Consequently, a wealth of digital contents is produced for the potential users through the DTT.

INTERACTIVITY AND USERS

The main element of this new media of social or massive communication is interactivity. It is this interactivity which distinguishes it from the analogical television and which allows the user not only to receive previously formatted information for the social/massive consumption, but playing an active role in the creation and consumption of information. This interactivity turns the digital television into an ICT, such as are: digital cinema, videogames, iPods, iPhones, Palms, etc. Besides, it includes other fundamental characteristics, such as: the democratization of an interface with millions of viewers.

The familiarity in the use of the television, and the remote control by almost all the users, whether they are digital native or not, added to the skills of handling multimedia information, in real time, is one of the main characteristics of the new digital social/massive communication media, Although sometimes it is used indistinctly, the terms massive and social in the television, it is necessary to differentiate it since the former refers to a unidirectional communication contents, whereas in the latter there is a feedback between the emitter and the receptor of the contents. An example is the social function of TV in distance education in countries such as Australia, Canada, New Zealand, etc. (Cipolla-Ficarra, 2010a)

Distance education may help to decrease the digital gap due to the lack of knowledge in the handling of the new technologies. The digital gap is the difference of diffusion of the use of the technologies of the information and communication in the daily activities which are presented among different groups of individuals belonging to the same community, countries or geographical regions. This gap in the diffusion of the ICT is due as much to the purchasing power of the latest technological novelties, whether in goods and/or services, as well as the lack of knowledge for the use of these technologies. In some studies, the authors claim that the DTTi can be a key instrument in the reduction of the digital divide (Compaine, 2001; Barclay, Duggan, 2008; Cipolla-Ficarra, 2010a, 2010b)

The applications that can be developed, added to the democratization of the obtained results, include the DTTi s a medium of social inclusion, if the human and/or social factors of a negative sign, which prevent going from theory to the practice. A social inclusion, whether it is from the technological point of view as well as between generations of potential users, due to the familiarity of the potential users with the classical TV, and to the great planet-wide diffusion of that means of social communication (Cipolla-Ficarra, 2010a).

However, the same as happens with the project One Laptop per Child (OLPC), many premises stay in the analogical supports (paper), or digital (online), in view of the reality of thousands and thousands of users in our planet, with a technological element indispensable to interact with this new technology such as the remote (Cipolla-Ficarra, et al., 2011; Cipolla-Ficarra, 2014).

CONTROL REMOTES IN THE DTTi: ERGONOMICS AND THIRD AGE USERS

One of the principles enunciated by Nielsen in usability engineering, is the ease of use of an interactive system (Nielsen, 1992). In principle, the use of the remote is something common or familiar among the viewers of the third age. However, we are in front one of the causes why many users of that age have stopped watching Tv in the south of Europe with the arrival of the DTTi. Although the DTTi is a new means of communication which does not require functioning knowledge, like a computer, that is, operative system or protection updating operations, such as can be the installation of antivirus, etc. Apparently on the TV screen the user must only select options and press the OK button. It is not even necessary to incorporate a "Qwerty" keyboard, to interact with the DTTi, especially for the group of users known as digital immigrants and digital ignorant, who in our study must be joined in the same set (Cipolla-Ficarra, Ficarra & Kratky, 2011; Cipolla-Ficarra, et al., 2012).

However, the economical factor (derived from the financial crisis of the new millennium) has prevented many homes in the south of Europe from choosing the new television models belonging to the DTTi. Many viewers have chosen a digital television adapter (DTA), or digital-to-analog, converter (set-top box), or commonly known as a converter box. In other words, it is a TV tuner that receives a digital television (DTV), transmission and converts the digital signal into an analog signal that can be received and displayed on an analog TV set. Now, the high demand of those products in so little time led models from Asia to be imported. In them, the cost-quality equation is present and also the ease of installation of the device, the speed of the software in detecting the available TV channels, etc. However, there is an ergonomic problem for the users of our universe of study: the reduced size of the remotes. This ergonomic factor is directly related to the design and realization of the product that has taken into account the physical aspects of the local hand, but not global.

Obviously making products of small size means saving costs in the used materials and, in some ways, it is the tendency of the computer electronic products, etc., since the late 20th century. However, those changes and the reduction of the production costs in the remote control of a DTA leads many senior users not to watch television anymore. If we analyze ergonomically some of the models made in Asia at the start of the millennium for the analogical television of international commercial brands such as Samsung

Figure 1. Models of remote commands to access analogical TV and DTA

or Sony, we can see the involution of ergonomics in our universe of study and consequently an involution of communicability, in view of the new ICT devices. In the figure a we have two models of remote control commands for analogical television and two for DTA in order to access the contents of the DTT.

The approximate sizes of the devices are:

- **Sony:** 230 mm x 50 mm, with a thickness of 20 mm. The rectangular shape is not ideal for a quick localization of the zone which must point at a reader of infrared beams of the TV and the remote.
- **Samsung:** 145 mm x 45 mm, with a thickness of 25 mm in the lower zone and 10 mm in the upper zone. The junction of a rectangle to rectangular trapeze has been a geometrical shape adopted by the remote commands of low cost DTA systems.
- **United:** 145 mm x 45 mm with a thickness of 20 mm in the lower zone and 12 mm in the upper zone.
- **Mpman:** 145 mm x 45 mm with a thickness of 20 mm in the lower zone and 10 mm in the upper zone.

The two latter models are practically similar from the ergonomic point of view (Salvendy, 2012). To this ergonomic aspect, we have to add the functional one, as it can be seen in each one of the keys, for instance, in the Figure 2 we have over 21 functions, aside from other remotes for other devices which still work in the TV, such as the DVD reader, video cassette, music equipment, etc. An example is the Figure 2.

In other words, the variegated aspect of the industrial design, the ergonomics of these technological products, as well as some fundamental principles of usability are not met. Indirectly, it also damages the communicability among

Figure 2. These commands require a fundamental principle of usability, that the functionality of each one of the keys should be easy to remember

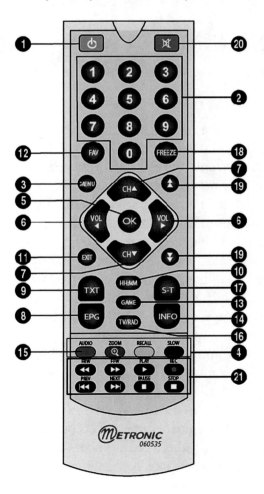

Figure 3. A multiple variety of remote commands which can exist in millions of homes who are 65 years old or over

the users inside a set of ages, in the era of expansion of communicability (Cipolla-Ficarra, 2010).

Starting from the current state of the art, a universe of study was established with people whose ages ranged between the 65 and 75 years, without any kind of physical or intellectual disability, split into three groups of 5 people each, in relation to the studies reached at the time: primary (P), secondary (S) and tertiary (T). Each group has been directed by a communicability expert to carry out the experiments, using as a main technique the direct observation in a HCI lab. Each one of the groups was presented with a video showing the functions of each one of the buttons of the Mpman remote and the channels where the 24/7 news programs were to be found (EuroNews –www.euronews. com). After a 30 minutes pause, they were assigned the task of turning on the television set and finding the news channel, which was made up of three numbers, within five minutes. The results obtained by each group can be seen in the following figure:

Although most of the users managed to switch on the television set quickly because they distinguished the red color key, then it was practically impossible to write quickly the three numbers of the news channel. After carrying out several attempts, some users switched off and switched on again the television set. Some belonging to the second and third group opted to

Figure 4. Over 73% of the users of the experiments did not find the news channel within 5 minutes

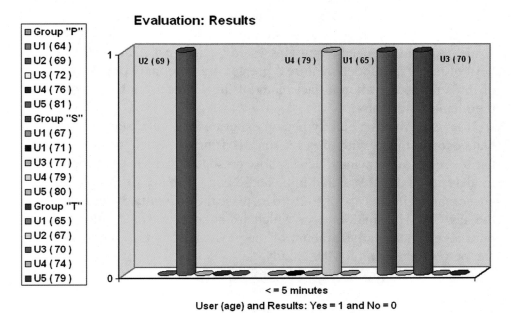

pass sequentially all the channels, until finding the news channel they had to locate. However, they repeated the operation several times, because they skipped the channel, because they were pressing the key in a continuous way. Another of the observed problems was that due to the scant space among the numeric keys, many users pressed two or more numeric keys at the same time without realizing it.

LESSONS LEARNED

The experiment carried out indicates that the digital divide has increased exponentially among the generations of users of the interactive communication media, generation Z, native digitals, and those illiterate or digital immigrants, whose age is over 65 at the moment of interacting with some remote commands. The economic factor, joined to the cognitive one, may bring about that the interaction with the new digital contents is practically impossible for many senior viewers, who watch the new television through a DTA. Some of them in the experiment made have claimed that they depend on other people to change the channels or tune in correctly the signal of the internal areal (avoid the continuous fluctuations of the signal, that is, the fading effect), etc. Before these viewers were more autonomous, with the remote commands of the analogical television, in spite of the high number of keys they had, and as a rule, they did not need to put glasses on to change a channel. Besides, the keys of the DTA models require a greater pressure and speed to write two or three numbers, when in fact many of the senior users have problems in their hands and limbs.

It is usual that the elderly person experiences loss of sensibility in their hands, for instance, with diseases such as arthritis, which makes difficult to use the remote commands such as those presented in the DTA models. These models are of small size and thin. These two attributes of industrial design are combined in our case of study to increase the difficulty of interacting with the new TV. The small buttons which are not easy to find, without glasses, but they need a relative amount of the greater strength to press. The latter can be very annoying for the elderly.

Another of the problems derived from the ergonomics and/or the industrial design is the high amount of compacted buttons in a small space resorting to the use of small letters, and illegible symbols at first sight for the third age users, with the purpose of indicating the function of each button.

It is necessary that the remote command has big buttons with a clear text to go with it, like for instance putting the volume up or down, for instance avoiding the use of a simple "+" or "-" to decrease. In contrast, it is positive to combine it with an abbreviation "Vol", which in English, Spanish, Italian, French, etc. means "volume". That is, the ideal combination is "Vol +" (increase) or "Vol -" (decrease).

Finally, it is necessary that the remote for these users do not have access to the configuration of the system because if they activate it by mistake, they are totally disoriented to go back to the previous interaction situation. A good example of the remote for senior users is in the figure 5, which has only seven programmable buttons.

The lack of access to television programming aimed at the news has generated in the universe of study that many users are not informed any longer in the audiovisual media. Although they mainly belong to the generation of the social communication media such as the press, radio and television (Reeves & Nass, 1996), they have lost the motivation towards the new television, which in spite of having a wider offer of channels, many elderly viewers must depend on other people to simply switch the channel or turning up the volume.

Figure 5. Universal remote command where there is an ease of use and boosts the communicability of the new technologies with the senior users

Consequently, the digital divide has not only increased, but there is also a lack of daily information which influences in a democratic system, for instance, since this universe of study keeps on participating in the political elections, for instance. In few words, a remote not adequate for these users has generated an increase of disinformation which makes difficult the wealth of criteria to cast a ballot vote, for instance. In a next study, we will examine how the digital divide out of ergonomic and economic reasons may have an influence among the elderly voters belonging to the set of digital illiterates and/or digital immigrants.

CONCLUSION

There is a digital divide between the third age users and the digital television, due to the instruments that allow the users to interact with the new audiovisual communication media. In those instruments, we have been able to detect failings going back to the 90s which belong to the principles enunciated by

Figure 6. The asterisk depicts the main areas that interact with the communicability at the moment of analyzing the remote commands in the current work

User* Centered Design	Design & Categories	Usability*	Design & Emotion	Software & Systems Quality
communicability				
Human Computer Interaction	Participatory Design	Critical Design	Cognitive Models	Human* Factors & Ergonomics

the usability engineering, and theoretically overcome in the current era of the expansion of the communicability. The triad simplicity, universality and ergonomics does not allow the access to DTT by 100% of potential viewers.

However, some models of DTA remote commands not only have bolstered the digital divide among the users of the interactive systems inside the ICTs, but they have also generated a greater isolation in regard to the social, local and global context where many senior viewers are to be found. Many of them, for economic reasons, have not been able to buy a new television set model before the implementation of the DTT system. At the moment of the switching off of the analogical television and in view of the impossibility of interacting with the DTA remote commands, of low cost but which have not been made in keeping with some quality criteria for this kind of users (ease to see the buttons, reduction of the number of buttons, vagueness and ambiguity of the symbols used in the buttons, etc.) have opted not to watch television in the south of Europe.

In few words, in the new millennium, the analogical switch off in the south of Europe, linked to the economic, ergonomic, industrial design and usability, factors has entailed the "switch off" of the reception of audio visual contents, interactive or not, for a myriad of senior users.

ACKNOWLEDGMENT

The authors would like to thanks a lot Maria Ficarra for her helpful advice on various technical issues examined in this chapter. Besides, Alejandra Quiroga, Mary Brie, Luisa Varela, Amélie Bordeaux, Giselda Verdone, Donald Nilson, and Carlos for the advice and comments.

REFERENCES

Barclay, C., & Duggan, E. (2008). Rethinking the Digital Divide: Towards a Path of Digital Effectiveness. In *Proceedings 41st Annual Hawaii International Conference on System Sciences*. New York: IEEE Press. doi:10.1109/HICSS.2008.376

Benoit, H. (2008). *Digital Television: Satellite, Cable, Terrestrial, IPTV, Mobile TV in the DVB Framework*. Waltham, MA: Focal Press.

Brown, A. (2004). *Digital Terrestrial Television in Europe*. London: Routledge.

Card, S., Mackinlay, J. D., & Shneiderman, B. (1999). *Readings in Information Visualization: Using Vision to Think (Interactive Technologies)*. San Diego, CA: Academic Press.

Cipolla-Ficarra, et al.. (2014). *Advanced Research and Trends in New Technologies, Software, Human-Computer Interaction, and Communicability*. Hershey, PA: IGI Global.

Cipolla-Ficarra, F. (2010a). *Quality and Communicability for Interactive Hypermedia Systems: Concepts and Practices for Design*. Hershey, PA: IGI Global. doi:10.4018/978-1-61520-763-3

Cipolla-Ficarra, F. (2010b). *Persuasion On-Line and Communicability: The Destruction of Credibility in the Virtual Community and Cognitive Models*. New York: Nova Science Publishers.

Cipolla-Ficarra, F. (2011). *Computational Informatics, Social Factors and New Information Technologies: Hypermedia Perspectives and Avant-Garde Experiences in the Era of Communicability Expansion*. Bergamo: Blue Herons Editions.

Cipolla-Ficarra, F. (2012). *New Horizons in Creative Open Software, Multimedia, Human Factors and Software Engineering*. Bergamo: Blue Herons Editions.

Cipolla-Ficarra, F., Ficarra, V., & Kratky, A. (2011). Computer Graphics for Students of the Factual Sciences. In *Proceedings Communicability, Computer Graphics and Innovative Design for Interactive Systems* (pp. 79–93). Heidelberg, Germany: Springer.

Compaine, B. (2001). *The Digital Divide: Facing a Crisis or Creating a Myth?* Cambridge, MA: MIT Press.

Livingston, J. (2007). ICT Design for Elders. *Interaction*, *14*(4), 20–21. doi:10.1145/1273961.1273977

Moragas-Spa, M. (1985). *Sociología de la Comunicación de Masas*. Barcelona: Paidòs. In Spanish

Nielsen, J. (1992). The Usability Engineering Life Cycle. *IEEE Software*, *25*(3), 12–22.

Palfrey, J. (2008). *Born Digital: Understanding the First Generation of Digital Natives*. New York: Basic Books.

Reeves, B., & Nass, C. (1996). *The Media Equation*. Cambridge, UK: Cambridge University Press.

Salvendy, G. (2012). *Handbook of Human Factors and Ergonomics*. New York: John Wiley. doi:10.1002/9781118131350

Veltman, K. (2006). *Understanding New Media: Augmented Knowledge and Culture*. Calgary: University of Calgary Press.

ADDITIONAL READING

Barrett, E. (1992). *Sociomedia: Multimedia, Hypermedia, and the Social Construction of Knowledge*. Cambridge: MIT Press.

Berger, P., & Luckmann, T. (1966). *The Social Construction of Reality: A Treatise its the Sociology of Knowledge*. New York: Anchor Books.

Brier, S. (2008). *Cybersemiotics: Why Information Is Not Enough!* Toronto: University of Toronto Press.

Carey, J. (1989). *Communication as Culture: Essays on Media and Society*. Boston: Unwin Hyman.

Geertz, C. (1973). *The Interpretation of Cultures*. New York: Basic Books.

Hackos, J., & Redish, J. (1998). *User and Task Analysis for Interface Design*. New York: Wiley.

Hiltz, S., & Turhoff, M. (1978). *The Network Nation: Human Communication Via Computer*. London: Addison-Wesley.

Ishizaki, S. (2003). *Improvisational Design: Continuous, Responsive Digital Communication*. Cambridge: MIT Press.

Lansdale, M., & Ormerod, T. (1994). *Understanding Interfaces: A Handbook of Human-Computer Dialogue*. London: Academic Press.

Lévy, P. (1994). *L'Intelligence collective. Pour une anthropologie du cyberespace*. Paris: La Découverte. in French

Maldonado, T. (1997). *Critica della ragione informatica*. Milano: Feltrinelli. in Italian

Marcus, G., & Fischer, M. (1986). *Anthropology as Cultural Critique: An Experimental Moment in the Human Sciences. Chicago: University of Chicago Norman, D. (2004). Emotional Design: Why We Love (or Hate) Everyday Things*. New York: Basic Books.

Norman, D. (2009). *The Design of Future Things*. New York: Basic Books.

Parekh, B. (2000). *Rethinking Multiculturalism. Cultural Diversity and Political Theory*. Basingstoke: Palgrave.

Raskin, J. (2000). *The Humane Interface: New Directions for Designing Interactive Systems*. Boston: Addison-Wesley.

Rheingold, H. (2000). *The Virtual Community: Homesteading on the Electronic Frontier*. Cambridge: MIT Press.

Rogers, E. (1971). *Communication and Innovation: A Cross-cultural Approach*. New York: Free Press.

Turow, J. (2011). *Media Today*. London: Routledge.

Warner, W., & Lunt, P. (1941). *The Social Life of a Modern Community*. New Haven: Yale University Press.

Warschauer, M. (2003). *Technology and Social Inclusion: Rethinking the Digital Divide*. Cambridge: MIT Press.

Wellman, B. (1999). *Networks in the Global Village*. Boulder: Westview.

White, C. (2012). *Social Media, Crisis Communication, and Emergency Management: Leveraging Web 2.0 Technologies*. Mahwah: CRC Press.

White, L. (1975). *The Concept of Cultural Systems: A Key to Understanding Tribes and Nations*. New York: Columbia University Press.

Williams, R. (1974). *Television: Technology and Cultural Form*. London: Fontana. doi:10.4324/9780203426647

Wood, L. (1998). *User Interface Design: Bridging the Gap from User Requirements to Design*. Boca Raton: CRC Press.

Zaphiris, P., & Kurniawan, S. (2006). *Human Computer Interaction Research in Web Design and Evaluation*. Hershey: IGI Global.

KEY TERMS AND DEFINITIONS

Communicability: A qualitative communication between the user and the interactive system, such as mobile phones, augmented reality, immersion multimedia, hypermedia, among others. The extent to which an interactive system successfully conveys its functionality to the user.

Design Model: The intersection between software engineering, interface design and human-computer interaction/communication into the interactive systems area.

Digital Terrestrial Television: (DTTV or DTT) is a technological evolution of broadcast television. A terrestrial implementation of digital television (DTV) technology uses an aerial to broadcast to a conventional television antenna (or aerial) instead of a satellite dish or cable television connection, for example.

End-User: In Information Technology (IT) context, the term end user is used to distinguish the person for whom a hardware and/or software product is designed from the developers, installers, and servicers of the product.

Generation Z: One expression used for the denotation of people born after the new millennial. There is no agreement on the exact dates of the generation with some sources starting it at the mid or late 1990s democratization of internet, or from the mid 2000s, to the present day.

Interactive System: A computer device made up by a CPU and peripherals, whose functioning requires a constant interaction with the user. Currently these systems tend to their miniaturization and/or invisibility, the mobility and wireless connectability among them.

New Media: Content available on-demand through the Internet, accessible on any digital device, commonly containing interactive user feedback and a constant participation with the end-users.

Chapter 8
Computer Animation for Ingenious Revival

Francisco V. Cipolla-Ficarra
Latin Association of Human-Computer Interaction, Spain & International Association of Interactive Communication, Italy

Miguel Cipolla-Ficarra
International Association of Interactive Communication, Italy

ABSTRACT

In this research work, we make known the excellent advantages of the use of computer animations in 3D with the purpose of transferring scientific heritage into paper support to the current generations of users of interactive systems. In it the archetypes factor is analyzed (semiotics perspective) and communicative inference of the analyzed examples. Besides, the main components of the layout category are analyzed, which are related to graphic computing and communicability inside the interface of the interactive system.

INTRODUCTION

Bi-dimensional (2D) and three-dimensional (3D) computer reconstructions may be an excellent solution in the context of the cultural heritage to solve the reproduction limitations of artistic works in copyright issues, for instance (Hughes, et al. 2014; Cipolla-Ficarra, 2014: Potter, 1995). In other cases, they can represent the scientific advances of civilizations through the images of objects, tools, mechanisms, etc., which have lasted across the centuries

DOI: 10.4018/978-1-5225-3437-2.ch008

in analogical support, as in the case of the "Book of the Secrets", published in the year 1,000 (Al-Muradi, 2008). In those illustrations are concentrated not only the mathematics, geometry, physics, chemistry, etc., but also an anonymous historical legacy, in many cases, but which has allowed inventions and/or discoveries of great importance in later centuries, thus boosting the development and the interrelation of the formal and factual sciences. Now both in geometrics and in physics, to mention two examples, an object is three-dimensional if it has a width, a length and a depth (Mortenson, 2006; Wrenninge, 2012; Lengyel, 2012; Akenine-Moller, & Haines, 2008). The two former constitute the 2D (abscises and coordinates, letters x e y) and the third depicted with the letter z. Currently, with these three numeric values, a dot can be depicted on a computer screen, inside an application aimed at generating three-dimensional animations. This minimal unit of information of digital graphics is what is called pixel. The space that surrounds the human being, at simple sight or under observation, is three-dimensional, but, in reality, there are more dimensions, as is the case of time. In the interactive design for multimedia systems it is a category which is called Panchronics (Cipolla-Ficarra, F., 2010). This category of design has its origin in the 90s, in the era of the usability of the interactive systems, when the synchronization between audio and video in the video, 2D and/or 3D animations, the locution of a text and the shifting of a cursor on the text, etc. (Cipolla-Ficarra, 2012), was nonexistent in a myriad commercial multimedia systems, which were distributed all across our planet, that is to say, there was no synchronism between the static and the dynamic means. It is a category of interactive design which in the era of the expansion of communicability is a qualitative component which must be present in the interactive process of the user and the multimedia contents, the Kaluza-Klein theory (Cipolla-Ficarra, 2012). Originally it posited a space-time of five dimensions, (which is space is four dimensions, one of which is compact or microscopic dimension). In other words, it is the general relativity theory, which was proposed by Theodor Kaluza (1919) and perfected by Klein (1926), through which it is intended to unify gravitation and electromagnetism, using a geometrical model (Armstrong, & Green, 1985). Simultaneously, in a conventional Euclidean space, a finite physical object is contained inside a minimal cuboid, whose dimensions are called wide, long and height, or depth and height. In other words, it is related to the axioms of Euclid in geometry. Moreover, when such physical phenomena as gravity are considered, the theory of relativity (Einstein, 1995) tells us that the universe is a tetra-dimensional entity which includes as well spatial dimensions as time and other dimensions. Different observers will perceive different "spatial sections" of that space-time so that the physical space is more complex than a three-dimensional Euclidean space. Although there are other theories about the dimensions, the role of the observer is important. In this sense, in the CAD systems, for instance (Zeid, & Sivasubramanian, 2009;), or others related to 3D animation (Solomon, 1994; Magnenat-Thalmann, 1985), there is always an option to see the scene from the geometrical perspective, through a virtual eye, which represents the observer (Laybourne, 1998; Childs, H. et al., 2013). In geometry, the following geometric figures are three-dimensional, divided into two great primaries:

1.   Curve surfaces: cylinder, cones and spheres.
2.   Flat-faced polyhedral: cube, pyramids and prisms.

These figures can be quickly generated from commercial applications of graphic computing, such as AutoCAD, Max, Maya, etc., where they are options of the 3D figures menu, although they can also be generated from the 2D and later on include the z coordinate, for instance (MacNicol, 1990; Levy, 1992; Robertson, 1995; Cipolla-Ficarra, et al., 2010). Besides, all of them can be included inside a three-dimensional Euclidean space. The same as in mathematics, in the applications, commercial or not, belonging to graphic computing, the three-dimensional system is represented in the Cartesian plane with the axis X, Y and Z. As a rule, these representations are handled in the geometrical forms of three dimensions such as the spheres, or the cubes in two dimensions using perspectives.

PERSPECTIVE AND 3D SIMULATION IN COMMUNICABILITY

The simulation and emulation of reality can be three-dimensional or bi-dimensional, analogical or digital. Both terms, simulation and emulation of reality are not synonymous, as can be seen in the Figure 1. Besides, the degree of realism of that simulation or emulation can be very high without using computers as is the case of the Figures 2 (a & b), where they are not digital or analogical photographs but paintings. Some claim that the art of the 3D graphics is similar to photography or sculpture, whereas the art of the 2D graphics is similar to painting. In the programs of computer graphics, this distinction is sometimes ambiguous, since some 2D applications use

Figure 1. Realism: simulation and emulation; classical representation of the human interaction through a computer (color screen-cathode ray rube)
www.calimero.com

3D techniques to reach certain effects such as illumination/shades, whereas some 3D applications make use of 2D techniques, especially in the computer animations for children on TV (Poynton, 2003; Dunn, & Parberry, 2011; Blain, 2012; Zink, Pettineo & Hoadey, 2011), such as is the case of Calimero, where there is a combination of 2D and 3D (Figure 3).

Since the late 20th century, qualitative simulation is possible through calculations based on the projection of three-dimensional environments on bi-dimensional screens, such as monitors or television sets. These calculations require a large load of process so that the computers and video consoles that since the 90s started to have available a certain degree of 3D graphic acceleration, through the use of devices developed for such an end, for instance, the 3D acceleration graphic cards (Dunn, & Parberry, 2011; Bolter, Engberg, & Macintyre, 2013; Cipolla-Ficarra, 2014). These devices are made up by one or several processors (units of graphic processing) especially designed to accelerate calculations implied by reproducing three-dimensional images

Figure 2. Excellent examples of how painting can simulate photography; in other words, these pictures are not photos.
Author: Iman Maleki, www.imanmaleki.com

Figure 3. Combination of 2D and 3D in computer animations aimed at the television children audience
www.calimero.com

on a bi-dimensional screen and in this way release the processing load of the central processing unit (CPU) of the computer, for other operations such as access to the graphic information stored in a local or remote database (through the Internet) for a virtual community, for example (Begel, Bosch, & Storey, 2013).

Other devices for the reproduction of those three-dimensional images can be helmets, glasses, etc., used in the virtual reality of the 90s and start of the new millennium. A virtual reality, where the same as in early action video games, the quality of the image remains on a second level, in view of the interaction of the virtual objects, or the action inside a video game. The democratization in the generation of the 3D graphics has boosted the application programming interfaces (API) to ease the processes in all the stages of the computer-made graphics generation. That is, these interfaces have demonstrated to be a priority for the developers of hardware for computer graphics, since the programmer can access the hardware in an abstract way, profiting from the advantages of the graphics accelerating card (Wrenninge, 2012). Currently some of the main interfaces for computer graphics and of a wider circulation among the programmers are (Cipolla-Ficarra, 2012): Open GL, RenderMan and Direct 3D (a subset of Direct X to generate interactive graphics in 3D).

In other words, that interaction was ahead of communicability in the 90s. The graphic quality of the "domestic" virtual reality (that is, that which can be accessed quickly and for financial reasons those interested in these technologies) has improved in the last decade (Cipolla-Ficarra, 2010). This improvement is due to the evolution of the hardware, the software and to the partial reduction of the production costs in the new millennium. However, currently there are studies tending to unveil the secrets of the functioning of the brain, through the virtual reality. However, these investigations leave in a second plane the resolution of a priority problem such as the issue of the loss of balance (vertigo or dizziness) experienced by the great majority of users of these devices which cover the head totally. Obviously emulating with not real images but in 3D, resorting to virtual reality, colours, textures, etc., which draw the visual attention, specially, of that which is intangible, which cannot be verified 100% such as the cognitive, emotive aspects, etc., of the human beings is easier and faster than solving the problems of computer science, electronics, etc., (Levy, 1992; Hodgins, Wooten, Brogan, & O'Brien, 1995; Childs, et al., 2013) at the moment of interacting/using that technology. In our days, and in the south of Europe, representing the intangible is still more productive from the financial and pseudo-scientific point of view. Fortunately, in other places of the planet, quantum computers, micro computing, robots, the contents of interactive multimedia, aimed at the preservation and the fostering of the natural and cultural heritage, etc., are the cornerstones to increase the communicability among the human beings, through the interactive systems, which are economically more accessible to a large part of the population, for instance.

In the generation of the components of a heuristic table for an analysis of the presentation of the information in the interface and the communicability, is briefly explained the creation of the dynamic and static graphics in 3D, through the commercial applications of graphic computing (AutoCAD, 3D Studio Max, Maya, Rhino, etc.) which can be summed up in the following set of activities: modelling, illumination and incorporation of textures, colours, etc., to the objects of the scene, animation and rendering (Cipolla-Ficarra, 2014). The first phase is the modelling which can be with 3D or 2D objects (incorporating later the z coordinate), consists in giving shape to each one of the objects that will later be used in the scene. Objects which can be generated from the start or incorporated from bookshops, to speed up the production process. There are different types of geometry for modeller with NURBS (Non Uniform Rational Basis Splines) and polygonal modelling or subdivision of surfaces (Blain, 2012; Mortenson, 2006; Zeid & Sivasubramanian, 2009). Besides, there is the image based modelling, which consists in turning a digital picture into 3D through the use of diverse techniques, from which the best known is photogrammetry.

In the set of the second stage is included the illumination which entails to generate lights of different kinds (directional, global, etc.), with different colours and properties; the inclusion of textures, colours, etc., of the objects which make up the scene and the interaction with the illumination, for instance. A great part of the 3D illumination requires the physical knowledge of light in reality: a knowledge which must spread from the global illumination down to the complex reactions of light such as its spread on surfaces, due to the effects of refraction, reflection, etc., for instance. In the option of global illumination, there is generally in the commercial applications a set of algorithms which try to simulate or approximate how the light sent by some source rebounds in each surface of the scene illuminating spaces which the direct light produced by the source would not illuminate. In this sense, the early algorithms of indirect illumination tried to simulate the light like photons. Consequently, since the 20th century, one of the most implemented algorithms in the commercial graphic software is the one called photon map. There are other algorithms such as the Quasi Montecarlo or algorithms based on irradiance caching, for instance, which depending on the render engine with which the software works have different names and implementations of their own. In the animation stage, is where the cameras are included (Wrenninge, 2012; Akenine-Moller, & Haines, 2008). The objects that make up the scene can be animated in several ways:

- The basic transformations in the three axes (x-y-z) that is, rotation, scale and translation, for instance.
- The use of deformers: whether they are deformation boxes (lattices) or any deformer which produces, for instance, morph, flex, etc.
- The shape, whether it is through skeletons: the objects can be assigned a skeleton, a central structure with the capacity of affecting the shape and movements of that object, such as can be a three-dimensional character. This speeds up the animation process, in which the movement of the skeleton automatically will affect the matching portions of the model. There are two main kinds of kinematics in this regard, forward and inverse, that is forward kinematic animation and inverse kinematic animation.
- Dynamics which are aimed at the hair simulations, movement of the textiles or clothes, etc.

It is in the rendering where the static or dynamic images in 2D are obtained, which can help to emulate or simulate reality. There are several techniques which tend to reach that goal: wireframe rendering, scanline rendering, raytracing, photon mapping, etc. The rendering process needs a great capacity of calculation by the computers, since they must calculate each one of the pixels of the scene, related to complex physical processes of reality. The capacity of calculation of the PC computers has increased quickly from 1995, allowing a high degree of realism in the renderings, without need of using workstations (Cipolla-Ficarra, 2014). In this sense, the render farm is a grouping of several computers which share the work of the rendering in the static or dynamic images, generated from a three-dimensional software such as can be K-3D, which interface and development is based on the Renderman, Blender standard, which has its own animations engine or interconnectivity/compatibility with the standard 3D Studio Max, Cinema 4D, Maya and Renderman, to mention some examples (Blain, 2012; Hughes, et al., 2014). The special effects of nature such as fire, explosions, rain, snow, fog, etc., increase the final quality of the result of the animation if they are included in a correct way, to increase the simulation of reality which surrounds the human being. An excellent example of their use is in the following figure, where the components of a water clock are broken down.

ARCHETYPES AND EMPATHY FOR 3D MULTIMEDIA CONTENTS

In semiotics, the notion of archetypes means an original type or exemplar upon which other things are modelled. Human communication entails predictions or expectations from the designer and the user with respect to the way in which communication creates feedback (Holzinger, 2005). While designing hypermedia/multimedia contents we simplify the potential users, and so there is a process of empathy regarding the communication between the designer and user. Empathy in communication allows us to differentiate between prediction and self-evidence (Cipolla-Ficarra, 2010). One potential application is in the design of cultural heritage hypermedia systems. An example is the multimedia offline "The Book of Knowledge of Ingenious Mechanical Device, or The Book of Secrets" (Al-Muradi, 2008). In the process of transferring the historical contents related to engineering, in an analogical support, to the digital with 3D animations, entails these two notions

Figure 4. A simple and effective interface for the interactive multimedia version of scientific mechanisms which were avant-garde in the 10th century

(archetypes and empathy) in the interactive design of the system, aimed at the potential users in the global village.

The "Book of Secrets" is a unique volume, kept in the Biblioteca Medica Laurenziana from Florence, Italy (Al-Muradi, 2008). It is a handwritten copy which was finished in Toledo in 1266. The original has as its author a Ibn Khalaf al- Muradi, who is regarded by some historians as an Andalusian engineer. The original book was written in Cordoba (10th-11th centuries) and it refers to automatic objects, created in Arabian culture in the 10th century. The screed is made up by 48 folios (96 pages, whose dimensions are 273x 200 mm). Donald Hill claims that the volume is a primary source of Arabic-medieval information about engineering. It is a book of mechanisms of complex precision. In 1206 Ibn al-Razzaz al-Jazari completed his work, whose title has sometimes been translated as "The Book of Knowledge of Ingenious Mechanical Devices" (Al-Jazari, & Hill, 1974). In the treaty by Al –Jazari appear drawings of machines to extract water, water clocks, musical automats and a pump which turned the rotating of a mill into the to-and-fro movement of a piston capable of pumping water at great pressure. Historians like Hill (Al-Jazari, & Hill, 1974) admit that Al-Jazari created the hydraulic pump three centuries before it was designed in the West, for instance. In short, some of his inventions went much beyond those described by Banü Müsa and his descriptions and diagrams are so detailed that the engineers of our days can reproduce his devices.

The new technologies have not only allowed the digitalization and translation of the text into several languages, but also that the schemes of the mechanisms have been built in 3D and animated, using graphic software such as 3D Studio Max, for instance. The designs have been examined and verified by the programmers in constant feedback between the model and the text, since each one of these elements is accompanied by an explanatory text of the mechanisms, for instance. Once the mechanic and/or geometric hypothesis had been obtained, they tested the obtained result. The functioning is verified and is compared with the text. That is to say, the strategy consisted in an interactive process, with a constant feedback, for each one of the components of the figures of the book. In view of eventual inconsistencies and mistakes, the process recommenced from the start, until the obtainment of the final machinery. Evidently, there are cases in which several reconstruction hypotheses are possible, and the one chosen was in keeping with the simplest and most correct possible functioning. Moreover, the designs in the text are not descriptive, since there was no notion of perspective in the writings of the 9th century. Now these machines have among themselves several common denominators which allow to establish five great sets:

- The clocks which are all hydraulic and with their movement set in motion all the gears. The hours are signalled with the emission of a metallic ball, of the movement of automat dummies and lamps.
- The small theatres or mechanical boxes with dolls. In them there are small wired dummies, with gears and twines, which move in function of pre-established routes. The goal of these movements is to tell a story.
- The war devices in the shape of extensible scissors, to reach elevated points of a construction such as a tower, for instance.
- The magic wells to pick the water in an original way.
- The meridians that indicate the passing of time and the hours through the sunlight.

Figure 5. Detail of the animation of a hydraulic clock and the fall of metallic balls at the moment of changing the hour

Figure 6. Advantage of the use of the computer animations to see the internal mechanism (frame a), since the clock has an external coverage (frame b)

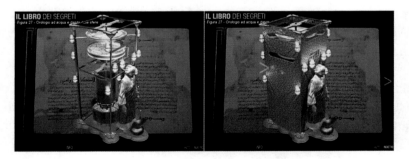

An analysis of the archetypes and empathy makes apparent that the lineal structure of the content facilitates the navigation among the different pages/frames which make up the interactive system. The sequentiality of the

Figure 7. A mechanic box which tells a fable

reading takes into account the origin of the text, with which the reading is made from the objects which appear on the index from the right to the left, as it can be seen in the Figures 10 and 11, for example. That is, it follows the same disposition as the pages (Figures 4, 5, 6, for example) with which it is preserved and projected in time, through the offline multimedia interactive system, the originality of an engineering work which belongs to the cultural heritage of humanity.

Aside from the great value that the movement contributes to the objects of the interactive system in a DVD-ROM support, in it is present one of the main attributes of the quality of a multimedia system, such as the naturalness of the metaphor (Cipolla-Ficarra, 2010; Cipolla-Ficarra, et al., 2012), since the pages are animated and it is as if the reader/user were really reading the book. This metaphor is of great importance, especially with the momentum of the social networks where the Z generation can't concentrate their attention on the traditional reading of universal classics, for instance.

Figure 8. The animation of a war weapon with an extensible scissors

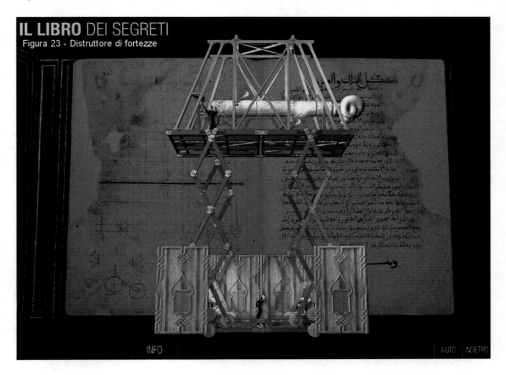

LESSONS LEARNED

The structure that is made up between the nodes and the links of the different contents of the dynamic and static means, boosts that the users lend more attention to the movement of each one of the 3D figures which make up the system. Moreover, the possibility of seeing a same figure in 3D from different perspectives thanks to the reusability of the visual information, has a high didactic value and boosts motivation, through which the communicability of the content will be increased, even if a thousand years have passed. Each one of the stages of the production of a 3D animation has been respected and presents an excellent quality from the selection of the textures for the different materials down to the rendering, including the special effects of the illumination.

The simplicity in the structure of the navigation where lineality prevails following the original text, but enriched in different ways the access to the

Figure 9. Sun clock with a water mechanism
(Approximate Translation: In the figure is the description of a sun clock with a water mechanism.)

information stored in the database, such as the index of the objects in figure 10, foster this interactive system to be used in other interactive supports such as an interactive whiteboard inside a museum. Having available a bigger size in the interface increases the educational function of the animations to better understand each one of the aspects of the presented devices. That is, the current interface can be perfectly adapted to an interactive interface of a bigger size without any need to make big changes from the point of view of the interactive programming of the device. Perhaps an option to slow down the animations might be included at the moment of the viewing. (With the current multimedia interactive system it is highlighted the validity of the traditional concepts at the moment of conceiving a system of a model, similar to the 90s, but using all the power of the commercial graphic software of the second decade of the 21st century, and with a low cost in the currently used hardware compared to the 90s. In short, a strategy of interactive design of the good quality off-line multimedia systems taken to our days.

Figure 10. The distribution of the figures in the index which allow to access the computer animations is laid in such a way that it allows a reading from right to left, that is, in the multimedia project the original layout of the book has been respected (Approximate Translation: Index of the figures)

Figure 11. The reading and/or translation of each one of the pages allows for the first time to understand all the details of the figures with the option of seeing those mechanisms from different perspectives

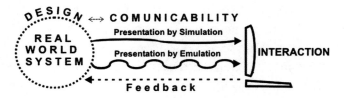

Figure 12. The icons and the aids make the interactive system ideal for the fruition of all kinds of potential users

(Approximate Translation: Help section for user navigation. The icons refer to the activation and deactivation of the music, pre-visualization of the figure in 3D, moving the magnifying glass area in any point of the page, visualize the original manuscript, and close help.)

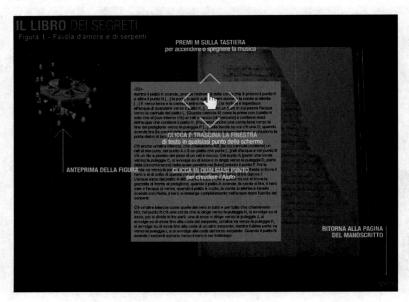

CONCLUSION

The use of graphic computing to depict the historical past of machines, for instance, has always been very positive since the early works where personal computers and commercial graphic software were used, since the mid 20th century. However, joining to the original text the translation into several languages and seeing on the computer screen machines in 3D function starting from sketches where the z coordinate was missing, make the analyzed system a good model to be followed in analogous situations. In the interactive system has been detected the presence of archetypes and empathy. A presence which can be examined in a binary way, through the presence or absence of the components which intervene/boost in the graphic dynamic/ static coherence whether it is in 2D and/or 3D. In other words, the designer/ programmer of the 3D animations of the analyzed system, for instance, has resorted to archetypes and empathy to achieve a higher acceptance of the content and the presentation of the dynamic and/or static information in the interface by the potential users of the offline multimedia system. Finally, the

Figure 13. Classical image of a hypermedia system in the decade of the 90s, where the text shifts in an automatic way as the locution advances

(*Approximate Translation: The history of the manuscript. The audio and the text narrate how a copy of the manuscript has arrived at the Biblioteca Medicea Laurenziana from Andalusia (Spain) to Florence (Italy).*)

communicability is very high, since other quality attributes of the interactive design have also been detected, such as the naturalness of the metaphor, and the reusability of the information, boosting the educational and informative character of the multimedia system.

The advantage of a correct use of the graphic static and dynamic computer science boosts the interaction of the contents and the dissemination of the contents with potential users whose previous knowledge of computer science may be very low or even none. In this sense, the lineal structure with guided links fulfills a very important function in the navigation and interaction with the dynamic media. These dynamic media go beyond the mere reproduction function of the real objects, including the didactical aspect at the moment of eliminating parts which hide the functioning of the mechanisms or switching the observer's point of view, to mention just two examples.

The image beats the text in this case to boost the interaction of the users. However, the inclusion of the original text, with its translation, where are described each one of the devices which make up the book, gives an additional value from the training and information point of view. This duality, deriving from the correct use of the graphic elements, boost the communicability not only interactively but also in the case that this content had to be presented in a classical audiovisual modality, such as video. This system constitutes an excellent diachronic and synchronic example of the presentation of the information in the off-line multimedia systems.

ACKNOWLEDGMENT

I would also like to show our gratitude to Maria Ficarra for sharing their pearls of wisdom with us during the course of this research. Besides, I thank Alejandra Quiroga, Jacqueline Alma, Mary Brie, Luisa Varela, Amélie Bordeaux, Pamela Fulton, Doris Edison, Sonia Flores, Julia Ruiz, Giselda Verdone, Jim Carré, Donald Nilson, and Carlos for assistence and comments that greatly improved the chapter.

REFERENCES

Akenine-Moller, T. & Haines, E. (2008). *Real-Time Rendering*. Natick: A. K. Peters.

Al-Jazari, I. A., & Hill, D. R. (1974). *The Book of Knowledge of Ingenious Mechanical Device*. Springer.

Al-Muradi, I. K. (2008). DVD-Rom, *The Books of Secrets*. Milan. *Leonardo*, 3.

Armstrong, W., & Green, M. (1985). The Dynamics of Articulated Rigid Bodies for Purposes of Animation. *The Visual Computer*, *1*(4), 231–240. doi:10.1007/BF02021812

Begel, A., Bosch, J., & Storey, M. (2013). Bridging Software Communities through Social Networking. *IEEE Software*, *30*(1), 26–28. doi:10.1109/MS.2013.3

Blain, J. (2012). *The Complete Guide to Blender Graphics, Computer Modeling and Animation*. Boca Raton, FL: CRC Press. doi:10.1201/b11922

Bolter, J. D., Engberg, M., & Macintyre, B. (2013). Media Studies, Mobile Augmented Reality, and Interaction Design. *Interaction*, *20*(1), 36–45. doi:10.1145/2405716.2405726

Childs, H., Geveci, B., Schroeder, W., Meredith, J., Moreland, K., Sewell, C., & Bethel, E. W. et al. (2013). Research Challenges for Visualization Software. *IEEE Computer*, *46*(5), 34–43. doi:10.1109/MC.2013.179

Cipolla-Ficarra, F. (2010). *Quality and Communicability for Interactive Hypermedia Systems: Concepts and Practices for Design*. Hershey, PA: IGI Global. doi:10.4018/978-1-61520-763-3

Cipolla-Ficarra, F. (2012). *Emerging Software for Interactive Interfaces, Database, Computer Graphics and Animation: Pixels and the New Excellence in Communicability, Cloud Computing and Augmented Reality*. Bergamo: Blue Herons Editions.

Cipolla-Ficarra, F. (2014). *Advanced Research and Trends in New Technologies, Software, Human-Computer Interaction, and Communicability*. Hershey, PA: IGI Global. doi:10.4018/978-1-4666-4490-8

Dunn, F., & Parberry, I. (2011). *3D Math Primer for Graphics and Game Development*. Boca Raton, FL: CRC Press. doi:10.1201/b11152

Einstein, A. (1995). *Ideas and Opinions*. New York: Crown Publishers.

Hodgins, J., Wooten, W., Brogan, D., & O'Brien, J. (1995). Animating Human Athletics. In *Proceedings of SIGGRAPH'95*. New York: ACM Computer Graphics. doi:10.1145/218380.218414

Holzinger, A. (2005). Usability Engineering Methods for Software Developers. *Communications of the ACM*, *48*(1), 71–74. doi:10.1145/1039539.1039541

Hughes, J. (2014). *Computer Graphics: Principles and Practice*. London: Pearson Education.

Laybourne, K. (1998). *The Animation Book: A Complete Guide to Animated Filmmaking –from Flip-Books to Sound Cartoons to 3-D Animation*. New York: Three Rivers Press.

Lengyel, E. (2012). *Mathematics for 3D Game Programming and Computer Graphics*. Boston: Course Technology - Cengage Learning.

Levy, S. (1992). *Artificial Life*. New York: Vintage Books.

MacNicol, G. (1990). 2-D Animation: Alive and Well. *Computer Graphics World*, *13*(3), 41–50.

Magnenat-Thalmann, N. (1985). *Computer Animation: Theory and Practice*. New York: Springer-Verlag. doi:10.1007/978-4-431-68433-6

Mortenson, M. E. (2006). *Geometric Modeling*. New York: Industrial Press.

Potter, C. D. (1995, January). Animation for Engineers. *Computer Graphics World*, *18*(1), 54–59.

Poynton, C. (2003). *Digital Video and HDTV Algorithms and Interfaces*. San Francisco, CA: Morgan Kaufmann Publishers.

Robertson, B. (1995). Toy Story: A Truimph of Animation. *Computer Graphics World*, *8*(18), 28–38.

Solomon, C. (1994). *The History of Animation: Enchanted Drawings*. New York: Wings Books.

Wrenninge, M. (2012). *Production Volume Rendering: Design and Implementation*. Boca Raton, FL: CRC Press. doi:10.1201/b12698

Zeid, I., & Sivasubramanian, R. (2009). *CAD/CAM Theory and Pratice*. London: McGraw Hill.

Zink, J., Pettineo, M., & Hoadey, J. (2011). *Practical Rendering & Computation with Direct 3D 11*. Boca Raton, FL: CRC Press.

ADDITIONAL READING

Alexander, R. M. (1983). *Animal Mechanics*. Oxford: Blackwell Scientific Publications.

Barford, N. C. (1973). *Mechanics*. New York: John Wiley & Sons.

Barrow, H. G., & Tenenbaum, J. M. (1981). In Proceedings Computational Vision. New York: IEEE, 69(5) 572-595

Bethel, E. W., Childs, H., & Hansen, C. (2012). *High Performance Visualization: Enabling Extreme-Scale Scientific Insight*. Boca Raton: CRC Press.

Bloomenthal, J., & Wyvill, B. (1997). *Introduction to Implicit Surfaces*. San Francisco: Morgan Kaufmann Publishers.

Cipolla-Ficarra, F. (2012). *New Horizons in Creative Open Software, Multimedia, Human Factors and Software Engineering*. Bergamo: Blue Herons Editions.

Cipolla-Ficarra, F. et al.. (2010). *Advances in Dynamic and Static Media for Interactive Systems: Communicability, Computer Science and Design*. Bergamo: Blue Herons Editions.

Cipolla-Ficarra, F., & Cipolla-Ficarra, M. (2009). Computer Animation and Communicability in Multimedia System: A Trichotomy Evaluation. In *Proceedings New Directions in Intelligent Interactive Multimedia Systems and Services* (pp. 103–115). Heidelberg: Springer. doi:10.1007/978-3-642-02937-0_10

Cipolla Ficarra, F., & Richardson, L. (2011). Photography and Computer Animation for Scientific Visualization: Lessons Learned. In *Proceedings First International Conference on Advances in New Technologies, Interactive Interfaces, and Communicability*, Heidelberg: Springer, 102-111 doi:10.1007/978-3-642-20810-2_11

Corso, J., Ye, G., Burschka, D., & Hager, G. D. (2008). A Practical Paradigm and Platform for Video-Based Human-Computer Interaction. *IEEE Computer*, *41*(5), 48–55. doi:10.1109/MC.2008.141

Cotton, W., & Anthes, A. (1989). *Storm and Cloud Dynamics*. New York: Academic Press.

Craig, J. (1989). *Robotics*. New York: Addison-Wesley.

Cutting, J. (1986). *Perception with an Eye for Motion*. Cambridge: MIT Press.

Frautsch, S. C., Olenick, R. P., Apostol, T. M., & Goodstein, D. L. (1986). *The Mechanical Universe*. Cambridge: Cambridge University Press. doi:10.1017/CBO9780511818493

Hainich, R., & Bimber, O. (2011). *Displays Fundamentals & Applications*. Boca Raton: CRC Press.

House, R. (1993). *Cloud Dynamics*. New York: Academic Press.

MacNicol, G. (1990). 2D Animation: Alive and Well. *Computer Graphics World*, *13*(3), 40–50.

Magnenat-Thalmann, N., & Thalmann, D. (1991). *New Trends in Animation and Visualization*. New York: Wiley-Interscience.

Mahoney, D. P. (1996). Riding the Wave of Motion-Based Movies. *Computer Graphics World, 19*(2), 30–31.

McFarland, D. (1971). *Feedback Mechanisms in Animal Behaviour*. London: London Academic Press.

McFarland, D., & Bösser, T. (1993). *Intelligent Behaviour in Animals and Robots*. Cambridge: MIT Press.

Prince, J. H. (1981). *How Animals Move*. New York: Elsevier/Nelson Books.

Szeliski, R., & Tonnesen, D. (1992). Surface Modeling with Oriented Particle Systems. *Computer Graphics, 26*(2), 185–194. doi:10.1145/142920.134037

Thomas, B. (1991). *Disney's Art of Animation from Mickey Mouse to "Beauty and the Beast."*. New York: Hyperion.

Thompson, W. (2011). *Visual Perception from a Computer Graphics Perspective*. Boca Raton: CRC Press.

Watt, A., & Watt, M. (1991). *Advanced Animation and Rendering Techniques*. New York: ACM Press.

KEY TERMS AND DEFINITIONS

Access Structure: The logical framework for locating and/or find data, for example, an index.

Animation: A set of static images 2D and/or 3D, joined together and show simultaneously so that they appear to move.

Communicability: A qualitative communication between the user and the interactive system, such as mobile phones, augmented reality, immersion multimedia, hypermedia, among others. The extent to which an interactive system successfully conveys its functionality to the user.

Emulation and Simulation of the Reality: Traditionally, from the point of view of the communication between the user and computer, it was noted that an emulation of reality exists in artistic models. As a result, the degree of realism is lower and this can, on occasions, impair an excellent interaction process. In a representation by simulation the degree of realism is greater.

Interactive System: A computer device made up by a CPU and peripherals, whose functioning requires a constant interaction with the user. Currently these systems tend to their miniaturization and/or invisibility, the mobility and wireless connect-ability among them.

Natural-ness of the Metaphor: The user's ability to understand the set of images that make up the structure of the interface. An image is natural when by itself it tends to suggest a single meaning. The naturalness of the image is in direct relation to the representation by simulation of the reality.

Chapter 9
Poiesis and Video Games for Adults:
A Good Example for the Cultural Heritage

Francisco V. Cipolla-Ficarra
Latin Association of Human-Computer Interaction, Spain & International Association of Interactive Communication, Italy

Jaqueline Alma
Electronic Arts, Canada

Miguel Cipolla-Ficarra
Latin Association of Human-Computer Interaction, Spain & International Association of Interactive Communication, Italy

Jim Carré
University of the Netherlands Antilles, Curaçao

ABSTRACT

The first studies of the social sciences aimed at the videogames of the 80s and the methods to evaluate the usability engineering of the 90s have highlighted a set of positive and negative aspects in the human-computer interaction which go from the ergonomic aspects of the devices down to the motivations to draw the attention of the users in the interaction process. In this research we present the results reached with adult users in relation to the communicability and the usability in a classical videogame for PC. We also present the elements of interactive design which boost the poiesis in cultural heritage that the analyzed videogame contains.

DOI: 10.4018/978-1-5225-3437-2.ch009

INTRODUCTION

The word *"poiesis"* stems from the Greek, which means "creation" or "production" (Nöth, 1995). One understands by *poiesis* any creative process. Iit is from this conception that, in the field of the arts, poiesis refers to the fascination provoed at the moment in which, through multiple associative phenomena contributed by perception, the different elements of a set interrelate and integrate to generate a new entity, called aesthetic, for instance. That is, a way of knowledge and also a playful way: expression doesn't exclude the game. For instance, in the categories of interactive design, the layout is the first of those categories related to aesthetics. However, the rest of categories (layout, content, navigation, connection, panchronic, and structure) also play an important role in reaching the highest aesthetics to foster and keep the attention of the user at the moment of interacting with the videogame. The notion of aesthetics can be linked to the notion of beauty in the arts (Beardsley, 1982). According to Plato, the arts can materialize to different degrees the quality of beauty. The beauty of the concrete things may change or disappear, it may exist for some and for others not. Beautiful things take very much into account the due proportion among the parts, through a mathematic calculation (Beardsley, 1982). In this sense, and with the passing of the centuries it sends us back to the notions of the *Divina Proporzione* by Leonarod Da Vinci (Figure 1) and/or *Sezione Aurea* (Figure 2), at the moment of disposing the elements that make up an interface, that is, the topology of the scrollbar, the icons, the illustrations, the text, etc. Now the qualities of the measures (metron) and the proportion (symmetron), constitute beauty and excellence. In this sense, Escher's works make up an excellent field of study, from the geometric point of view of the impossible figures (Schattschneider & Emmer, 2005; Escher, 1996). In the beauty and excellence interrelation,

Figure 1. The Divina Proporzione and the interface space

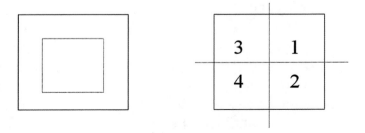

Figure 2. The Sezione Aurea

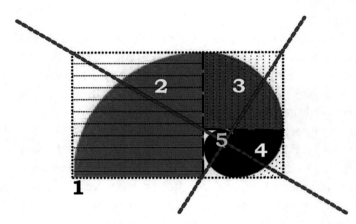

since it depends on measure, beauty is assigned a high post in the final list of the good things. In other words, these thoughts by the classical Greeks are interesting at the moment of evaluating the usability of an interactive system, generating a set of quality metrics, for instance (Figure 4).

If the diagonals are drawn as in the figure where they cross we have a very important focal point for the youngest television viewers or computer users in the Western world. In the succession of quadrants the so-called logarithmic spiral is achieved. Now the artistic works made since Antiquity in Persia, Egypt, China, etc., had their basis in the observation of nature. It was Leonardo Da Vinci in the Renaissance who unravelled the keys in the flora and fauna, for instance. That is why that they are also in the logarithms spiral present in the shell of a snail, shell of the nautilus, entrepreneurial logos, etc. A good example of the multimedia interface is the Figure 4 (Attica Cybernetics, 1994) because it is present the *divina proporzione*.

However, the measurement of quality in usability engineering (Nielsen, 1993) hadn't been considered at the moment of the implementation of the notion at the end of the 80s and early 90s as it can be seen in the Figure 4. What is more, the author of the notion considered that it wasn't possible to measure it (Nielsen, 1996). Those were mistaken statements because both usability engineering and the techniques used to measure them have components of the social sciences (Nielsen & Mack, 1994). Besides, it is feasible through the through the quality notions of the software engineers, human-computer interaction, the design models of the interactive systems, semiotics, etc., to establish heuristic quality attributes, the interdependence of said attributes

Figure 3. Escher: interactive system off-line

and lastly the metrics (Cipolla-Ficarra, 1997; Cipolla-Ficarra, 1998; Cipolla-Ficarra, 2002). Quality attributes, metrics, techniques and methods have been developed for the heuristic evaluation of usability and communicability. Both notions, usability and communicability, aren't synonymous. Nor should usability engineering and semiotics engineering (Sieckenius-de-Souza, 2004). In this latter case, we see how the mercantilist factor of scientific-educational knowledge edges out science epistemology. Semiotics is not an engineering because it belongs to the context of the social sciences. The mercantilism in the factual sciences on the part of the formal sciences is due to a human factor which tries to justify the inclusion of people in a set of activities to which they do not belong because of their academic training or professional

Figure 4. This interface is a good example because it has the Divine Proporzione at the moment of disposing the elements that make up an interface.

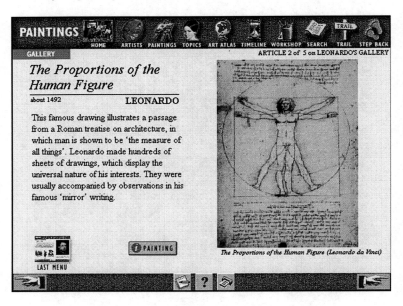

experience. In public, private and hybrid universities of southern Europe, it is very beneficial to them from the financial point of view to attract new students to courses, seminars, etc., where the qualitative aspects of the game, such as playability, learning, such as learnability, etc., are "canned and sold", in the academic training offer, as an innovating engineering. This is one of the reasons because of which there is a misguided attempt to turn semiotics into an engineering. In few words, that transformation does not derive from a creative or transversal process of the different disciplines of the social and/ or factual sciences, but rather from human factors linked to the economics (in the short run) in the university context.

Establishing quality attributes, metrics, etc., applying semiotics, for instance, to a new discipline in the computer environment, such as usability engineering, has proved to be with the passing of time a source of conflicts stemming from the human and social factors in an academic context. As a rule, they are professionals hailing from the formal sciences who aim at including the set of the social sciences in their studies (Cipolla-Ficara, et al., 2012). They do it in the least possible time and disregarding the advances from the social sciences towards the formal sciences. In the study of metrics for interactive systems there are a myriad cases in the format of scientific

Figure 5. In the main principles enumerated by Nielsen in the usability of a computer system (1989) [6], the aspect of generating quality attributes to measure the usability of an interactive system was not regarded, for instance.

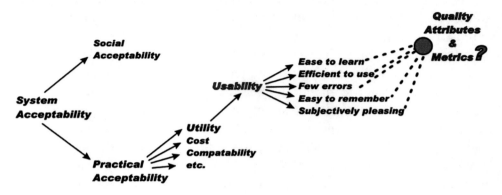

articles and/or website. The common denominator of those deviations is to prevent that the factual sciences occupy a prevailing place in the current era of the expansion of communicability through the ICTs.

COMPUTER ANIMATION: TEAMWORK EVOLUTION

As Beardsly claims, "Animation has always required a close collaboration between artists and scientists, poets and engineers. Current trends in computer animation have made successful and effective teamwork a necessity. To address these issues we have developed an interdisciplinary computer animation course for artists and scientists that focuses on team work and contemporary issues in computer animation" (Ebert & Bailey, 2000). In that statement we find three terms: artists, scientists and interdisciplinarity which have been extrapolated from the USA to southern Europe without making any cultural adaption, for instance. The results have been negative with the passing of time, especially from the point of view of the human factors. For instance, currently the job stability of self-styled "renaissance" artists in Spain, against the perennial instability of the scientists; the use of the term interdisciplinarity to conceal the meteorite or antimodels factor, in the Catalan university education (students who accumulate six or even more university titles in a decade, without there being a common link among them, and simultaneously holding posts of managers in firms alien or not to the university where they get those degrees), and a long etcetera.

A reality which contradicts the principles of the animators of the Warner Brothers, who between 1930 and 1950 have produced animated cartoons regarded as the most famous of the 20th century (Maltin, 1987). In those animations existed an interrelational collaboration among the directors, animators, storyboard writers, technicians, artists and musicians, obtaining an excellent result of the project. Consequently, the notion of interdisciplinarity in the computer and/or analogical animations carried out in the educational context should foster team work, where the practices should serve to learn the ones from the others, that is, among students, including the professors. A learning process where the notions of software, hardware, esthetics and art should constantly interact among themselves, as Karen Sullivan contends. From the point of view of the 3D, aside from knowing the technique, it is necessary to be able to tell a story. An action which is the second decade of the new millennium, the creative aspect, can be omitted or go unnoticed by the addressees or users of the video games, for instance. "Computer animation is largely not about hardware and software. Unquestionably, computer animators must become proficient with technology. They must be willing to develop the patience to spend long hours in virtual spaces doing very detailed work. But knowing specific software will not secure success (or employment). The single major problem (…) is how to allow technology to support the idea" (Sullivan, 2001). That is, that we are facing the technical aspect lacking in inventiveness or creativity. To reach that creativity it is necessary to develop it in a planning process which goes through the communicability process, the study of art history, the interest towards constant experimentation and a down-to-detail work in each one of the elements which make up an animation or video game.

PLANIFICATION AND GRADUAL EVOLUTION: THE KEYWORDS FOR CONTINUOUS VIDEO GAMES

The term planification has always been associated to any project since the beginnings of computer science, irrespective of the dimension of said project, the financial resources available, the total of members of the programmers team, systems analysts, software engineers, etc. Those who do not plan, even if they have large sums of money in the centennial industrial environment, only generate productive anti-models although they may be labeled as R&D or the international image of the commerce of a country, with the famous "made in…" (Cipolla-Ficarra, Nicol, & Cipolla-Ficarra, 2010). One of the best examples in the planification, development and international diffusion of the multimedia video games for computer is SimCity (Electronic Arts, 2013).

Briefly, SimCity is a video game which is included in the set of the simulation video games. The videogame consists in creating a new city, shaping up the orography of the territory (rivers, mountains, lakes, etc.) or starting from an existing town. The first commercial version is from 1989, in a floppy support, and it worked in the PCs with the MS-DOS operative system. Originally, it was developed in a Commodore 64. Starting from this first version, other versions were developed which evolved with the available software and hardware for the multimedia contents: SimCity 2000, SimCity 3000, SimCity 4, the SimCity reboot, the Streets of SimCity spinoff, SimCity societies, SimCity iPhone (Cipolla-Ficarra, et al., 2013), down to the current SimCity 5 (Electronic Arts, 2013). In 2008 Electronic Arts (owner of the copyrights) and following the project One Laptop per Child, distributes the source code in GPL 3, turning this videogame into an open source project under the name of Micropolis.

In the videogame, the player becomes a mayor, and has to manage the whole city. A city which he will build or modify in relation to the requests of its inhabitants (called Sims) and the available budget. If it is decided to start the city from scratch, he/she can dispose of the territory at his/her will to build the power stations, the neighborhoods, the factories, the schools, the libraries, the stadiums, the shops, the squares, etc. Now in this construction and management process of the city a series of difficulties come up that must be faced by the mayor, his/her administration, the sims, etc., such as flooding, fires, tornados, earthquakes, etc. It has a superior global visual –an isometric vision (Saucan, 2012).

The possibility of changing the perspectives in the visualization of the city, like the option of getting closer or further away to analyze certain areas, are positive elements to increase the simulation of 3D realism and the motivation of the human computer interaction. It is also a positive feature the distribution of the components in the user's interface, such as are the icons that allow the navigation through the different areas of the videogame, the statistic resources of the evolution of the city, the presentation of the interactive information stemming from the social media, etc. All these components belonging to the interactive design categories (layout, content, navigation, structure, etc.) have stayed constant with the passing of time, in the different versions of the videogame. Keeping a constancy in the structural elements of an interactive system and improving them with the passing of time in relation to the advances of the graphic software, for instance, denotes a good planification of the production of the videogame and connotes the existence of users who evolve with the new versions. In the current work we have shaped up our group of users with those who since the 90s have been playing with this videogame, whether in all its versions or some of them. We have also included users who for the first time interacted with the latest commercial version of 2013.

USERS, EXPERIMENTS, AND RESULTS

Although our main goal is to determine the poeisis of the videogame, which is related with communicability, we have included some aspects of the usability of the system, such as its installation in several computers by the users. The users have an age which oscillates between the 40-50 years. These users have been split into three groups of 5, those who have interacted with all the versions of the SimCity, those who have interacted with some of them and those who interact with it for the first time. The experiments have been divided into two stages. The first is related to the usability and the second with communicability. Each of the groups has had a new version of the videogame which they have had to install in their PC in an autonomous way, avoiding the use of the Internet, that is, with the instructions of the videogame. Once the installation of the videogame has been carried out, each user was assigned the task of locating quickly three elements related to cultural heritage. The experiments were carried out in a human-computer interaction lab, where evaluators of communicability intervened. The evaluation techniques used were the video sections for the installation of the videogame, direct observation and users surveys to determine the poiesis. The results are in the following graphics:

The results obtained make apparent that both from the point of view of usability and from the communicability it is an excellent system. The values are in seconds and represent the average of the values obtained inside the group. The time used for the installation of the videogame in the first group of users, it adjusts to the standard values which the computer requires to record the files in the hard disk. Although one of the requisites of the system is to be wired to the Internet, some users have used the dictionnary of technical terms which they didn't know beforehand. Besides, the computers used are PCs with the Windows XP operative system, wired to the Internet and they meet the requirements specified by the manufacturer of the videogame. The systems requirements are:

Figure 6. Time used in the installation of the videogame

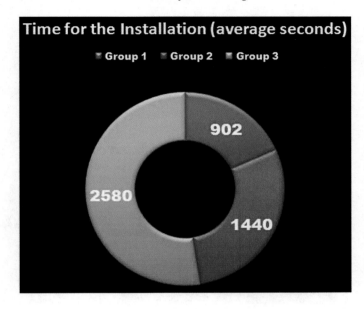

Figure 7. Use of the Internet (help) for the installation of the videogame (total people)

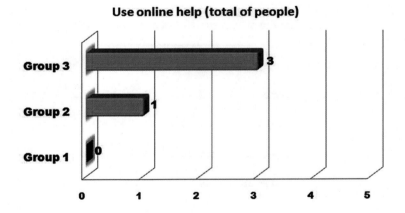

- **Operating System (Minimum):** Windows XP, Windows Vita, Windows 7 or Windows 8.
- **CPU:** AMD Athlon 64x2 Dual-Core 4000+ or better or Intel Core 2 Duo Processor 2.0 GHz or better.
- **RAM:** At least 2Gb.
- **Disc Drive:** DVD drive.

Figure 8. Time used to find three elements related to cultural heritage

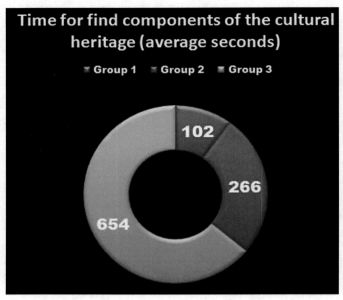

Figure 9. Elements which determine the presence of poiesis (total of the users)

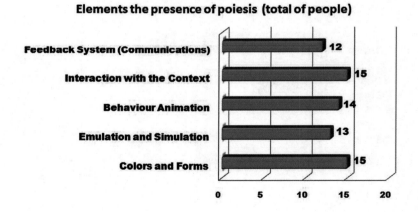

- **Hard Drive:** At least 10 Gb or free space.
- **Video:** ATI Radeon HD 2400 or better, NVIDIA 7800 or better, Intel HD Graphics or better.
- **Broadband Internet:** Minimun 256 kbps download, 64 kbps upload.

Only 3 people of the third group of users have had to resort to the Internet to carry out some definitions related to the hardware because it was the first time in their lives that they installed an interactive system in their computers.

The localization of the elements of the cultural heritage has required implicitly an additional set of activities related to such task, as were some of the rhetoric questions which have been asked to 80% of the participants of What is cultural heritage?, Can cultural heritage and tourism be considered jointly?, and Can nature also be included in the cultural heritage of the city? The users of our experiment have established that the monuments, the museums, the libraries, the schools, the universities, the plazas and/or gardens that make up basically the cultural heritage of a city. That is, that these groups of users of SimCity, find in the cultural heritage strong interrelation nexuses of interrelation with the education and nature.

Finally, poiesis can be found in the combination of the colors and the "warm" shapes (primary colors + curves) of the buildings and other constructions, the simulation and emulation of the city, especially in the animated components (the movement of transportation, respecting the traffic rules, sea waves, the effe+ùncs<cts of nocturnal lighting, such as the shadows, the glinting on the glass, etc.), lthe possibility of coming closer to a structural problem and getting far from it at the moment of carrying out a work to understand the impact on the area, constantly having statistic or global information of the city and its denizens, the communicative feedback system between the mayor, the sims and the user (module of news about daily life, resorting to transparencies and blurring to present textual information, using the emoticons, etc.). Ranking by order of importance from major to lesser the four interactive design categories we have in the first place the layout or presentation, followed by the navigation and the content, and finally there is the structure.

LESSONS LEARNED

The poiesis of the SimCity has been found in the current study in the realism of the futurist architecture of the construction and in the interactive dialogue system and in the informative textual-iconographic. Mainly in the static image and with panoramic views. Although the poiesis refers to the presentation of the information and the content, in the system of the analyzed video game it interrelates with the navigation and the structure that underlies at the moment of having access to the different dynamic and/or static data that are in the hyperbase. From the point of view of usability engineering the ease of use has been confirmed at the moment of the installation of the system in the computer. Usability engineering has been overcome, as the users of the 90s have interacted daily with the PCs, whether with working, educational, pastime or games purposes, etc. Currently we are transiting in the age of the expansion of communicability, essentially with micro computing applied to the multimedia mobile phones. An era that requires that the poiesis is increased exponentially in the contents of the multimedia systems.

Finally, another of the important aspects of the current videogame is how the users locate not only the presence of elements of the cultural heritage, but also the necessity of merging it with nature and education, for instance. That is, to generate a single bidirectional triadic entity between cultural heritage, nature and education. Now when a content from an interactive system is aesthetically excellent and fulfills a function of utility such as can be the help to the promotion of cultural heritage, through a videogame, the relationship of its main function with its aesthetic character is something important. The controversy about the functioning in the art or architecture, for instance, has a lot to do with the relation with the practical functions for a correct navigation In the system and the esthetics of the interface, for instance. The central issue of the dichotomy is whether the form should always follow the function, or if the form of the object should be considered with a relative independence from the practical function it has. In the current videogame analyzed this

Figure 10. An excellent example of the presence of the poiesis in a static image of SimCity 5, where the rendering boosts the 3D image

Figure 11. The style of the curves, the transparences, the combination of primary colors strengthen the poiesis in the interface of the SimCity
(Approximate Translation: The video camera. In the information it is assured that it looks like a quiet town, but it has some problems and it invites the user to visit the city hall, for which she has to press the left button of the mouse and pull it to turn the camera.)

Figure 12. The information style stays, typical of the social media, and prompts the interaction of the user with the videogame
(Approximate Translation: In the figure of the balloon of the comic, in the left lower area, the user is being asked to create a residential area. Meanwhile in the lower central part appears the image of the residential area tool.)

Figure 13. Switching from the global or panoramic view to the foreground of the details of a problem, is a means to draw the user's attention and boost the navigation of the videogame, such as can be the resolution of a last minute problem
(Approximate Translation: The area shown the region where the city is. Besides, it is indicated that each one of the cities may have a different mayor, or the same mayor can rule them all.)

Figure 14. The animations inside the videogame emulate the daily reality of the denizens of the city, such as stopping before a red traffic light
(Approximate Translation: Electricity. There you have it! That coal truck brings coal to the power plant. When it arrives, the power plant will start to supply electricity to the city.)

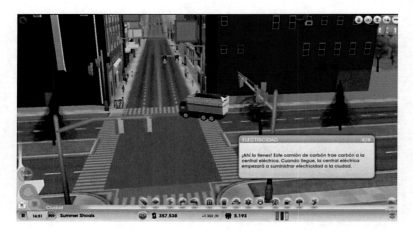

problem does not arise because the poiesis makes that the components of the interactive design, irrespective of the category to which they belong, exists without any need of enclosing new functions to the elements that make up the whole of the interactive system.

CONCLUSION

The esthetics of SimCity is to be found in each one of the categories of interactive design: layout, content, navigation, conection, panchronic, and structure. This is an esthetics that, although it has evolved with the passing of time, it has kept masterfully a fundamental value: the freedom of creating and managing the content, that is, a city. From that point of view, the poiesis duplicates itself because on the one hand, we have the resources of navigation that the system offers to the user in each moment to adapt to daily reality, but it also boosts the creativity of the user to manage resources stored in the database of the system. In this freedom of choice is to be found the core of computer science in decision-making which acquire the written form of "if… then…", "if…then…else…", "while...when", etc. in the several programming languages. In the dots are included the operators or Boolean values. Operators which boost the logical programming that a computer program entails. The resources of traditional semiotics, linked to the work of the communicability experts, has demonstrated once again to be a valid tool to detect quickly and with very low costs the quality of the design of an interactive system, in this case, aimed at pastime or entertainment. The poeisis of SimCity has evolved through time, in each one of the different versions of the videogame and it stills boosts the motivation of the adult users all around the world.

ACKNOWLEDGMENT

We would like to extend very warm thanks to Maria Ficarra and all those who have played a part in this research: Luisa Varela and Valeria Villarreal.

REFERENCES

Attica Cybernetics. (1994). *Great Artists CD-Rom*. London: Attica Cybernetics.

Beardsley, M. (1982). *The Aesthetic Point of View*. Ithaca, NY: Cornell University Press.

Cipolla-Ficarra, . (2013). *Advanced Research and Trends in New Technologies, Software, Human-Computer Interaction, and Communicability*. Hershey, PA: IGI Global. In Print.

Cipolla-Ficarra, F. (1997). Evaluation of Multimedia Components. In *Proceedings International Conference on Multimedia Computing and Systems*. IEEE Computer Society. doi:10.1109/MMCS.1997.609769

Cipolla-Ficarra, F. (1998). Method for evaluation of hypermedia usability. In *Proc. 7th IFAC/IFIP/IFORS/IEA Symposium on Analysis, Design and Evaluation of Man Machine Systems and Human Interface*. Kyoto: Elsevier.

Cipolla-Ficarra, F. (2002). Homepage and Communications: Quality Metrics. In *Proceedings Eight International Conference on Distributed Multimedia Systems*. San Francisco: DMS.

Cipolla-Ficarra, F. (2012). *Computer Engineering and Innovations in Education for Virtual Learning Environments, Intelligent Systems and Communicability: Multimedia Mobile Technologies, Experiences in Research and Quality Educational Trends*. Bergamo: Blue Herons Editions.

Cipolla-Ficarra, F., Nicol, E., & Cipolla-Ficarra, M. (2010). Research and Development: Business into Transfer Information and Communication Technology. *Proceed. First international conference on Advances in new technologies, interactive interfaces, and communicability*, 44-61.

Corbalán, F. (2010). *La proporción áurea: El lenguaje matemático de la belleza*. Barcelona: RBA. (in Spanish)

Ebert, D., & Bailey, D. (2000). Collaborative and Interdisciplinary Computer Animation Course. *Computer Graphics*, *34*(3).

Electronic Arts. (2013). *Simcity Limited Edition DVD*. Redwood: Electronic Arts.

Escher, M. C. (1996). *Escher Interactive CD-Rom*. New York: Harry N. Abrams.

Maltin, L. (1987). *Of Mice and Magic: A History of American Animated Cartoons*. New York: Plume.

Nielsen, J. (1993). *Usability Engineering*. London: Academic Press.

Nielsen, J. (1996). Usability Metrics: Tracking Interface Improvements. *IEEE Software*, *13*(6), 12–13.

Nielsen, J., & Mack, R. (1994). *Usability Inspection Methods*. New York: Willey. doi:10.1145/259963.260531

Nöth, W. (1995). *Handbook of Semiotics*. Bloomington, IN: Indiana University Press.

Saucan, E. (2012). Isometric Embeddings in Imaging and Vision: Facts and Fiction. *Journal of Mathematical Imaging and Vision*, *43*(2), 143–155. doi:10.1007/s10851-011-0296-9

Schattschneider, D., & Emmer, M. (2005). *M. C. Escher's Legacy: A Centennial Celebration*. Berlin: Springer.

Sieckenius-de-Souza, C. (2004). *The Semiotic Engineering of Human-Computer Interaction*. Cambridge, MA: MIT Press.

Sullivan, K. (2001). Concept Development for Computer Animation. *Computer Graphics*, *35*(2).

Chapter 10
Quo Vadis "Interaction Design and Children" in Europe?

Francisco V. Cipolla-Ficarra
Latin Association of Human-Computer Interaction, Spain & International Association of Interactive Communication, Italy

Valeria Ficarra
Latin Association of Human-Computer Interaction, Spain & International Association of Interactive Communication, Italy

ABSTRACT

In the current appendix are presented the results of a heuristic study about the lack of educational control related to the new technologies and the future generations, especially children. A set of examples make known the real factors which increase the digital divide among the European population of 2020. Finally, a heuristic equation is presented to detect quickly and easily the professionals who currently tend to be misleading in their interactive design for children.

INTRODUCTION

While the European statistics indicate a vertiginous drop in the children population, especially in those countries known economically as "the European engine" (Figure 1, "Germany remains without children"), in India, a very special phenomenon is taking place in the reshaping of the population pyramid, turning into a diamond (Bijapurkar, 1979; Bijapurkar, 2006), as it can be seen in the Figure 2. This means that the parents of the children population

DOI: 10.4018/978-1-5225-3437-2.ch010

Figure 1. Information with regard to the lack of births in the Old World, for instance, in Germany

(Approximate Translation: "The government tries to correct the demographic decline with financial help, but does not succeed in convincing the families to have children") Source: El País (www.elpais. es –09.06.2013).

will have the necessary financial resources to offer to their children the latest technological breakthroughs. In contrast, in the Old World, the digital divide will keep on increasing since there will be no population renewal (Angelo & Pinna, 2008). In the midst of this reality of the statistics of the population growth, a series of deviations can be seen in the R&D projects, subsidized or not, by local, regional and Pan-European governments tending to design a non-existent future in the context of the ICT, for the children who won't exist in 2020, 2030, 2040, 2050, etc.

Figure 2. Socio-economic metamorphosis of the population in India

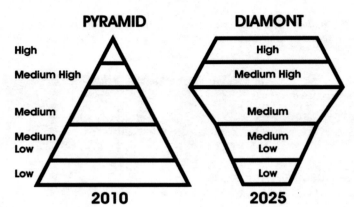

In that context of realities, the current computer science sector is trying to collect as much information as possible in the least possible time and with a cost equal to zero from the children educational sector through R&D pseudoprojects. The term "pseudo" refers to the fact that the scientific research is practically non-existent both from the theoretical and the practical point of view. From the theoretical point of view because data-gathering techniques of the traditional mass media are used, once World War II finished. That is, the opinion surveys, the filling of forms, the phone interviews, etc. (Moragas-Spa, 1985). That is, that the future that is contained in these projects, many of them financed from Brussels, entail a leap back in time of 75 years.

From the practical point of view, we go back to the mid-nineties, because it is just a matter of making simple containers of digital information, that is, databases. The fields of their records can be compiled or seen on the computer screen, through special formularies. These are forms that do not take into account the essential aspects of the interfaces design aimed at the user, in this case, basic education or primary school teachers. The function of those teachers is to provide the managers of the website with free information.

However, that way of compiling data is very similar to the PGI (General Information Program) of UNESCO in the 70s in order to compile the library information of a great part of the American continent (UNESCO, 2000). The result of that project was practically null.

Summing up, from the theoretical point of view we go back 75 years, from the practical point of view t o25 years, and from the point of view of other similar experiences, taken as example, to almost 35 years. Consequently, we are in the face of a flash back and not a flash forward, from the timeframe point of view.

In this introduction to the problem at hand, a myriad rhetoric questions arise which make up the structure of the current work.: What sectors of education, scientific research, technology transfer, etc., are fostering the inertia or return to the past in Europe of the R&D? What is the profile of those alleged professionals of the ICT in the educational environment.? What modus operandi do they use, that is, techniques or methods to reach their primary and/or secondary goals? Is it feasible to measure the performance of those pseudo professionals who deviate the main goals in interactive design for children?

Each one of these questions has an answer and at the end are presented the learned lessons and the conclusions. Lastly we point out the use of a special language (combination and techniques of the social sciences) that we are developing at the moment of presenting and/or analyzing the topics where there are human and/or social factors.

HUMAN-COMPUTER INTERACTION FOR CHILDREN: THE EUROPEAN STYLE

One of the techniques used in the marketing of the European textile sector, for instance, is changing the term "made in" by "style", since the production (that is, the looms) are located beyond the European borders, in countries like Egypt, Turkey, India, China, etc. [6]. However, they need the European country to get economic subsidies from the EU, whether it is in a blatant or disguised way. It doesn't matter if the invoicing of those centennial firms has 9 yearly digits of euros, they need to finance each one of the activities they carry out inside their half-empty offices or factories through fictitious R&D projects (Cipolla-Ficarra, 2011). The notion of ghost or fictitious projects refers to the professionals of the sector of software engineering and its derivations: computer science, systems, telecommunications, etc., which back that modus operandi, turning into a bridge from the firm to the university, through the alleged transfer of technology. The virtuality and unreality of the bridge and the technological transfer is due to projects that are stranded at the design and or planning stages but are never ended, because the funds have been spent 100% before starting the execution stage. The reader interested in this aspect can find a wide description in the following references (Cipolla-Ficarra, Ficarra, & Cipolla-Ficarra, 2011; Cipolla-Ficarra, Ficarra, & Kratky, 2011).

In the case of the universities, it suffices to analyze the professor staff of the masters or continuous training courses to detect the presence of that "ghost style" [9]. For instance, in Spain the high unemployment rates force many scientists to emigrate for a second time to the USA, describing the scientific hardships in open or public letters addressed to the Prime Minister, we have Catalan universities where the ICT, audiovisual departments, etc.,

Figure 3. The adulteration of the sciences in the ICTs and/or audiovisual departments in Barcelona (Catalonia), Spain university, for instance
www.upf.edu

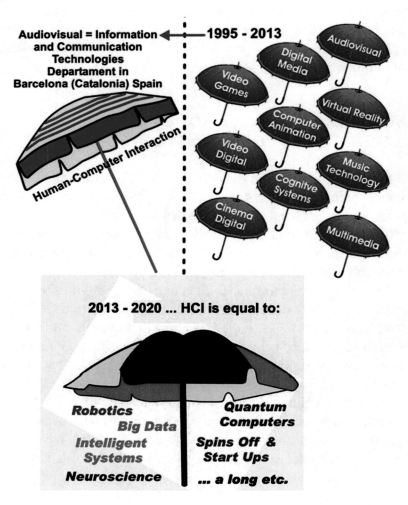

Figure 4. Trivial projects to trivialize the computer graphics, interfaces, computer art, etc.

devote themselves to make water mills for children as scientific projects of technological avant-garde (figure 4).

This debasement of the sciences takes place in those institutions under the cover of such terms as "interdisciplinarity", transversal knowledge, highly qualified experts, and a myriad similar terms which through the publicity agencies and press rooms (Cipolla-Ficarra, Ficarra & Kratky, 2011), located in those very same university departments, turn fleetingly into fads providers. All of this is feasible because in those university departments several disciplines of the scientific knowledge of the 90s have converged towards a kind of big parasol under the title of human-computer interaction.

In other words, the notion of human-computer interaction is used in some Catalan educational centers with mercantilist purposes (Cipolla-Ficarra, et al., 2011). A mercantilism raised to its highest level, as can be verified in the mass media, on which it exerts its power (for instance, the commercial magazines of the sector or the technological sections of the local, regional and national newspapers), or to the associations of the international computer sector (ACM, IEEE, etc.), to foster those deviations which do not only damage scientific epistemology, but also increase the statistics of the unemployed (Cipolla-Ficarra, 2012).

A way to draw the attention of the potential attendees to those courses related to children are the games topics and the high chances that their works are exhibited in computer art festivals, music, etc., the participation in national and international contests (whose awards have been granted beforehand by the jury), a long list of irregularities which haven't changed with the passing of time in those educational contexts because they amount to a modus operandi.

The problem of the working opportunities they offer once those masters, specialization courses or continuous training crash courses are finished, etc. is solved by hiring as directors of those courses entrepreneurs of individual companies who have got contracts with multinational firms of the video game sector. Obviously, the academic training of that kind of staff is equal to zero, but the publicity appeal is high, and may cover the failings of the course.

Theoretically, they train ICTs experts in a semester, without any previous knowledge in computer science, interfaces design, computer animation, digital video, storyboard, etc., in the programming of videogames which work with the latest hardware technologies in the multimedia sector. In some way they keep the pedagogic, publicity structure, etc., of the 90s applied to the audiovisual environment (computer animation project) and which is depicted in the following Figure 5. The interested reader can find a larger description of that deceitful strategy in the following bibliographical references (Cipolla-Ficarra, Ficarra & Cipolla-Ficarra, 2011; Cipolla-Ficara, et al., 2011; Cipolla-Ficarra, et al. 2012)

THE FOSTERING OF THE DIGITAL DIVIDE IN EUROPE

The lack of control in the university educational context of the ICTs implies that the potential future users of the interactive systems may or may not have access to the latest technological breakthroughs, to low quality experiences, whether from the usability or from the communicability point of view. This lack of quality is due to the fact that in the experimentation stage of a myriad

Figure 5. The horizontal line indicates the moment at which the making of the animations meant extra hours for the lab assistant

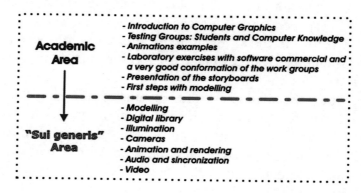

Figure 6. Students in an overcrowded small classroom in order to allegedly hand in their final projects, which have not been carried out 100% with the knowledge/practice acquired inside the classroom or the computer labs of the university course they paid for learn

projects subsidized from the EU are carried out by the relatives of those who receive said subventions. For instance, in the "Interaction Design and Children", the theoretical and/or practical aspects derive from observations, experiments, etc. beyond the usability labs, human-computer interaction, etc, of those who present results in the magazines, international congresses, etc., that is to say, their parents, uncles, etc. A way to detect that shortcoming in the naturalness of the users is the video recording of the moment of interacting with installations of virtual reality or increased reality for children, such as can be an interactive toboggan. Where there are no children but rather teenagers or youth miming the natural behaviour of a kid. In this sense the Youtube website allows to watch the videos of projects, subsidized with European public money, which do not resolve the digital divide in Europe or the overall figures of the unemployed in Spain or Portugal, for instance. That is, projects with a zero in technological transfer (Cipolla-Ficarra, 2011). A rhetoric question in this sense which any entertainment industry engineer would ask himself/herself: How many interactive toboggans have been sold? The origin of these blunders can be investigated within the context of the butterfly effect of the training of those promoters of the digital divide (Cipolla-Ficarra, 2010; Compaine, 2001; Barclay & Duggan, 2008). Promoters who have been directed even by industrial engineers and theoretically should have taught the practical aspect of the projects and not the playful aspects of the pastime, which increases the digital divide between the current and the future generations. The butterfly effect takes place when in scientific research originality is equal to zero. An example is the following figure, where is presented as original the vagueness of concepts. In the following references are detailed the butterfly effect in education and research (Cipolla-Ficarra, 2011; Cipolla-Ficarra et al., 2010).

Figure 7. Originality equal to zero in Catalan "butterfly" research, for instance

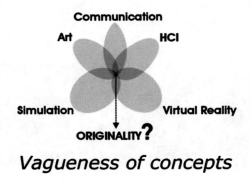

A way which the promoters have to hide their origins belonging to the butterfly effect is by resorting to parochialism to attack originality, creativity, quality, the low costs in R&D, the independent non-subsidized work, etc. (Cipolla-Ficarra, et al., 2011), which has been acquired and developed with the passing of time the real professionals of the ICTs sector. That is, on the one side we have true professionals of the technological avant-garde belonging to the set of the ICTs and on the other groups of individuals who exert a perennial destructive power through the human and the social factors through the Web or face to face communication, with colleagues of the interactive design sector, hypermedia, the human-computer interaction, virtual reality, augmented reality, etc.

THE BUTTERFLY EFFECTS IN ICTS: SOME EXAMPLES

Another strategy of the butterfly effect constituted at the end of the 90s and early 2000s in Spain, consisted in setting up akin societies directly and indirectly with the human-computer interaction (AIPO –www.aipo.es, Alzado –www.alzado.org, Cadius, etc.), from the public Catalan and Basque universities where their associates paid a pertinence fee to those associations (Cipolla-Ficarra, et al., 2012; Cipolla-Ficarra, et al., 2010), similar or superior to associations of great international prestige such as ACM (Association for Computing Machinery, www.acm.org) and IEEE (Institute of Electrical and Electronic Engineers, www.ieee.org) based in the USA. Simultaneously organizations external to the universities were launched, theoretically non-profit. However, in reality they worked as real corporations. One of their main goals consists in attracting potential associates and contacting with the media to turn into a fallacious source of news related to the new technologies and all their derivations. That is, they succeed in excluding the real professionals of the ICTs sector. With the passing of time, those associations, Spanish organizations, have become very influential power groups when it comes to making decisions in issues related to the R&D, in the educational, industrial, social fields, etc. In less than a decade (2001–2007) the experts in scientific information in the Spanish territory were totally excluded. These associations still apply those methods in emerging countries of the American continent, for instance. Resorting always to the same strategy. That is, the associates pay monthly fees, even if they are symbolic figures, contacting with the media to introduce the news that it is in their interest to spread in spaces related to the new technologies, using issues like disabled users, children, the elderly, etc. (i.e., Aitadis). In few words, the butterfly effect is fostered by people lacking originality in approaching the issues of the human-computer interaction and who only seek the greatest financial profit, in the shortest possible time and with the least personal effort.

THE TROJAN HORSE IN THE "INTERACTION DESIGN AND CHILDREN"

If they are studied in detail, the human and social factors in the context of computer science it is feasible to detect the presence of a kind of Trojan horse (Cipolla-Ficarra, Ficarra, & Cipolla-Ficarra, 2011; Cipolla-Ficarra, et al., 2011; Whitman & Mattord, 2011). A set of examples is to be found in the following rhetorical questions:

- How is it possible that young professors who don't even have scientific publications reach the role of university dean?
- How is it possible that in the European future of 2020 for the children and the design of interactive systems theories and experiments are worked upon that were surpassed in the social sciences decades ago?
- How is it possible that the "Garduña Factor" in the European university education has grown exponentially with the financial crisis and those directly responsible for the migration of hundreds of thousands of graduates, engineers, doctors (PhD), etc. beyond the European borders

are still unmovable in their lifelong posts, in the public, private and hybrid universities?

- How is it possible that the European university endogamy is not wiped out in the 21st century?
- How is it possible to find the same authors in the scientific works in congresses related with the European Interaction design and children, excluding all those who do not belong to Western culture?
- How is it possible that the participants in congresses related to childhood, education, interactive design, mobile phones, e-books, peace in the world, etc. decide as a bloc to opt out of the scientific committees of similar events and who had previously accepted in writing their pertinence?
- How is it possible that a destructive power is exerted in the scientific environment of those who allegedly foster the international project One Laptop for Children, the human-computer interaction for the disabled, etc.?
- How is it possible that a Byelorussian student, for instance, wins a contest in Trento (Italy) to take a PhD in computer science without knowing the language, and later on takes a post-graduate in the same university without having learned Italian in all that time?
- How is it possible that in the EU those who have a PhD can't even teach in the primary school because of the autonomic academic legislation, in each country that is a member of the EU?
- How is it possible that a young politician of the Lombardy regional government gets a college degree in an European country without having finished high school in his country?
- How is it possible that centennial industries force the European public universities to sing collaboration agreements in the ICTs with those foreign universities that are favourable to their business interests?
- How is it possible that the public universities are governed by religious groups?

Obviously it is a list that might be widened indefinitely. However, the inception has to be found in academic training. For instance, a graduate in physics occupying the post of coordinator of an audiovisual department, an atomic engineer taking care of children education, a mathematics graduate organizing seminars for her friends about the design models aimed at children, a former technician in avalanches in the Alps examining the behaviour of the teenagers in the social networks, an English philology graduate connecting wires to verify cognitive models of the robots, a fine arts graduate setting up tiny windmills for the kids, in front of a wall, and a long etcetera (the interested reader can find other examples in the following references (Cipolla-Ficarra, Ficarra, & Kratky, 2011; Cipolla-Ficarra, et al., 2011; Cipolla-Ficarra, et al., 2012; Cipolla-Ficarra, et al., 2010).

It is also mistaken to claim that those people carry out those operations contradicting their educational training because they have had an excellent academic record, is it can be read in the final average of the university degree. In this regard, and in contrast to what happens in the Hispanic or Anglosaxon world, in the Italian university context at the moment of submitting a final project,, the end average of the qualifications register obtained by the student can be increased by the panel at the moment of submitting the project orally. That is, raising the average to the highest value: "110/lode". Consequently, the maximum degree that can be read in the CVs of graduates, engineers, etc. in Italy are not synonymous with their having been brilliant students in all the subjects, during the whole university cycle. Evidently, these last minute modifications are unthinkable in the Spanish speaking countries, for instance.

In short, these individuals, with or without "110/lode" or other analogue classifications in the EU act inside the Interaction Design and Children project like the so called Trojan horse viruses. Now a Trojan is not in itself a computer virus, even if theoretically it can be distributed and function as such. The fundamental difference between a Trojan and a virus consists in its purpose. For a program to be a Trojan (Whitman, & Mattord, 2011) it only has to access and control the host computer, without being warned, usually under an innocuous appearance. On the contrary, a virus is a "destructive guest", but the Trojan doesn't necessarily cause damages because it isn't its goal. The main goal is to offer the attacker a remote access to the infected equipment, without need of a permit. The actions that an anonymous user can carry out in the remote equipment depend on the privileges that the legitimate user may have, in the remote computer and the characteristics of the Trojan. Some of the many operations that can be carried out in the remote computer and which we include in a parallel, as some examples of the human factors in computer science, are:

Using the computer as part of a botnet (participating in the international events to discredit them once they are finished).

Theft of personal information: keys to access the email, security codes for the access to bank accounts online, credit cards, etc. (theft of personality, the research topics, the working methods, the collaborators, etc, of the person who is the target and to be destroyed);

Erasing, modification or transfer of files (elimination of the sources where they get information for their daily works, such as the erasing of online information –works carried out, pertinence to the professors staff, etc.– of the victims, since their attacks may last for decades).

Monitoring of the system and follow-up of the user's actions (constant control of the activities of their victims to plagiarize them, for instance).

TOWARDS A FIRST EQUATION

The individuals who increase the "digital divide" in the current research work have the same way to introduce themselves as the Trojans in the context of the viruses. That is, a Trojan presents itself to the user of the computer as an apparently legitimate and harmless program. However, it is obvious that they are not. A heuristic equation to detect quickly and easily the professionals who currently disorient the interactive design for children is in the graphic of figure 8, where in the axis of the abscises is quantified the training in keeping with the workplace, in the coordinates the tasks that he currently develops in the

Figure 8. A heuristic equation for the professional activities in an autonomous way

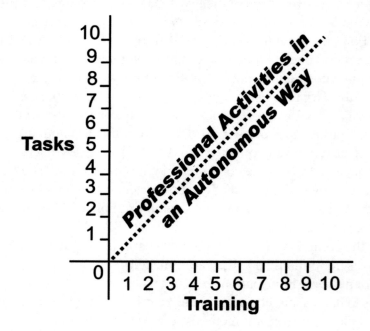

working structure (that is, university, research and development centre, etc.) and the line is the trend of the professional activity in an autonomous way.

Consequently, this line will grow if there is a working and training affinity between the training received and the post that the person holds, and vice versa. In other words, it is a bidirectional relationship which in the current work the human and social factors of the "Interaction Design and Children" is to be found in the negative area, because of the professionals of the sector in Europe.

This equation makes apparent the high financial costs entailed by the deviation observed in the "European Interaction Design and Children." These costs originate from the professional teams that actually carry out the works in the R&D projects, for instance, through subcontracts or outsourcing. In the university classrooms would be the collaborators, who are hired to keep ad aeternum the ghost professors in the software field, for instance. Here is one of the reasons why endless battles are started against all those who work in an autonomous way and without subsidies, whether it is funds stemming from the EU or the local, provincial, regional, state governments, etc. Simply that way of doing autonomous and independent research can't and mustn't exist within the EU boundaries.

LESSONS LEARNED

In view of the rhetorical question: Quo vadis? the current work has two actions: the first is to withdraw it, because the Interaction Design and Children in Europe is inexistent from the point of view of the neutrality of the intersection of the formal and factual sciences. The second is to apply it to the future scientists who are currently leaving the old continent as a result of the described reality belonging to the human and social factors in the university, scientific, technology transfer and digital divide, etc., inside the European borders. Analyzing certain international events related to the future generations and interactive designed, it can be detected the typical behaviour of parochialism of their members who act under the Garduña Factor (Cipolla-Ficarra, et al., 2013).

A factor that is changing some of the origins of the social factors in the problems of the youth in view of the job market or working after finishing their study, such as can be a "high rate of unemployed" in the south of Europe and "the migration towards the north or central Europe", with the equation "migration in search of lower costs to study in the universities

Figure 9. Disguising the lack of work for the young university graduates with a migration previous to the situation, through the search of universities where studying is cheaper.
(Approximate Translation: "Studying abroad pays", with the subtitle "The reputation of the foreign universities, the lack of job prospects and the a more promising future attract more and more students".)
Source: El País (www.elpais.es –09.14.2013).

(Figure 9). However, the university training knowledge, the working skills demonstrated across time with financial resources equal to zero, the creative competences elaborated in an autonomous and original way, if they have not been considered in the recent past of the ICTs, they will be even less in the European present and future.

A future where not only the birth rate is scarce, but also the stagnation of the purchasing power of a great part of the population towards the acquisition of the new multimedia mobile or services devices compared to that of India, for instance. That is, they will switch from a normal pyramid to a diamond in those issues of potential users of interactive systems online and offline. Whereas in the Old World, those pseudo scientists who have children, nephews, etc. to carry out international gatherings will present as a novel goal in children education the compiling of information in digital containers, (databases with online access), etc., for the alleged good of the future generations in 2020, obsolete theories or concepts since they are even 75 years old in the framework of the US or Canadian mass/social media communication, for instance. It is a reality that will not change while those individuals enjoy a perennial permanence in their positions of power, within and without the university classrooms. The solution lies in revoking the lifelong status of the university posts when the foster the Garduña Factor in Europe.

Finally, in the current work we have continued with the use of a special language which we will keep on developing to present human factors in computer science and all its derivations.

CONCLUSION

Approaching disparate topics such as can be the children or childhood, the interfaces design, contents, etc., children pedagogy, the online and offline interactive systems, etc., by people who do not have a training in keeping with these topics is not positive. With the passing of time, these shortcomings have a repercussion on society. Currently it is not an easy task to detect them because they shield themselves disguisedly under the terms of interdisciplinarity, human-computer interaction, human-computer interface, human-computer communication, human-centered technology, etc. Besides, the study of the diachronic reality has verified individual or group patterns of behaviour with a below zero professional ethics. Some negative values where runs the line of the professional activities in an autonomous way. That is, when the results of the equation generated in the current work are analyzed, where there are individuals who jumble together childhood, education, interactive design, the new technologies and a myriad areas in the formal and/or factual sciences with mercantilists purposes but presented under formula of R&D projects. Those projects where participate the children, nephews, etc. of early age, of those who usually make those research in the field of the ICTs, with which the scientific objectivity of the results reached is nil.

REFERENCES

Angelo, P., & Pinna, L. (2008). *Perché dobbiamo fare più figli*. Milano: Mondadori. (in Italian)

Barclay, C., & Duggan, E. (2008). Rethinking the Digital Divide: Towards a Path of Digital Effectiveness. In *Proceed. 41st Annual Hawaii International Conference on System Sciences*. New York: IEEE Press.

Bijapurkar, R. (1979). *We are like that only understand the logic of Consumer India*. London: Penguin.

Bijapurkar, R. (2006). *Winning in the Indian Market: Understanding the Transformation of Consumer India*. New York: Wiley.

Cipolla-Ficarra, . (2010). *Quality and Communicability for Interactive Hypermedia Systems: Concepts and Practices for Design*. Hershey, PA: IGI Global. doi:10.4018/978-1-61520-763-3

Cipolla-Ficarra, . (2013). *Advanced Research and Trends in New Technologies, Software, Human-Computer Interaction, and Communicability*. Hershey, PA: IGI Global.

Cipolla-Ficarra, F. (2010). *Persuasion On-Line and Communicability: The Destruction of Credibility in the Virtual Community and Cognitive Models*. New York: Nova Science Publishers.

Cipolla-Ficarra, F. (2011). Software Managment Applications, Textile CAD and Human Factors: A Dreadful Industrial Example for Information and Communication Technology. *Proceed. First international conference on Advances in new technologies, interactive interfaces, and communicability*, 121-131.

Cipolla-Ficarra, F. (2011). *Computational Informatics, Social Factors and New Information Technologies: Hypermedia Perspectives and Avant-Garde Experiences in the Era of Communicability Expansion*. Bergamo: Blue Herons Editions.

Cipolla-Ficarra, F. (2012). *New Horizons in Creative Open Software, Multimedia, Human Factors and Software Engineering*. Bergamo: Blue Herons Editions.

Cipolla-Ficarra, F., Ficarra, V., & Cipolla-Ficarra, M. (2011). New technologies of the information and communication: analysis of the constructors and destructors of the european educational system. *Proceed. Second international conference on Advances in new technologies, interactive interfaces, and communicability*, 71-84.

Cipolla-Ficarra, F., Ficarra, V., & Kratky, A. (2011). Computer Graphics for Students of the Factual Sciences. In *Proceed. Communicability, Computer Graphics and Innovative Design for Interactive Systems –CCGIDIS 2011* (pp. 79–93). Heidelberg, Germany: Springer.

Compaine, B. (2001). *The Digital Divide: Facing a Crisis or Creating a Myth?* Cambridge, MA: MIT Press.

Moragas-Spa, M. (1985). *Sociología de la Comunicación de Masas*. Barcelona: Paidòs. (in Spanish)

UNESCO. (2000). Retrieved from http://unesdoc.unesco.org/images/0012/001203/120374E.pdf

Whitman, M., & Mattord, H. (2011). *Principles of Information Security*. Boston: Course Technology - Cenage Learning.

Chapter 11
Anti–Models for Architectural Graphic Expression and UX Education

Francisco V. Cipolla-Ficarra
Latin Association of Human-Computer Interaction, Spain & International Association of Interactive Communication, Italy

Jim Carré
University of the Netherlands Antilles, Curaçao

Alejandra Quiroga
Universidad Nacional de La Pampa, Argentina

Valeria M. Ficarra
Latin Association of Human-Computer Interaction, Spain & International Association of Interactive Communication, Italy

ABSTRACT

We present the main motivations why the excellence of the university education related to architectural CAD, graphic art/expression, and UX may be inexistent in Spain, by focusing exclusively on graphic design. A set of online examples allows to orient the potential users of computer systems, user experience (UX), electronic information systems and generators of original multimedia contexts towards the epistemological principles of the formal and factual sciences. Besides, we detected an educational anti-model and the mercantilism in CAD, architectural graphic expression, art and UX education with a semiotic analysis of the dynamic and static media in university websites.

DOI: 10.4018/978-1-5225-3437-2.ch011

INTRODUCTION

Computer-Aided Design (CAD) allows to order and process the information related to the characteristics of a material object (Demel & Miller, 1984). In architecture CAD serves to build an analogous model of the building, for example (Newman & Sproull, 1979). Although it is true that in interactive design it may start with a folio and a pencil, this does not mean that the designer of the 21st century has to be a graduate in fine arts or an illustrator to carry out their tasks. One of the advantages of CAD is what prevents the need from working with the hand, that is, the architect or the civil engineer decides what things are like and the CAD shows how they are seen (Newman & Sproull, 1979). Currently there is a very wide variety of commercial programs or systems, which allows to draw lines and store them in bitmap files or vectorials. Starting from these lines and sketches it can be imported in another set of commercial programs with worldwide circulation (AutoCAD, DataCAD, TurboCAD, etc.) to turn them into 2D and/or 3D objects. In this work, the notion of object refers to a building or to the component thereof, for instance, a door, a window, a plant, etc. In other words, CAD takes care of the exclusive design tasks, such as technical drawing and its documentation. However, with the passing of time, some commercial products have included the animation to architectural CAD (Van Welbergen, et al. 2006). For instance, in the transit from the 20th to the 21st century, the 3D Studio Viz of Autodesk (www.autodesk.com) included the day light phenomena. Now although a CAD system, commercial or not, it may adopt a myriad algorithms of graphic computing which allows it to work in many different ways, there are some common elements, which all share and which have been adapted as rules: it is spatial, Cartesian and vectorial.

Traditionally, in Spain graphic illustration has been more aimed at the fine arts rather than at architecture. However, there are university contexts where the exception to the international academic rules is always a constant practice in some departments or members thereof. Now the exception to the academic rules doesn't mean that we are talking of excellence. As a rule, the expression "transversal discipline" is fashionable in some pedagogic academic environments where allegedly the students attend master or educational excellence classes whether it is in situ that is, within the classroom, or virtually thanks to the new ICT (Information and Communication Technology).

Irrespective of whether the architectural CAD education is carried out inside the classroom or in e-learning, the new technologies play an important role for the practices, review of the main notions, the fostering of teamwork, etc. In our days, not even the last generation virtual agents aimed at education, with an excellent communicability level and a high realism in the gestural movements, voice and movement synchronism, etc. have been able to replace 100% the whole human team of professors to obtain a degree or a technical engineering, for instance (Cipolla-Ficarra, 2005). In other words, the new technologies must be considered as tools which facilitate the learning process. The problem arises when there is a mercantilist use (disguised or manifest publicity in each one of the social communication media) from the university educational environment.

SEMIOTICS FOR WEB ANALYSIS

Greimas' narrative semiotics (Nöth, 1995) approaches the study of narration from the analysis of what the calls the narrative structure of text (Nöth, 1995). It is precisely its theoretical origin which guarantees the solidity of the construction of the objects he handles. The generative route is a theoretical construction which tries to model the way in which is generated and articulated the sense in a text, for instance a résumé of an online college professor. The generative route of a website where we find a curriculum contains two great levels: the level of the discursive structures and the level of the semio-narrative structures. The level of the discursive structures is the level of the textual manifestation, in other words that which we deal with when we "read" the text. The level of the semio-narrative structures is a more abstract level whose constituents do not directly show in the website, but are rebuilt through analysis. The level of the semio-narrative structures is to be found subdivided in two sublevels: a deep sublevel and a surface sublevel. The deep level of the semio-narrative structures is the most abstract one. It is the level where for the theory take place the first articulations of sense, that is, where the least elaborated and most elemental terms of signification appear: knowledge-ability, master-slave, authoritarian-democratic, etc. These units are presented in simple binary oppositions (0 and 1) which on the whole give place to a purely logical plot whose main structure links us to the primary semantic level of computer language, for instance. The minimal units, constituents of the primary semantic level of the deep level (that is, fundamental semantics) are organized in relation to elementary oppositions which may be described through a universal outline which is called by the theory semiotic square (Nöth, 1995).

In the semiotic square are expressed several kinds of relationship: relations between opposite terms or contrarian. For instance, the relation between the terms /master/ and /slave/ on the one hand and the relation between the terms /non-master/ and /non-slave/, for instance, and between /non-master/ and /non-slave/. Besides, there are the relationships between terms called subcontrarians (between the terms /master/ and /non-slave/ and similarly between the terms /slave/ and /non-master/, called implication relationships. Now the content of a website (with texts, images, sounds, etc.) at the deep level may be regarded as a net of elementary significations only articulated by relationships as those mentioned: contrariety, contradiction, implication. This descriptive level, as can be seen, is highly abstract. It tells us, above all, that a narration is legible because it speaks (redounds) and certain basic meanings ("the master", the power", etc " and which in general terms deals with exploring the meanings that are associated to these basic significations.

In the components of a website, the minimal units do not appear disorganized. This organization may be attributed to a taxonomic component of the deep level which allows to organize the elementary structure of signification through the instauration of semiotic squares. The generation of new terms through given minimal units is the product of the action of an operational subcomponent of the main syntax. For instance, from the term /freedom/ can be generated the contradictory term /non-freedom/ thanks to a fundamental operation which is negation. Another operation, assertion, allows the appearance of terms situated in the axes of the contraries and subcontraries: the assertion of the negation of the term /freedom/, that is, the assertion of the term /non-freedom/ causes the term /slavery/ which is its opposite, the assertion of the negation of the term /non-slavery/ causes the term /non-freedom/ which is its subcontrary). In this way are obtained oriented operations which allow from any of the terms generate the others. The readers interested in other operations of the semiotic square, narrative, etc. can look up the following bibliographical references (Nöth, 1995; Colapietro, 1993)

The master-slave, freedom-slavery, authoritarian-democratic, knowledge-ability, among others, make apparent that the educational structures in the 21st century are made up by human resources which should never have been incorporated for a correct educational system in each one of the teaching levels of a community and with the purpose of preventing situations of a high unemployment rate. A way to detect those social factors is by investigating the curriculum vitae of the professors. In this regard we find those who not only already exercise the master-slave relationship, but also stalking towards all the other eventual slaves who have broken their chains with the ignorant master, but with all the red tape requisites of the autonomous community where the college is located, which enables them to teach classes on a lifelong basis, for instance. One of the key elements which can be read in the curriculum vitae of someone who fosters slavery in the educational context is the presence of comments with references to the tyrants who dictatorially have ruled for a period of the history of a nation. It is a way the master has to present himself/herself as a victim for not having been born in the territory where he/she works as a professor, although linguistically he/she speaks the language of that regional community.

VIRTUAL OR REAL LINGUISTIC BARRIERS FOR CAD EDUCATION, GRAPHIC ART/ EXPRESSION AND UX IN SPAIN?

One of the ways of not practicing teaching is by raising linguistic barriers. This is a strategy followed by those who need to learn before, foreign colleagues with rubbish contracts and even of their students, because they do not know the issues, for which they hold a post in the universities. A classical example is the endogamy in the universities of the south of Europe or the inheritors of the Garduña –Toledo, 1412 (http://en.wikipedia.org/wiki/Garduña; Peñalva, 2011). Not for nothing there are in the context of the Catalan computer graphics, for instance, heads of department with vertical structures who literally forbid their immediate subordinates (professors and researchers) the interrelations with the rest of the members of departments of that university. These prohibitions may entail the exclusion from the working group for all those who do not abide by this invisible but latent rule. Now it is widely known in the Spanish public universities that all those who hail from other countries can't write correctly, with which the time to submit their final work, that is career final project, doctoral thesis, etc., will double or triple. Now there are exceptions to this rule and inside the context of the European zone, and with the implementation of the Bologna plan, such as can be the Italian autonomous regions that border on Austria and Switzerland. Consequently, we may have a Bielorussian who without speaking Italian obtains his/her doctor thesis in a computer science department. This is a common denominator in universities of cities like Bolzano or Trieste in Italy.

How is it possible that in Catalonia an architect, engineer, graduate, physician, etc., from Latin America in whose countries of origin Spanish is spoken, has to suffer for years the negative consequences of the master-slave relationship because theoretically he/she can't write in Spanish? How is it possible while in other European regions those who obtain their doctorates in the field of computer science, for instance, do it without knowing the official language of the state that will issue their certificates and/or academic diploma? These two rhetoric questions make apparent educational contradictions in the UE zone, under the rule of the Bologna plan. Another way to test this are the university students who with the purpose of ending quickly the cap of credits needed to start to develop their career final project register in subjects of other universities, outside from the country of origin of the EU zone. As a rule, the university professors automatically passed those students since the linguistic knowledge was very low in the written examinations.

Now in these examples students hailing from other countries have been considered. What happens in those countries where the state or official language coexists with other autonomous regional languages? In the Spanish case, we can find Andalusian professors who from Majorca claim to the rest of the citizens that there are no linguistic barriers to practice their teaching profession. When the legal reality imposes teaching in the regional languages. These situations are those that we call in the current work "the sirens song" (the Ulysses myth) which are localized in the university departments among people charged with issuing press communiqués, constantly to all the traditional communication media, such as television, radio, the newspapers, specialized magazines, etc., and the new Web 2.0 media communication.

It is the umpteenth strategy used to boost the master-slave relationship deceiving Spanish and foreigners to the fact that there are no problems in the use of languages in the classrooms but once inserted in the island's daily life they must put up with carrying out technical activities (lab practices, such as can be the programming of multimedia systems, for instance) because since they do not know the local language they can't teach lessons. The "sirens song" phenomenon is fostered by those who have benefited from a great favor inside the department to which they belong such as can be the obtainment of a master or even a doctorate, without any knowledge of the degree they received. One example is a graduate in fine arts who receives a PhD in mathematics and computer science.

That is, from the theoretical point of view he/she lacks the knowledge in those areas of science. From the practical perspective, a graduate in the fine arts will devote himself to what he/she has studied in his degree, that is, illustrate and paint walls in bars, hotels, hospitals, etc. In parallel he/ she will set up a virtual shop for the sale of his/her products such as can be bags, sandals, etc., and will investigate the commercial marketing, etc. In other words, he/she will turn into a commercial brand. Obviously from the Majorca commercial structure and without costs in offices or staff for his/ her personal activities (Cipolla-Ficarra, Nicol & Cipolla-Ficarra, 2011). This last fruit of the slaves that he/she has at his/her disposal for linguistic reasons. In the Figures 1, 2 and 3 we can find summarized all the negative aspects that destroy the image of the Spanish educational system. That is, in

Figure 1. Fine arts graduate, doctor in mathematics and computer science devoted to the mass media (fostering the sirens song within and without the Spanish borders), commerce, marketing, illustrations, and a very long etcetera
(Approximate Translation: Website of the staff of the University of the Balearic Islands, where among others are the following data: category [tenured professor of a college school], department [sciences, mathematics and computer sciences], area of the department, [graphic expression in architecture), website and contact.]

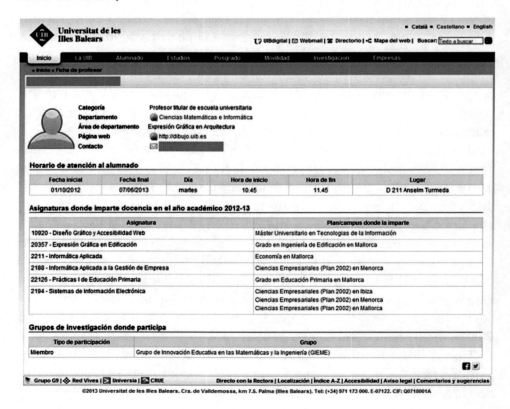

Figure 2. Some definitions about the application of the ICT and the education which do not follow the epistemological parameters of the sciences, starting by pedagogy

Figure 3. The Paraguayan tucan is best described by having a big beak and a very small head. This article is a lousy example for those who intend to reach educational excellence in Europe: digital newspaper "El Mundo"
(Approximate Translation: Article of the Spanish newspaper El Mundo - Balearic Islands (Spain). Title: Teaching 4.0, the didactic "short".) www.elmundo.es 06.26.2012.

it concentrate all the negative variables which make educational excellence in the Spanish territory equal to zero.

TEACHING 4.0 FOR CAD, UX AND GRAPHIC ART?

With the passing of time, the degree of knowledge and/or experiences of graduate in fine arts in his role of dynamic persuader can be detected, when he/she makes up 4.0 education and makes it known in format of publicity shorts or didactic short films. In parallel he/she calls the Majorcan press to spread the word of his/her participation in international congresses in Valencia, invitations from abroad (California), alleged statistic data of access to the video online, his/her website has got over 79.000 visits during this course (he/she has only 63 students).

Countries such as Mexico, Canada, Russia or Uruguay appear as the most interested in his/her project. Some hardly reliable statistic data on the Web 2.0, like some definitions about e-learning shape to us the profile of the professor –PhD in mathematics and computer science: "If we undestand traditional teaching as 1.0, the use of participatory networks fund in web 2.0, tools and the combination of both by using digital content availble in Internet as 3.0, we could create the concept of "Teaching 4.0" if we put all together and produce the material by ourselves both in traditional media, offline, as well as material produced using thte information and communication technologies, online" (Figure 2). In few words, and resorting to humor, we are in the face of the "Paraguayan tucan phenomenon" (Cipolla-Ficarra & Ficarra, 2011) that is, a very big beak and a very small head, as can be read in the online content of the continuation of the alleged revolutionary project in online education (Figure 3).

This is the umpteenth provoking publicity add with a negative sign of a dynamic persuader (Cipolla-Ficarra, 2010), who defines himself/herself as a frustrated journalist, that is, the umpteenth role of those who appear listed in the Figure 3. This is a classical phenomenon of those people who only seek to draw attention to themselves without measuring the economic or social consequences (Washburn, 2005) as it has been seen in the examples of the current working place reality in Spain and the migration abroad of ICT engineers, for instance (Figure 4).

The Figures 1, 2, and 3, depict in a synthetic way the antimodel of educational excellence in the south of Europe. The credibility of the Majorcan public university is very challengeable. In this case, it has granted doctorate

Figure 4. The high rate of unemployed in the south of Europe fosters migration towards other places of the planet. The Spanish emigration and immigration. Digital newspaper "El País"
(Approximate Translation: Article of the Spanish paper El País with the title "I have a grandson in America" and with the subtitle "Over 40.000 people have left Spain this year". Graphics with migration and immigration in Spain (2009-2012).) www.elpais.es –07.18.2012.

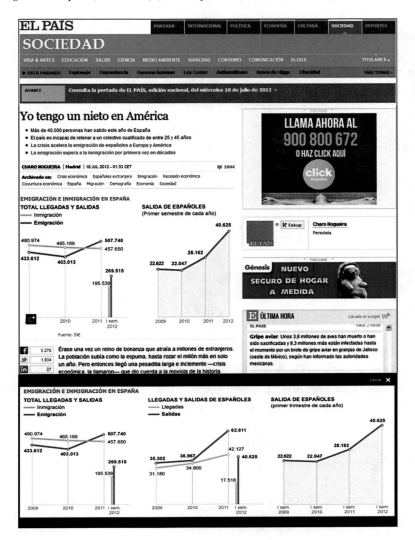

degrees to its school teachers, without ever having published a mathematics and/or computer science in an international scientific environment of great prestige (with anonymous evaluators) at the moment of the defense of the doctor thesis, for instance.

The false linguistic barriers are created inside a university to foster the discredit to university educational teaching, boosting the new equation "working and not studying", as well as human inequality, through the master-slave relationship. In the last two decades the implemented control mechanisms such as can be the evaluation of educational quality have also given negative results.

LESSONS LEARNED AND FUTURE RESEARCH

The semiotic analysis of the dynamic and static media of the websites (university portals such as the digital information of the new media), linguistics, social psychology, sociology, pedagogy, marketing, etc. has allowed to carry out a set of premises which have been verified with the studies of the analysis of the text of the documents gathered along time. We have also resorted to other heuristic evaluation techniques such as the interviews and observation. Although they are techniques of use for the communicability experts, they must constantly adapt to the different supports of digital information, following the isotopic lines that are being studied. Each one of the incorporated figures shapes a first map of those websites, where educational excellence is non-existent.

In future works will be generated a set of attributes to measure the bidirectional relationships between study and work. The examples from the south of Europe can be taken in some specific cases in Northern Europe. A geographical environment which has been excluded in the current work but may be an interesting line of research for future works from a sociological point of view to compare the functioning of parochialism and the endogamy in the university structures, for instance. Semiotics once again may be a valid instrument to detect anomalous situations in the educational structures –Architectural CAD education, and systems which allegedly belong to excellence.

CONCLUSION

In the relation of the semiotic square used by Greimas, using two terms such as "master-slave" one cat get the current map or state of the art which has prevailed in the last 25 years in the educational context of the highest level: the university. The high unemployment rates deriving from financial reasons in Europe, like a myriad variables which damage two of the main cornerstones of the developed countries, such as education and healthcare, will take longer to be solved, because in the universities there is no melting pot of ideas stemming from other places of the planet in the making of decisions. That is, the power summit has been cut down to those who play the role of masters because of simple linguistic issues or parochialism, etc. All the presented examples show the failure of trying to correct these deviations even in the paneuropean context such as can be a macro plan like the Bologna plan.

Computer science, telecommunications, off-line hypermedia systems, online databases, democratization of the Internet, etc., of the 20th century have opened a wide range of disciplines in the universities of the late 20th century. The intersection of the formal and factual sciences has allowed the arising of professionals to foster the quality in the user-interactive system communication, such as the evaluator of communicability (he/she can detect the presence or absence of quality in an interactive system, in short time and without need of labs or special instruments, for instance), the webmaster of the portals, the safety expert of the networks, etc. This is about intersections and not unions of knowledge which it is very usual to come across in the multimedia engineering curricula, graduates or audiovisual engineers, etc. Such intersections must be very clear about the notions of interdisciplinarity, transdisciplinarity, etc. which even from the pedagogical point of view are used as synonymous when in fact they are not. Many of the problems that pull away university educational excellence are due to mistaking educational excellence with the handling of the new technologies, excluding for instance theory from the set of teachings. Handling latest generation technologies in CAD education does not allow the professionals to have a 360 degrees vision that enables them to overcome the constant changes deriving from the daily evolution or revolution of the software and the hardware of the ICTs. This global vision is counteracted by the alleged educational excellence oriented at the mercantilism of knowledge.

ACKNOWLEDGMENT

The authors would like to thank Maria Ficarra, Sonia Flores, Jacqueline Alma, Pamela Fulton, Doris Edison, Mary Brie, Luisa Varela and Carlos for their helps and contributions.

REFERENCES

Cipolla-Ficarra, F. (2005). Heuristic Evaluation of Animated Help in Hypermedia. *Proceedings of the HCI International*

Cipolla Ficarra, F. (2010). *Persuasion On-Line and Communicability: The Destruction of Credibility in the Virtual Community and Cognitive Models*. New York: Nova Science.

Cipolla-Ficarra, F., & Ficarra, V. (2011). Software Managment Applications, Textile CAD and Human Factors: A Dreadful Industrial Example for Information and Communication Technology. In *Proceedings First International Conference on Advances in New Technologies, Interactive Interfaces and Communicability, ADNTIIC 2010*. Heidelberg, Germany: Springer. doi:10.1007/978-3-642-20810-2_13

Cipolla-Ficarra, F., Nicol, E., & Cipolla-Ficarra, M. (2011). Research and Development: Business into Transfer Information and Communication Technology. In *Proceedings First International Conference on Advances in New Technologies, Interactive Interfaces and Communicability, ADNTIIC 2010*. Heidelberg, Germany: Springer. doi:10.1007/978-3-642-20810-2_6

Cipolla-Ficarra, F., Nicol, E., & Cipolla-Ficarra, M. (2011). Vademecum for Innovation through Knowledge Transfer: Continuous Training in Universities, Enterprises and Industries. In *Proceedings Innovation through Knowledge, Transfer 2010* (pp. 139–149). Berlin: Springer. doi:10.1007/978-3-642-20508-8_12

Colapietro, V. (1993). *Semiotics*. New York: Paragon House.

Demel, J., & Miller, M. (1984). *Introduction to Computers Graphics*. Boston: PWS Engineering.

Newman, W., & Sproull, R. (1979). *Principles of Interactive Computer Graphics*. New York: McGraw Hill.

Nöth, W. (1995). *Handbook of Semiotics*. Bloomington, IN: Indiana University Press.

Peñalva, J. (2011). *Corrupción en la Universidad*. Madrid: Ciudadela. (in Spanish)

Van Welbergen, H., Nijholt, A., Reidsma, D., & Zwiers, J. (2006). Presenting in Virtual Worlds: An Architecture for a 3D Anthropomorphic Presenter. *IEEE Intelligent Systems*, *21*(5), 47–53. doi:10.1109/MIS.2006.101

Washburn, J. (2005). *University, Inc.: The Corporate Corruption of Higher Education*. New York: Basic Books.

ADDITIONAL READING

Barrow, J. (2009). *Le immagini della Scienza*. Milan: Mondadori. In Italian

Card, S. (1993). The Psychology of Human-Computer Interaction. New Jersey: Hillsdale

Ching, F. D. K. (2010). *Design Drawing*. Hoboken: John Willey.

Ching, F. D. K. (2014). *Architectural Graphics*. Hoboken: John Willey.

Cipolla-Ficarra, F. (2005). *Interazione uomo-computer nel XXI secolo: Analisi e valutazione euristica della qualità per la comunicazione e l'usabilità*. Bergamo: Blue Herons. In Italian

Cunningham, D. W. (2011). *Experimental Design: From User Studies to Psychophysics*. Boca Raton: CRC Press. doi:10.1201/b11308

Ficarra, F.V.C. (1994). Mallorca: Una isla de animaciones infográficas y multimedia. *Imaging* (12), 20-35 Barcelona: PressGraph. *In Spanish*

Ficarra, F. V. C. (1999). Artes gráficas e infográficas en el siglo XXI. [In Spanish]. *Chasqui*, (68): 30–33.

Ficarra, F. V. C. (2005). Interacción persona-computador: Sálvese quien pueda. [In Spanish]. *Chasqui*, (91): 72–79.

Ficarra, F. V. C. (2006). El byte y el pixel: Interacción persona-computador. [In Spanish]. *Chasqui*, (94): 74–81.

Ficarra, F. V. C. (2007). Interacción persona-computador. ¿Quo vadis ética y estética? [In Spanish]. *Chasqui*, (97): 68–75.

Furnas, G., Landauer, T., Gomez, L., & Dumais, S. (1987). The Vocabulary Problem in Human-System Communication. *Communications of the ACM*, *33*(2), 964–971. doi:10.1145/32206.32212

Gervautz, M., & Schmalstieg, D. (2012). Anywhere Interfaces Using Handheld Augmented Reality. *IEEE Computer*, *45*(7), 26–31. doi:10.1109/MC.2012.72

Hainich, R., & Bimber, O. (2011). *Displays: Fundamentals and Applications*. Boca Raton: CRC Press.

Holtzblatt, K. (2011). What Makes Things Cool? Intentional Design for Innovation. *Interaction*, *18*(6), 40–47. doi:10.1145/2029976.2029988

Laurel, B. (1990). *The Art of Human-Computer Interface Design*. Massachusetts: Addison-Wesley.

Raymond, E. (1999). *The Cathedral and the Bazaar*. Sebastopol: O'Reilly & Associates.

Salpeter, M. (2011). *Social Networking for Career Success: Using Online Tools to Create a Personal Brand*. New York: Learning Express.

Senge, P. (1990). *The Fifth Discipline: The Art and Practice of the Learning Organisation*. London: Random House.

Smith, P., & Ragan, T. (2004). *Instructional Design*. New York: Merrill.

Tufte, E. (2006). *Beautiful Evidence*. Cheshire: Graphics Press.

Weinberg, T. (2009). *The New Community Rules: Marketing on the Social Web*. Sebastopol: O'Reilly Media.

White, C. (2003). *Language Learning in Distance Education*. Cambridge: Cambridge University Press. doi:10.1017/CBO9780511667312

Winograd, T., & Flores, F. (1987). *Understanding Computers and Cognition: A New Foundation for Design*. Reading: Addison-Wesley.

Wood, L. (1998). *User Interface Design: Bridging the Gap from User Requirements to Design*. Boca Raton: CRC Press.

Zaphiris, P., & Kurniawan, S. (2006). *Human Computer Interaction Research in Web Design and Evaluation*. Hershey: IGI Global.

KEY TERMS AND DEFINITIONS

Architectural Expression: The graphic subject that introduces the people to drawing as the basic language for the architect, and as the required tool (for example, a 2D/3D commercial software, i.e., AutoCAD, DataCAD, etc.) to develop capabilities of understanding, conception and expression of architecture.

CAD: It is also known as computer-aided design. CAD is a computer technology that designs a product and documents the design's process.

Communicability: A qualitative communication between the user and the interactive system, such as mobile phones, augmented reality, immersion multimedia, hypermedia, among others. The extent to which an interactive system successfully conveys its functionality to the user.

Interactive System: A computer device made up by a CPU and peripherals, whose functioning requires a constant interaction with the user. Currently these systems tend to their miniaturization and/or invisibility, the mobility and wireless connect-ability among them.

Semiotics or Semiology: A name for the general theory of signs, sometimes supposed to be a science of sings.

User Experience: It includes the human emotions about using a product, system or service. It is not a synonymous of communicability or usability. Besides, generally, it includes the practical, experiential, affective, meaningful and valuable aspects of human–computer interaction and product ownership.

Chapter 12
Free Emails in Bad Portals

Francisco V. Cipolla-Ficarra
Latin Association of Human-Computer Interaction, Spain & International Association of Interactive Communication, Italy

Alejandra Quiroga
Universidad Nacional de La Pampa, Argentina

Valeria M. Ficarra
Latin Association of Human-Computer Interaction, Spain & International Association of Interactive Communication, Italy

ABSTRACT

The possibility that millions of users have a free access to a website to send and receive multimedia messages has contributed to the democratization of the Internet since 1995 in the south of Europe. We present how those websites in the second decade of the new millennium tend to a radial and vertical structure of online services. A heuristic and diachronical analysis of the main design categories of Yahoo Spain has been carried out in a human-computer interaction lab whose results are presented in the current research work. The informative aspects of the dynamic and/or static media have also been analyzed, especially in the content and also in the presentation of the online information, on the PC and tablet screens.

INTRODUCTION

A browser is a computer system that seeks files stored in web servers, through the spider or web crawler (Melies, 1996). In other words, they are websites which put at the disposal of the users programs capable of carrying out automatic

DOI: 10.4018/978-1-5225-3437-2.ch012

searches based on key words (Hall & Papadopoulos, 1990). Basically, we have an interface where the user can interact with databases, connected among each other, through the phone network, for instance (Conklin & Date, 1990). The momentum of the browsers took place at the end of the last century, with the democratization of the net. In this democratization process took place an evolution of the hypertext towards the hypermedia of the contents (Mitchell & McCullough, 1995), as the ability increased to transmit data in the phone networks, that is, from the classical copper cable until the optical fiber, down to the current wireless nets. It is a process that has entailed a structural change in the telecommunications and in the design of the databases for online access in split seconds (Date, 1990; Mitchell & McCullough, 1995). However, many elements remain constant is spite of the advances of the last two decades, whether it is in the databases or the interfaces (Date, 1990; Apple, 1992), for instance. In the former we can make references to the Boolean operators, and or, etc, and in the latter the text, as a greater communication speed among the users. Currently a good example are the Twitter messages in the social networks, being so that the current infrastructure for telecommunications in the great cities of the EU also allows a quick sending and reception of the dynamic data, such as videos, computer animations, songs, etc. Now both the static and the dynamic texts, linked to the illustrations, have been essential in the expansion of the browsers thanks to the possibility of opening for free e-mail accounts (Cipolla-Ficarra, et al. 2011).

In the 90s an easy way to classify the browsers was dividing them into national and international, as can be seen in the Figures of Appendix 1. That is, those that carried out their information searches inside the country itself from those who did it in the whole web. Some examples belonging to Italy are, for instance, Ciaoweb, Supereva, Tin, Virgilio, Kataweb, lol, Tiscali, etc. In contrast, as international engines in this decade are: Google, Yahoo, Excite, Altavista, Msn, etc. Many of them offered since the start the free email service, but limiting the available space in the user's account, generally between 50 and 100 Mb. Those who wanted more space could hire the services, in the same website, paying an annual fee for said service. Obviously, with the passing of time has taken place a metamorphose in the brands and/or logos of all those services firms. Browsers that in the early 90s with the notion of virtual firms take an important place in the market of the computer services (Cusumano & Yoffie, 2000), surpassing even the fabrication of the hardware of the servers, for instance. Besides, through the interrelations of their logos can be seen how they have grown and evolved in this sector, establishing a wide set of interrelations among themselves, due to the metamorphose of the services offered to the users, whether it is for free or paying for them.

BROWSERS: A COMMERCIAL AND INFORMATICS EVOLUTION

In a summarized way are presented some of the main evolutional characteristics of he browsers that appear in the Figure 1. The goal is to know the origins of the evolution of the current computer sector and some of the outstanding technological and commercial characteristics of the current websites (Cusumano & Yoffie, 2000).

Google was founded in 1998 by two PhD students from Stanford (Cusumano & Yoffie, 2000: Ryan, 2013). The goal was to get relevant information through an important amount of data. They created an algorithm for data search called PageRank. This technology would later turn into the core that would make Google work. In that very same year, 1998, Microsoft presented the MSN Search, which consisted of a search engine, index and web tracker. At the start it used the Inktomi search results. Later on it showed the Looksmart listings mixed with the results of Inktomi. The images search was bolstered by the Picsearch firm. The service also allowed that its search results were visible from other websites of search engines. All of this was due to the competition that already existed in the field of the virtual businesses related to the browsers.

The first version of the Windows Live Search goes back to 2006. The new search engine offered the users the ability to search specific types of information through search files which included the web, news, images, music, Microsoft Encarta encyclopedia (Microsoft, 1997). A configuration menu was

Figure 1. Variegated result of the exploration of images of the search engines

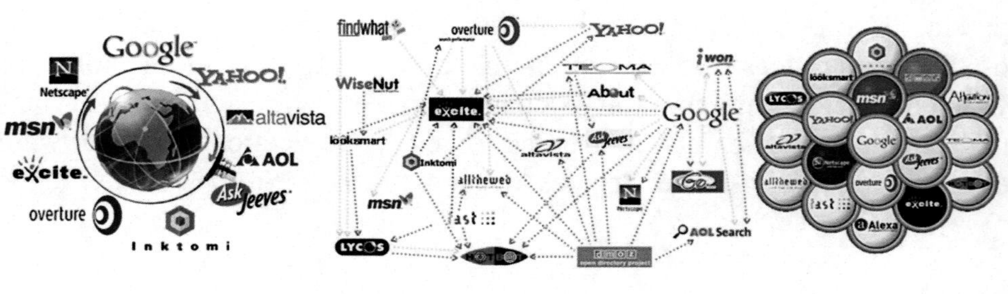

available in Internet Explorer to change the predetermined search engine. In the switch from MSN Search to Windows Live Search, Microsoft quit using Picsearch as its search provider of images and started to carry it out by itself, fed with its own search algorithms. In 2007 Microsoft announced it would separate the search development from the family of services of Windows Live, rebranding the service as Live Search. The term "live" would lead to a series of changes out of marketing reasons until in 2009 a new identity is created for the Microsoft search services. That is, Live Search was replaced by Bing in 2009.

In 2009 Microsoft and Yahoo! Announced that they had made a deal for 10 years in which the Yahoo! Search engine could be replaced by Bing. According to that agreement, Yahoo! Obtained 88% of the revenue coming from the sales of search ads, in tis website, for the first five years of the operation and they would be entitled to sell ads in some Microsoft sites. With this agreement, the disappearance of the Alta Vista network was scheduled. Said portal was bought by Yahoo! In 2003 abd had to use the latter's engine from 2004.

Finally, three other names in the context of the international browsers: Alta Vista search, Lycos search and Infoseek search. Alta Vista is a powerful browser. When a web signs up to Alta Vista automatically it is visited to read its content and register all the most meaningful words. This shows that the key that we look for can be found in thousands of webs but Alta Vista will present them all. Alta Vista does not have directories or categories available. It responds with a list of the webs where can be found what is looked for, which may have different presentation formats. When one presses the link of the web one wants to see, one will go straight towards that web. Lycos search is a set of searchers made up by search instruments stemming from A2Z, Point and Lycos itself. Each one has a database with different characteristics. Lycos is a conventional searcher with directories from theme categories, A2Z searches in the most popular places of the Web, and Point stresses the commercial capabilities of the Web. The presentation of the information is well structured. There appear summing-ups of the selected webs and abstracts of the content.

Infoseek Search presents the information in a detailed and structured way in theme directories. Besides, the search can be limited in sections with FAQs, e-mail addresses or News. Also, and together with the links towards the webs where the information that is searched can be found, is presented a specially written roundup or an automatic abstract of the content. In the directories are located other webs which, even they may not have the key on, possibly deal with the same subject that is being searched.

Briefly, it has been verified that the mergers of the websites aimed at offering free services such as the search of information or the possibility of having an email address. Besides, the influence that those websites currently have in the context of the software and the hardware from a financial point of view that fosters or not certain R&D projects. Projects which tend to be aimed at the traditional digital communication media, and especially towards the circulation of news. However, with an information management which denotes the inexistence of editors, due to the scarce or non-existent professional value of the work presented online (Cipolla-Ficarra, 2010), as is the case of Yahoo España!

TEXTUAL INFORMATION NEWS PLAGIARISM AND MANIPULATION

One of the advantages of the democratization of the Internet was the creation of a myriad new working activities in the field of the ICTs, whose professionals developed their activities in the work offices or from the home, such as webmaster, webdesign, webcontent, etc. Now the issue of generating own contents, original and qualitative, has been sidelined in an endless string of commercial websites in southern Europe, since those contents were literally plagiarized in the 90s from other information websites (Cipolla-Ficarra, et al. 2013). Information which might be found in the same local language, or rather translated from English, French, Italian, etc.

Evidently, it was an easy way to generate revenue in websites where the publicity spaces were sold to banners, interviews to business managers, propaganda, etc., in the websites and the production cost of the information was practically equal to zero, because they were as a rule activities developed by the secretaries of those virtual firms. Exceptionally the services of external collaborators to the virtual newsroom were hired as freelance, who followed the same methodology followed in these virtual firms, that is, what in Spain is called "sofrito de noticias" (news rehash). The Spanish legal loophole surrounding these virtual information businesses was due to the fact that there wasn't in the legislative body of the 80s absolutely no law to tutor the digital freelance journalists. In 1993, in the city of Barcelona (Spain), a group of local and foreign journalists, created a journalists union (SPC –www.

sindicat.org) to protect those workers and curb the rehash on news online, for instance. However, in the last years, in view of the high rate of Spanish unemployed, Yahoo España!, which is based in Barcelona, carries on with the same practices or modus operandi as in the early 90s, that is, the news rehash. A domain where misinformation, plagiarism, manipulation, xenophobia, etc., is the common denominator which can be appreciated in the news website, for instance. Some examples are in Appendix 2.

VISUAL DESIGN: TOPOLOGY OF THE INFORMATION ELEMENTS IN THE USER INTERFACE AND INTERNATIONAL CONNOTATIONS

The color of the interface is essential to draw the visual attention of the users [6]. Since the beginning of the new millennium options have been incorporated to change the color of the websites and the distribution of the information in columns. For instance, in the Figures 2 and 3.

In 2013 Yahoo España! has introduced a series of changes in its website, resorting to a set of escamotages, but following Lampedusa's "The Leopard" saying, that is, "to change everything so that nothing changes" (Di-Lampedussa, 2007), especially in the modus operandi to group and present news in their Spanish website. One of the most remarkable changes is the incorporation of the purple colour.

Figure 2. Portal with two columns and grey background
(Approximate Translation: Italian website, www.email.it with the possibility of having two kinds of email boxes, personal (free) or entrepreneurial (with a yearly fee). The entrepreneurial, email.it business is regarded as the ideal solution for businesses and has internet connection with free dial-up access.) Source: www.email.it –2008.

Figure 3. Now the portal has three columns and a green background
(Approximate Translation: Italian website, www.email.it regarded as the email service leader in Italy,
whether it is in its personal modalities (private) or entrepreneurial. In the case of the personal can
be stressed with its several options, email, fax service, internet access, Hosting/ISP. SMS and phone
service.) Source: www.email.it –2008.

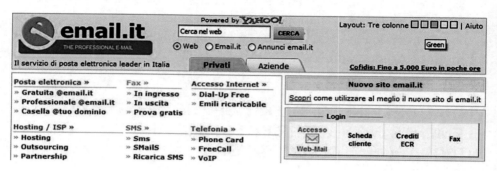

Through the colour of the interface components, we can reach a higher
or lower coherence (Cipolla-Ficarra, 2008). The element of the interface
where a single colour is more predominant is the background of the interface,
especially if the background is a colour and not a structure. The background
colour or screen base can be grouped basically in primary and secondary
colours. The use of colours must be analyzed previously during the design
stage of the interface as they have different connotations (Murch, 1984;
Travis, 1991). Besides, there is a conceptual evolution of colurs in relation
to the field of study (psychology, art, etc.), use industrial design, fashion,
publicity, communication, etc.) and transformation of meanings with the
passing of time. We can see the colours preferences and dislikes between
different people, as well as *the principal concepts used Italian industrial
textile design and remarks of Vasili Kandinsky and Rudolf Steiner.* Lüscher
and Jung –reflections and conclusions. *A violet fabric is sophisticated, refined,
fanciful, original, in some ways disturbing. Its weight varies according to
its brightness. "Violet is a colour that until some time ago was not really
appreciated because it was too much linked to ideas of "repentance" and
"suffering" and even if recently other symbolisms have superimposed, many
people still have that sense of uneasiness deriving from its liturgical use that
makes it an unfavourable or anyway improper colour (...) the fondness for
violet expresses a strong desire for individuality, eccentricity and fascination,
together with creativity and artistic talents* (Riedel & Farben, 1999).

Historicity, power, magic, passion, hedonist, transgression. For the
reader interested in these notions they are widely explained in the following

reference (Cipolla-Ficarra, 2008), where is presented an interactive table called "COCOHO" –Correct Colours for Homepages. The main areas of formal and factic sciences used by COCOHO are in the following figure:

Now the selection of the violet colour on a white background in the Spanish popular sport culture connotes a football club like Real Madrid F. C. Obviously, here we have a negative element to gather users around a website. In this sense, the studies carried out from the point of view of usability, communicability and cultural tourism in the Trentino Tourism Official Website and the soccer clubs (Murch, 1984), also show negative results in touristic promotion, for instance.

AN ANALYSIS OF THE CONTENT OF THE WEBSITE BY COMMUNICABILITY EXPERTS

First of all the universe of study of the website Yahoo España! has been determined through a random selection of the sections to be analyzed or entities which make up the home page of the website: news, sports, cinema, finances, etc. Once the entities of the analysis have been determined, in our case: news, sports and cinema, we have proceeded to compile the daily information, since January 2013 until September 2013. Generating a file with

Figure 4. COCOHO and the factic and formal sciences intersection

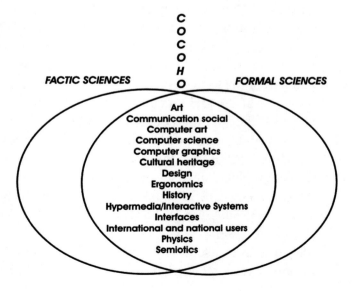

Figure 5. The violet is the new color in Yahoo España! For instance, home page for meteorological information and Email.
(Approximate Translation: The Yahoo meteo service at the moment of accessing the email box, where it is said that "The forecast is magnificent" [a completely new way to check the weather] and the user is invited to find out the weather forecasts.)

those news. Later on a set of negative criteria has been established which are related to the news and the social/human factors (stalking, xenophobia, copy & paste, wording failings, omission of the information sources, etc.). Once the corpus of analysis has been determined, we have gone on to examine what part of the news had to be studied. In this sense, we have followed the model of structuring a news item in the shape of the inverted pyramid and divided into four areas. The first is called lid. It is the main one, and where a summary or conclusion of the topic is presented, in no more than 30 words. The second, explanation of the main idea and development of the eventual sub-topics. In the third, there is the contextualization of the information. In the last, there is an enlargement of the lid. In the current work we have focused on the titles, the first and the third section. The reason for the third section was to find geographical nexuses. In this sense we have followed the precepts of the critical analysis of discourse (Nöth, 1995; Greimas, 1984; Eco, 1979; Barthes, 1985; Saussure, 1983; Dalmasso, 1992; Veron, 2004; Van-Dijk, 1993).

Traditionally, the analysis of discourse delves into that which even if obvious has not been thoroughly researched (Greimas, 1984; Eco, 1979; Barthes,

Figure 6. A negative home page for international tourism promotion because it has components of soccer
(*Approximate Translation: The tourism website of the Italian region called Trentino [the whole name is Trentino-Alto Adige], with the logo of the German football club "FC Bayern München" and the news of the presence of said football players in that region in the summer vacations.*) *Source: i.e., F.C. Bayern Munchen –July 2010.*

1985; Saussure, 1983; Dalmasso, 1992; Veron, 2004; Van-Dijk, 1993), that is, into the fact that the multimedia messages are specific types of the text and speech, linked to the human-computer interaction. The techniques and methods of these messages require new professionals. Besides, the analysis of the discourse is a multidisciplinary task which may relate its structural content to several proprieties of the cognitive and social context.

As Teun A. Van Dijk rightly contends, the critical analysis of the discourse is a special approach in the analysis of the discourse which focuses on the discursive conditions (Van-Dijk, 1993), in the components and in the consequences of the abuse of power exerted by dominant groups and institutions (elite). The critical analysis of discourse carries out this task in opposition to those groups and institutions which abuse their power and in solidarity with the dominated groups. For instance, by unveiling discursive domination and cooperating in the increase of the power of the dominated. Tasks and goals which can be achieved through the analysis of discourse, aimed at theory and description, eluding the impressionism of an interface and the shallowness of the textual contents, such as can be Yahoo España!. An example of the impressionism of the interface of Yahoo España! is when they emit online the same news from Euronews, with the goal of lending seriousness to the website, in their section of news in video format.

The shallowness of the contents goes from the self-promotion of the website down to a myriad mistakes in the wording of the news, that is, in the titles that do not match the lid, the spelling mistakes, the lack of a style in the wording of the text, the errors in the names of persons, geographical places, historical dates, etc. Many of these failings are pointed out by the readers, in the comments section, making fun of who publishes the news. This comments section is very interesting to compile subjective information of the negative views, deposited towards the virtual team of the generators and

Figure 7. Reuse of an "Euronews" news with the purpose of increasing the credibility of the website
(Approximate Translation: Website Yahoo News in Spanish where the video of a Euronews journalist has been included which presents the news "The Pope's Resignation [Joseph Ratzinger-Benedeto XVI], skyrockets the sale of objects with his image. That is to say, it isn't a news from Yahoo Spain but the European news channel Euronews.)

manages of the news, and which can be an interesting line of study for future research works. Another element which shows the poverty of the website in the news section is the constant reusability of the images, as it can be seen in Appendix 2 (figure abc and which is the same picture in the figure abc). In other words, the reusability of the same picture in the smearing campaign towards a soccer player.

RESULTS AND LEARNED LESSONS

The three communicability evaluators, using computers and PCs tablets in a human-computer interaction lab have carried out the examination of the website in keeping with the predetermined tasks and areas of analysis of content. They have focused on the notions of objectivity of the content without mistakes (T1); precision of the structure of the inverted pyramid in sections 1 and 4, with relation to the heading of the news (T2); neutral and original self-promotion of the website (T3); persecution of actors, sportsmen, etc. (T4); smearing campaigns towards third countries (T5). These tasks have been coded with the letter "T", accompanied with a number. The analyzed information has been

Figure 8. Self-promotion of Yahoo Mail! where it is claimed that it has the latest local, national and international news, but which in reality stem from other media sources (Approximate Translation: Promotion of Yahoo as a news channel at the moment of accessing the email. The text makes apparent that Yahoo "Allows you to enjoy easily what matters most to you in your world" Besides, it continues with "Yahoo! Mail the best mail in its class, with last hour local, national and international news, finance, sports, music, movies, and much more. You will enjoy the web ... and life.")

Figure 9. Request to the user of turning Yahoo into their main website through the news
(Approximate Translation: Promotion of Yahoo as home page at the moment of accessing the Internet.)

divided into two groups: dynamic –"D" (video, audio, computer animation, etc.), and static – "S" (texts, graphics, sketches, illustrations, pictures, etc.) and are graphically depicted in the following Figure 10.

The quality of the dynamic means surpasses that of the static means. This is due to the fact that the former are usually generated outside the human team of the website, whereas the latter, especially the text belong to the newsroom team of the portal. In both cases, the copyrights of both the authors and the images, video, etc., that is, the source of information is sometimes not mentioned in the website. In accordance with the notion of the critical analysis of discourse [26] as in section 1 and 3 of the inverted pyramid, in a short lapse of time (24 to 48 hours), has made apparent the presence of xenophobic elements towards such countries as Peru and Argentina (see figures abc and bcd –Appendix 2), excluding other countries of the South Cone such as Brazil, Bolivia, Paraguay and Uruguay. This denotes the presence of Chileans in the management of the Barcelona-based Yahoo España! website in Barcelona. Oddly enough, these latent and sometimes manifest attacks are towards those countries with which it has geographical boundaries.

The news section of the Yahoo España! website constitutes an informative antimodel when the news use static means. They are also antimodels because they constantly draw the attention of the reader not because of the quality

Figure 10. There are low indexes in the tasks T1, T2 and T3. Tasks T4 and T5 have reached a high index of presence in the universe of study

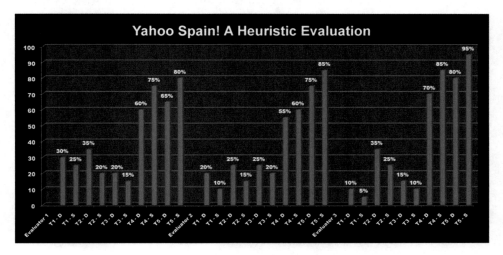

of the content, but because of the provocation. Provoking headlines which are not related to the text of the news. This continuous provocation, as well as the publicity resources in the interactive design (for instance, the use of the purple colour) etc., connotes the presence of a kind of destructive parochialism. Carrying out an analysis of the localization of the headquarters of the website and the interrelations with the Catalan university sector, we are in the presence of the Garduña Factor. In few words, the negative factors detected in the current work override the goal of information and formation of the information sciences and digital journalism.

Besides, those are working environments where the ethical rules of the profession are not respected, and it can also be inferred that the contractual conditions of the workers of the sector of the digital information in the era of the expansion of communicability aren't respected either.

CONCLUSION

The possibility of having free access to a free email address in the 90s meant a great advance in McLuhan's global village, because it was an important part of the democratization process of the Internet. However, the mercantilist factor soon made its appearance, becoming virtual firms where that service was offered for free, thanks to the publicity that was inserted in the websites. Later on, with the advances of the multimedia software and hardware, the telecommunications (for instance, the increase of the bandwidth to broadcast contents of the dynamic media), etc., some of those websites have turned into multimedia browsers, including the internal management of news as in the analyzed website. A website that for linguistic reasons (the Spanish language) has a potential of over 400 million users in the whole world. The obtained results do not only denote a low quality of the news service, but also a set of negative connotations from the point of view of social communication, such as the human and social factors with a negative sign, the lack of respect to the professional deontology of the digital information sector, the promotion of plagiarism and the manipulation of information. Adjusting to the new technological devices as can be the PCs tablets, multimedia mobile phones, etc. is positive for the advance of the ICTs, but previously the contents must be studied in each one of the categories of interactive design, starting by the contents. Contents which should be generated in a qualitative, autonomous and independent way, without boosting the Garduña Factor in the south of Europe, for instance.

ACKNOWLEDGMENT

We would to express our gratitude to Maria Ficarra. Besides, we should like to thank all our colleagues for their contributions: Sonia Flores, Mary Brie, Luisa Varela, Amélie Bordeaux and Valeria Villarreal.

REFERENCES

Apple. (1992). *Macintosh Human Interface Guidelines*. Addison-Wesley.

Barthes, R. (1985). *L'aventure sémiologique*. Paris: Seuil. (in French)

Cipolla-Ficarra, . (2013). *Advanced Research and Trends in New Technologies, Software, Human-Computer Interaction, and Communicability*. Hershey, PA: IGI Global.

Cipolla-Ficarra, F. (2008). HECHE: Heuristic Evaluation of Colours in HomepagE. Proceed. Applied Human Factors and Ergonomics.

Cipolla-Ficarra, F. (2010). *Persuasion On-Line and Communicability: The Destruction of Credibility in the Virtual Community and Cognitive Models.* New York: Nova Science Publishers.

Cipolla-Ficarra, F. (2011). *Emerging Software for Interactive Interfaces, Database, Computer Graphics and Animation: Pixels and the New Excellence in Communicability, Cloud Computing and Augmented Reality.* Bergamo: Blue Herons Editions.

Cipolla-Ficarra, F., Nicol, E., & Cipolla-Ficarra, M. (2010). Usability, Communicability and Cultural Tourism in Interactive Systems: Trends, Economic Effects and Social Impact. *Proceed. of the First International Conference on Human-Computer Interaction, Tourism and Cultural Heritage,* 100-114.

Conklin, J. (1987). Hypertext: An Introduction and Survey. *IEEE Computer,* *20*(9), 17–41. doi:10.1109/MC.1987.1663693

Cusumano, M., & Yoffie, D. (2000). *Competing On Internet Time: Lessons From Netscape And Its Battle With Microsoft.* New York: Free Press.

Dalmasso, M. (1992). *La imagen y el sentido. Las paradojas de lo verosímil. Teoría y Crítica de la Manipulación* (Vol. 2). Córdoba: Universidad Nacional de Córdoba. (in Spanish)

Date, C. (1990). *An Introduction to Database Systems.* Addison-Wesley.

Di-Lampedussa, G. (2007). *The Leopard.* New York: Random House.

Eco, U. (1979). *A Theory of Semiotics.* Indiana University Press.

Greimas, A. (1984). *Structural Semantics: An Attempt at a Method.* University of Nebraska Press.

Hall, P., & Papadopoulos, S. (1990). Hypertext Systems and Applications. *Information and Software Technology,* *32*(7), 477–490. doi:10.1016/0950-5849(90)90163-L

Melies, H. (1996). Toward the Information Network. *IEEE Computer, 29*(10), 69–78.

Microsoft. (1997). *Microsoft Encarta.* Seattle, WA: Microsoft.

Mitchell, W., & McCullough, M. (1995). *Digital Design Media.* New York: ITP.

Murch, G. (1984). Physiological Principles for the Effective Use of Color. *IEEE Computer Graphics and Applications*, *4*(11), 49–54. doi:10.1109/MCG.1984.6429356

Nöth, W. (1995). *Handbook of Semiotics.* Bloomington, IN: Indiana University Press.

Riedel, I. F. (1999). In Religion, Gesellschaft, Kunst und Psychotherapie. Stuttgart: Kreuz Verlag. (in German)

Ryan, J. (2013). *A History of the Internet and the Digital Future.* London: Reaktion Books.

Saussure, F. (1983). *Course in General Linguistics.* New York: McGraw-Hill.

Travis, D. (1991). *Effective Color Displays: Theory and Practice.* London: Academic Press.

Van-Dijk, T. (1993). *Elite Discourse and Racism.* Newbury, CA: Sage Publications. doi:10.4135/9781483326184

Veron, E. (2004). *La semiosis social. Fragmentos de una teoría de la discursividad.* Barcelona: Gedisa. (in Spanish)

APPENDIX 1

Figure 11. The Italian interface of Google in 2001 for the online search
(Approximate Translation: Interface of Google Italy with the options of web search, images, groups, and directories. In the right margin of the rectangle to write what one wants to search, are the alternatives of advanced search, preferences and instruments for the languages. Below are among others the search options in the whole web or only in the Italian pages.)

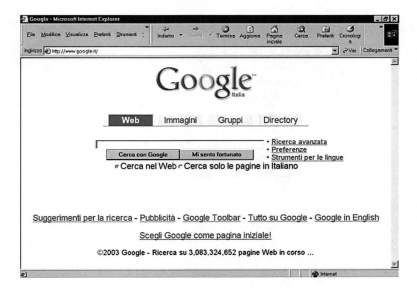

Figure 12. The advanced search option where are used more Boolean operators to localize the information in a specific and accurate way
(Approximate Translation: Interface of Google Italy with the breakdown of the advanced search [upper zone] to find results [inclusion of all the words, inclusion of the following sentences, one of the following words and exclusion of the words]; language; file format; dates; domains, etc. In the lower area is the specific search with the similar pages or the links.)

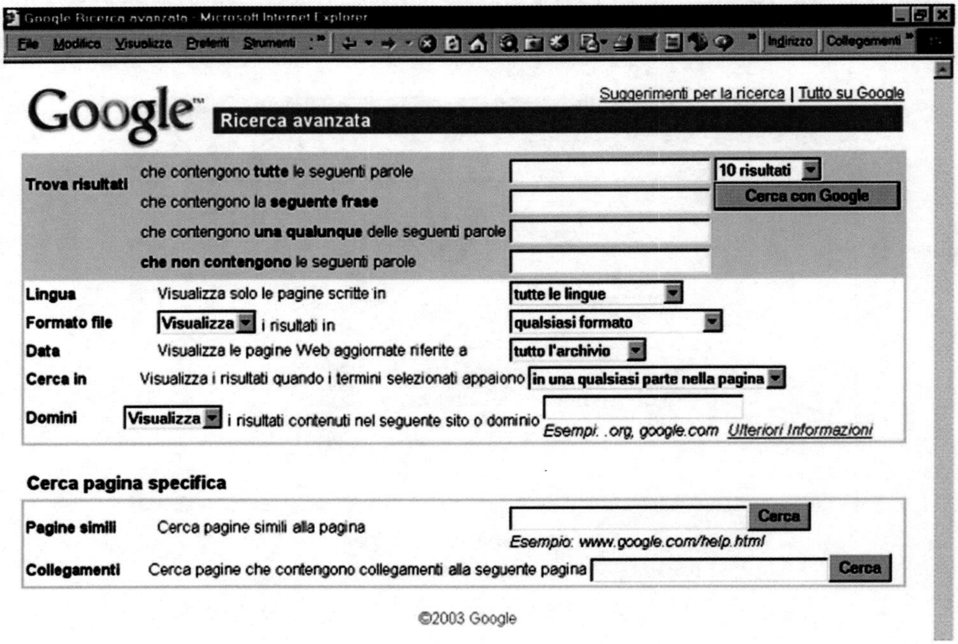

Figure 13. The Yahoo Italy interface and the tendency towards the information website, through the use of the hypertext (2001)

(Approximate Translation: Interface of the Yahoo Italy website with the searcher, the services of Yahoo [News, Purchases, Communication, Entertainment, Access, Organization of an agenda, Notebook, etc.], below is the email service. On the right side and vertically is to be found a virtual and personal assistant, Yahoo publicity [travels, etc.], and a listing of last minute news.)

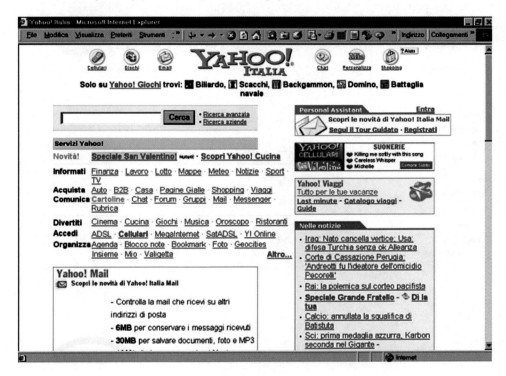

Figure 14. The Yahoo advanced search option with inferior options to those offered in Google

(Approximate Translation: Interface of the website Yahoo Italy with the advanced search, with the options for the search in the Web [all the words, some of the words, excluding terms, etc.] Below are the other options with regard to the language, the nation, the date, etc.)

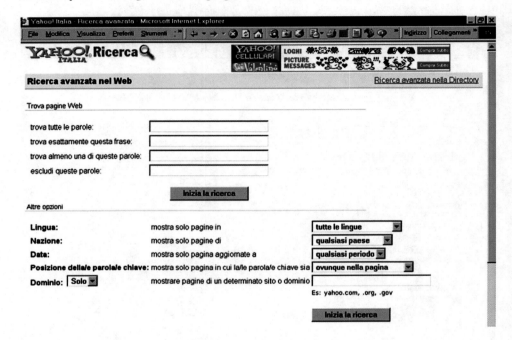

Figure 15. The 2002 Lycos website where the graphical elements of the interactive design are superior to those used in the home page of Google and Yahoo. Besides, news online are present

(*Approximate Translation: Interface of the Lycos website, with the search options in the web, news and shopping.*)

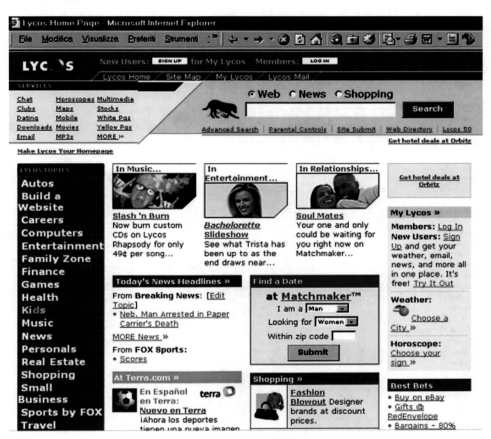

Figure 16. The Italian website of 2001 where the free email service for all is accompanied with a commercial website, where there is news and a tendency towards the current Yahoo España! website from the point of view of the structure of the home page
(Approximate Translation: Interface of the Italian website Virgilio, with the main options on the left margin of the page [weather, horoscope, last edition of the news, etc.] and in the upper part, accompanied with a wide service of the latest news, economy, sport, international news, etc.)

Figure 17. A website dedicated to the browsers existing in the Italian national and international market of the first decade of the new millennium
(Approximate Translation: Interface of the Italian website "Search Engines" with the following areas: Main, research, links, suggestions, inclusion on the websites, news and newsletter.)

Figure 18. Today, the violet is the constant color for options in Yahoo España! (last version). For example, the links into home page.
(Approximate Translation: Interface of the Yahoo website in Spanish, in the option active registration, and where there is a self-promotion slogan: "Yahoo Mail. Your ideal corner.")

Figure 19. The violet color for options in Yahoo España! –mobile phone, for example
(Approximate Translation: The Yahoo Mail application in the mobile phones, whose self-promotion is synthesized if the following way: "Attractive, easy to use, and ultrafast". Besides, stress is laid on the possibility of sending easily high-resolution pictures, changing from an inbox to another and start a safe session without passwords.)

La aplicación Correo Yahoo

Figure 20. The violet is present for the email icons of the tools
(Approximate Translation: The icons of the options for the Yahoo Spain email with the invitation to the user of "Explore your functions. All the tools you need to give a fresh air touch to your experience with the mail". The options of the icons are: novelties, inbox, search, write, calendar, contacts, storage and safety.)

APPENDIX 2

Figure 21. Smearing and persecution campaign (stalking) towards F C Barcelona players such as Messi, using such headlines as "Olympics: Lionel Messi said no to Madrid 2020" (08.29.2013)
(Approximate Translation: The Yahoo Spain, section Spain-Sports. In the text is the news of the refusal by Leo Messi to the president of the Spanish Olympic Committee, Alejandro Blanco, to participate in the promotional video of the Madrid candidacy as location of the Olympic Games in 2020.)

Figure 22. Romario "Messi has Asperger syndrome", for instance (09.09.2013)
(Approximate Translation: The Yahoo Spain, section Spain-Sports. In the text is the news of the Brazilian Romario where it is claimed that the Asperger syndrome, a variation of the autism of Messi. Besides, it claims that Einstein and Newton also suffered it and that Messi has overcome it and is a football star.)

Figure 23. Denounce of racism by an Argentinian model/dancer towards a Peruvian child in a television program (08.06.2013)
(Approximate Translation: Yahoo Spain – in the photo news title "I can't hide how racist he is". In the text of the news is told the controversy in Peru for the lack of respect from a female dancer to a four-year-old.)

Figure 24. Presence of carnivore worms in the ear of a British tourist who had visited Peru (08.06.2013)
(Approximate Translation: Yahoo Spain – in the picture news titled "Eight Larvae Nested in his Ear". In the text of the news it is indicated that the tourist Rochelle came back from her vacation in Peru with a weird headache and some disgusting guests.)

Chapter 13
Inverted Semanteme Into Financial Information Online

Francisco V. Cipolla-Ficarra
Latin Association of Human-Computer Interaction, Spain & International Association of Interactive Communication, Italy

Valeria M. Ficarra
Latin Association of Human-Computer Interaction, Spain & International Association of Interactive Communication, Italy

Miguel Cipolla-Ficarra
Latin Association of Human-Computer Interaction, Spain & International Association of Interactive Communication, Italy

ABSTRACT

In the current work is presented the strategy of the "inverted semanteme" to analyze the lack of veracity of the financial information in the Spanish websites, which have a ISO certification. A set of real examples accompany this semiotic analysis of the interactive design to indicate an inappropriate use of the certification quality of logos in the Internet. An inappropriate use which breeds discredit towards the human team of small and middle size technological firms which have ceased their activities. Besides, the social factors are researched of the damage towards the communicability and the online credibility stemming from the promotion of false information in the financial context.

DOI: 10.4018/978-1-5225-3437-2.ch013

INTRODUCTION

The global financial crisis of the new millennium has made apparent the need to resort constantly to the new technologies to enlarge the institutional image of Banks, credit institutions, government bodies and so on. Thanks to the democratization of the internet in the 90s, currently the banks, savings banks, etc., offer a myriad enticements to carry out financial operations from the home or the working place, counting with a maximun of online safety and speed in the transactions (Zhong, Liu, & Yao, 2007; Andriole, 2010; Cipolla-Ficarra, 2012; Cipolla-Ficarra, 2014). Those automation services have economic costs, and these vary in view of the relationships between the customer and the financial institution with which he/she is interacting (Chandramouli, et al., 2010; Pons, 2006). Within those services there are eventual aids offered to the potential customers who decide to open a small or middle size business. That is, a kind of promotional help with a cost equal to zero from the financial point of view at the moment of starting the entrepreneurial activities. Activities which may be aimed or not at the goods and/or services in the ICT (information and communication technology) sector, for instance (Begel, 2013).

Now, how can it be that a firm that has totally ended its activities at the start of the global financial crisis, that is, at the end of the first decade of the 21st century, currently appears in one of those websites as an active commercial institution and invoicing in-between a million and a half-three million euros per year? (Figure 3).

The Figure 3 depicts an example of what we call in the current work inverted semanteme. Semanteme is a unit of meaning, a linguistic element that it self expresses a concept and, in turn, is combinable with other such elements (Colapietro, 1993). In the current work one of those elements is the transparency of meaning, which constitutes a quality attribute of the online and/or offline multimedia information. An attribute of quality whose origins are related to the notions of linguistics and semiotics (Saussure, 1983; Eco, 1977), but which influence each one of the design categories of a multimedia system. In the current study aimed at online financial information.

Figure 1. Virtual firm of online services to find out the financial information of real firms

(Approximate Translation: Interface of the Axesor Portal [First Spanish Rating Agency] with the main options of business information, virtual gallery, marketing services, fees, directories, access and registration.) www.axesor.es

TRANSPARENCY OF THE MEANING

The transparency of meaning analyzes the use of terms (mainly), images and sounds inside the interface, which do not generate ambiguities between the level of content and the level of expression. These two levels are related with the notion of significant and signification. Moreover, both concepts have their origin in linguistics and which later on have been studied in semiotics or semiology (Eco, 1977; Eco, 1984).

Figure 2. Website where by paying a small figure in euros (42, 24, etc.) one has access to the confidential information of the directors of a firm

(Approximate Translation: Location of the Alfacis S.L.l firm in Barcelona in the Axesor website with the Google map. The information presented of the firm on the screen refers to the legal form, the address and the CIF (fiscal code), the activity to which it devotes itself, how long it has been active, etc. There are also the different fees to obtain financial information, commercial, etc, of the firm: 360°, credit report, commercial profile of the firm.)

The elements that make up the interface are interrelated accomplishing a function of anchoring or underpinning of the signification. The elements refer to the terms (regarded as a chain of characters), images (static or dynamic), and sounds. In the figure 4 has been observed how the components of the interface with their matching titles bolster the meaning of "artist" (Focus Multimedia, 1998). Next are analyzed a series of notions related to the semateme, accompanied by educational examples stemming from offline

Figure 3. Into the Spanish website "Axesor" there are falses financial and commercial information online
(*Approximate Translation: Interface of the Axesor Portal with the fake data from the Alfacis S.L. firm, where is declared a social capital of 100.000 euros, with an amount of employees ranging between 11 and 50, and a yearly billing between 1.500.001-1.000.000 euros.) www.axesor.es*

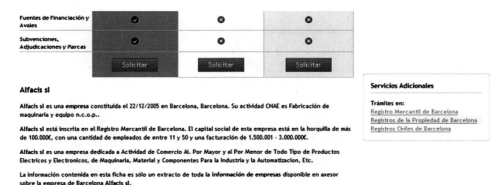

multimedia systems, many of them regarded as "classical" because they have signaled frequent errors of the interactive design and usability, and the eventual solutions to those issues.

In the notion of sign defined by Saussure we find that a linguistic sign joins a concept with an acoustic image (Saussure, 1983). This acoustic

Figure 4. An excellent example about the contents which do not generate ambiguities between the level of content and the level of expression

image is not the material or physical sound, but what Saussure defines as a "psychic trace", that is, the representation on the senses of the human being. The concept and the acoustic image are linked between themselves, they are arbitrary and are reciprocally interrelated. The graphic representation of sign given by Saussure is in the Figure 5.

The sign designates the whole, whereas concept and acoustic image were replaced with the passing of time by signification and significant respectively. In the Figure 6 there is the representation of this transformation.

If the link that binds the signification and the significant is arbitrary, then the sign is arbitrary. That is, it depends on a set of pre-established rules across time, such as is the case of a language. But to the acoustic image defined by Saussure must be added the grammatical image in the field of the significant, as Hjelmmslev claims (Nöth, 1995). This correction has allowed to overcome the idea of significant as a mere phonic sequence (expression). However, in the division of two levels by Hjemslev, such as are the expression (significant) and the content (signification) it is observed that there also exists between its components a bidirectional relationship, just the same as in the saussurian notion of sign. Without going into the methodological binomial form/substance that Hjelmslev applies, in the current research we have focused on the transparency of Saussirian concept or signification or the content of hjemlesvism to avoid ambiguity. An ambiguous content is that in which outside any context it is possible to assign two or more interpretations. The triangle of Baldinger (Nöth, 1995) serves to watch a case of ambiguity with the term "piano" in several languages, which depending on the context

Figure 5. The components of the sign according to Saussure

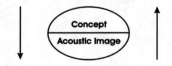

Figure 6. Evolution of the sign concept

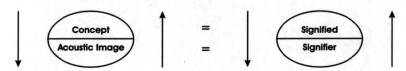

Figure 7. Triadic relationship between signification, significant and object

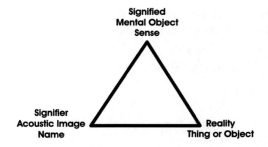

might seriously affect the communicability and the usability of a system, for instance.

The spelling of the word "piano", as the pronunciation in Spanish, French, English and Italian is identical. Besides, it refers to the same musical instrument. But in the case of Italian, the relation between the significant and the signification is "richer", that is, aside from the musical instrument it connotes several "elements" of reality: Walking or treading slowly; Whispering; Floor of a building. Flat surface. Map of a building or a region; planning of activities or work.

This phenomenon of connotations or of wealth of content is in relationship with the notion of boundless semiosis by Pierce (Eco, 1977; Nöth, 1995).

Figure 8. Semiosis representation

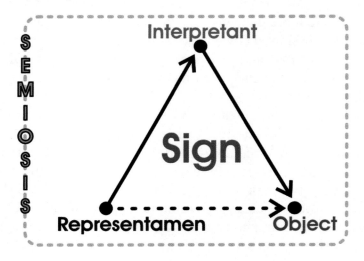

De Saussure and Hjelmslev regard the sign as bilevel (dualistic) but with Pierce a triad is established between an object (real or imaginary), the representation (material expression, such as a word) and the interpretation (content). In the interrelation interpretation and representation is where takes place the boundless semiosis. Boundless semiosis is a normal event in the evolution of a language.

For instance, this is the reason why in a multimedia system whose goal is the learning of several languages, unless images are inserted of the object to which they refer, a term in an isolated way may prompt confusion at the moment of the interaction of the user. The image in this case accomplishes the function of anchoring of the sense (Nöth, 1995). Besides, the ambiguity of the signification in the online and offline multimedia contents is presented to the user as a disjunction between two or more different interpretations and an orientation is missing. It is important to point out that the ambiguity is basically a problem of signification rather than of the significant.

In regard to the wealth of the content are observed two situations: one positive and another negative. On the one hand, it may complicate the "decoding" of the message given the abundance of data in front of the user, and on the other hand it facilitate the decoding by reducing the number of interpretations. In spite of this the user finds himself/herself in front of several interpretations and does not know what sense to choose. The context offered by a natural metaphor of the interface facilitates the task of picking the most consistent interpretation among the several alternatives that have been presented (Fairclough, 2003).

There is a kind of ambiguity called phonic (Nöth 1995; Cipolla-Ficarra & Cipolla-Ficarra, 2008) which affects the dynamic means of the multimedia systems. They are those elements of audio in which the synchronization of the emission of the slowed down locution brings about incomprehension by the user. They constitute a set made up by messages that although they may occasionally receive an identical phonetic articulation possess differentiated phonological descriptions.

It is not the same the locution in Spanish of "de mente joven" (with a young mind) as "demente joven" (demented young person). An usual mistake and detected with quality attributes, metrics, method and techniques, heuristic evaluation, communicability, etc. (Cipolla-Ficarra, 2010a): MEHEM (Methodology for Heuristic Evaluation in Multimedia), MECEM (Metrics for the Comunications Evaluation in Multimedia) and HEDCDEH (Heuristic Evaluation Disk for Communication and Design in Hypermedia) in a set of CD-ROMs for the young whose translation was made in an Anglophone country. Generally this ambiguity may be reduced if an animated text is included, that is, as the speaker speaks the listened words are illuminated or highlighted (this method has been called "karaoke"). Finally, related to the ambiguity these two notions are found:

1. The vagueness. A term is vague when its limits of designation are inaccurate. In the following definition of the language "C" in Spanish of the Encyclopaedia of Science –a classical examples of off-line multimedia (DK Publishing, 1997) the expression *"es un lenguaje de programación más extendido"* –it is a more widespread programming language", the term *"extendido"* by itself does not establish accurately the reason of the extension, such as can be the following factors: by the ease of use, the compatibility with the other programming languages, seniority, etc. In such circumstances there are always realities which can be denoted both by the term and by neighbouring signs in the system. Vagueness is a phenomenon of designation, not of signification. This phenomenon has its origin in the inaccurate limits which the designative class that the signs of a language posses or of a natural language. The significations within it are established through oppositions of concepts. The signs of the natural languages posses a high degree of vagueness. The scientific language which tries to be accurate and exact must avoid it as much as possible. This precision is a goal to be achieved and achieving it has its inconveniences, since in the definitions of scientific language terms of the natural language are used.

2. Indeterminacy is the lack or poorness of the information. The user wants to know more data than those conveyed in the message. In the indeterminacy the signification is unique, there is no signification duplicity or multiplicity. It is a resource used to bolster the advance in the computer assisted teaching system, where the contents are presented to the user in a fractioned way. Next a classical example of the multimedia offline course Windows 95, where the concept of edition of the Paint is presented in three parts (CD-ROM Windows, 1995). The briefly described actions allow us to determine whether in an interface the content is 100% truthful and which elements are used to give veracity to a false information. The following bibliographical references allow us to broaden these concepts.

Figure 9. Example of a "vague" term
(Approximate Translation: In the definition of the programming language "C" in the first sentence it can be read "is the most widespread programming language".)

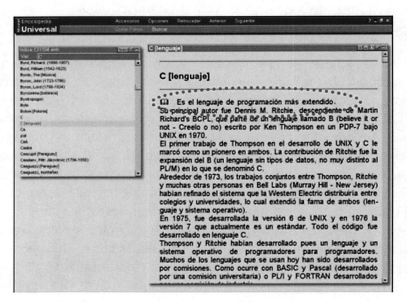

In the previous example the fragmentation of the content of the information at the moment of the presentation has educational purposes. However, there are definitions in the system The Universal Encyclopaedia (DK Publishing, 1997) where the poorness of the information is observed and without a solution to this kind of problem, since the offline multimedia system did not have an online connection to access another database.

In the example of the Figure 11, it can be seen how the indeterminate information reduces the motivation to a user in the self-learning process of an operative system, through the multimedia systems. There are also cases in which the correct access to the information can be damaged if the relationship between the signification, the significant and the object does not encompass all its meanings. This failure takes place generally in some systems of the encyclopaedia kind which have been translated from other foreign languages and which usually include a dictionary of Spanish, but which do not take into account all the alternatives of the relationship signification, significant and object. Such is the case of the first system Larousse multimedia Encyclopaedia (Larousse, 1998). This failure was non-existent in the system Dictionary of the Spanish Language of the Espasa-Calpe firm which were developed contemporarily (Espasa-Calpe, 1998).

Figure 10. Example of a solution in the indeterminacy of signification on three screens
(*Approximate Translation: Fragmentation of the content in the explanation of the functioning of the Paint of Windows. In section 1 [red box]: Through the edition menu it can undo or repeat the last action carried out in his work. In section 2 [green box]: With the options cut. copy and glue it can move or copy selected areas of its drawing. Besides, the copy option allows it to copy an area selected as an independent file. In the section 3 [red box]: Go to the menu "see" pressing the right cursor key.*)

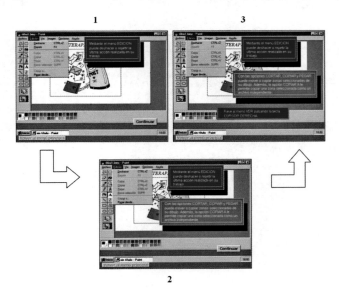

THE STRATEGY OF LINGUISTIC INVERSION

De Saussure had established a bidirectional relationship between signification and significant. However, when the quality attribute such as the transparency of the content is missing, as it can be seen in the Figure 3, a strategy of inverted relationship can be established between the texts and the images that appear in the interface of an interactive financial system.

On the one hand, are grouped the elements that bolster the visual content, such as the use of the logos and on the other hand we have the elements that decrease the veracity of the information, such as the texts. For instance, in the Figure 12, we can see the logos of Spanish banking institutions such as Santander (www.santanderbank.com) and BBVA (www.bbva.com), multinational firms such as Mapfre (www.mapfre.com), Endesa (www.endesa.com) and Iberdrola (www.iberdrola.es), and private healthcare institutions such as Sanitas (www.sanitas.es) or humanitarian organizations such as the Red Cross (www.cruzroja.es). All of them are presented as "guarantors or

Figure 11. Indeterminate or "poor" definition of the BASIC language
(Approximate Translation: In the definition of the "BASIC" programming language it says that it is an acronym of the English expression Beginners Allpurpose Symbolic Instruction Code. It is a symbolic conversation language and without any specific application used in the computers.)

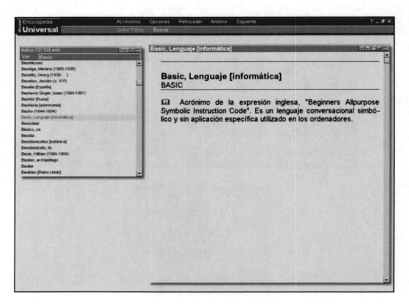

backers" (anchoring function) of the information because they are under the title "they trust us".

Other elements which bolster that phoney information are the logos, in the lower part of Figure 12. The first one refers to AENOR –Spanish Association for Standardisation and Certification (it is a leading institution in the certification of management systems, products and services, and responsible for the development and diffusion of the UNE rules (*Una Norma Española*) and within the guidelines ISO 9001: 2008, that is, drawn by the International Organization for Standardization (ISO). In other words, it lays down the requirements for a system of management of quality (SGC). The second one is the Certified Management System (distinctive of quality to the excellence). The third "Trust Online" is a public-private self-regulation system of Spanish reach under a the juridical form of an association. The private promoters of this system are the Association for the Self-Regulation of Commercial Communication and the Spanish Association of Digital Economy, whereas the promoter on behalf of the public sector is Red.es (www.red.es).

Figure 12. Use of logos of local, national and international prestige (right area) to underpin the image of the Spanish website which sells phoney financial information to the potential customers
(*Approximate Translation: Free access to the Axesor website, with reports of Positions and Directors plus, with the two registration options to access the product and purchase without registration. In the upper part of the interface below the sentence "they trust us" are the icons of those firms.*)

Although in the context of the design of the interfaces of interactive systems, authors such as Regis Debray claim that the image is dead (Debray, 1992) because they can be manipulated or retouched with commercial applications such as Photoshop, that is, they do not depict reality at 100%. Therefore, it is necessary to go back to the text. Now in the context of the financial information of the new millennium, we also find that the text does not guarantee either a veracity of the information at 100%. In the Figure 3, we can read that it is a one-person firm (*S.L. sociedad limitada*, Ltd. Society) that is, with a single person who has the function of only administrator and employee at the same

Figure 13. False utilization of logos which certify a high quality in a website, when in fact they are offering to the potential customers who hire those services untruthful financial information about the firms that they have stored in the databases
(*Approximate Translation: In the figure aren't only the quality certificates of the service, but also the slogan "Axesor, to know to decide".*)

time. Now how can there appear a total of employees ranging between 11 and 50? And in the same vein, how can there be an allocated capital of € 100,000 when legally they were constituted with less than € 5,000? (Figure 3). That is, within the category of the Spanish minimum legal for the limited companies. These two rhetorical questions underline the vagueness in the textual information and denote a false online information.

The vagueness and the falseness of the online information bring about in the wealth of the content of a multimedia system an inversion in the decoding of the message. There are two situations: one positive and another negative, where in principle the online information is presented as true by the static and dynamic elements of the interface (graphics, drawings, animations, video, etc.), but the falseness of the textual data inverts the decoding process. Although there is in the interface an abundance of data which may complicate the decoding of the message, making it appear as truthful, on the other hand, the text facilitates the decoding by reducing the number of interpretations. In spite of this, the user finds the first time that he/she access the website several interpretations due to the importance of the logos, as a function of the anchoring of the veracious meaning. However, once the falsehood of the information is detected, when it is verified in the real world that the firm is no longer active, the user does not know anymore what sense to choose, when he/she checks again the same screens. That is why the context provided by

Figure 14. The information into Axesor does not guarantee either a veracity of at 100% about ex-Alfacis S.L.
www.axesor.es

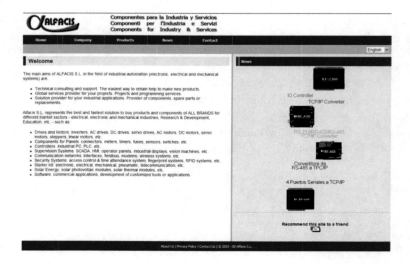

a natural metaphor of the interface facilitates the task of picking the most consistent interpretation among the different alternatives that have been shown to the user for the first time.

LESSONS LEARNED

The global financial crisis has not only brought forward great negative structural changes as to purchasing power and access to multimedia information of the potential users due to the increase of the digital divide, for instance, but it has also destroyed a myriad personal firms (small and middle size) regarded since the industrial revolution of the 19th century as the real productive, economic and financial cornerstone within one of the four European economies regarded as an European engine: Catalonia (Cipolla-Ficarra & Ficarra, 2011; Cipolla-Ficarra, 2010a). A myriad personal firms aimed at the ICT sector were literally swindled by employees of savings banks, banks and so on which not only haven't helped the promotion of their productive activities or services at the moment of the opening, such as can be the free promotion inside the databases of the customers of those financial institutions, namely a newsletter, but they have had to do in the realization of those totally illegal activities if they are compared to other European realities. In the first case, they have neglected sending a simple file in a ASCII (American Standard Code for Information Interchange) format where the opening of the firm is mentioned with the activities it will potentially carry out. In the second case, they have turned the entrepreneurial losses into personal losses of the single administrators of those firms through the credit cards. That is, they have jeopardized through a hustle in disguise the future of the potential entrepreneurs. This modus operandi in Catalonia, like in many other places of the Spanish territory, are totally illegal in many countries of the EU. In few words, and from the social perspective, there is not only the financial destruction of those single administrators of the small firms, but there is also a kind of virtual attack from the perspective of the new technologies. The analyzed examples in the Internet highlight the destruction of the credibility (Cipolla-Ficarra, 2010b) of those victims of the Spanish financial fraud by purporting that their businesses still remain active, with a staff of employees and invoicing figures beyond the € 1,000,000. The heuristic analysis, where there is an intersection of the formal and factual sciences, the notions of linguistics, semiotics ande communicability allows to locate in a fast and efficient way the anomalies of the interactive design in the online financial sector.

CONCLUSION

In the same way as the bit is the minimum unit of information in computer science, the semantemes detect quickly the veracity of the online audiovisual contents, in the banking or financial system. Although they are profit organizations, the financial global crisis of the first decade of the new millennium has brought about the crumbling in the institutional image of those centennial institutions, with regard to the small and middle-size entrepreneurs as is the case of the denizens of Catalonia. Those businessmen are doubly victims, from a temporal and ICT perspective. In the past, through the analogical and digital information of those institutions and the publicity with propaganda purposes to take loans in the short, middle and long term, without any responsibility whatsoever in the last five years, for the issuers and promoters of this fraudulent system who resorted to the new technologies to recruit their possible victims. In the present and in the future, not only because of the financial-economic damage caused, by turning the entrepreneurial debts into personal debts, but also through websites that discredit thousands of those victims, by selling false information about businesses that closed down five years ago, for instance. These examples make up an investment in the credibility of the online information when allegedly the democratization mustn't only allow the access to the information but to a veracious information, especially that information related to the financial institutions which ethically and aesthetically belong to the swamp of illegality. Financial institutions that make an effort to revamp their websites with the latest technological breakthroughs, but the problem is not the interactive design, but the transparency and reliability of the information about the services that are offered to the users, within and without their offices. Finally, that lack of veracity of the online information doesn't only affect those financial institutions, but also the quality system of the online information of the state, since they include the ISO certification logos, like those belonging to non-profit humanitarian organizations which enjoy a great international prestige such as the Red Cross. Through the analysis of the semantemes of those websites can be detected a lack of control in the quality system of the online information which hugely damages the image of the country in the global and local village of the ICT.

REFERENCES

Andriole, S. (2010). Business Impact of Web 2.0 Technologies. *Communications of the ACM*, *53*(12), 67–79. doi:10.1145/1859204.1859225

Baecker, R., Moffatt, K., & Massimi, M. (2012). Technologies for Aging Gracefully. *Interaction*, *79*(3), 32–36. doi:10.1145/2168931.2168940

Begel, A., Bosch, J., & Storey, M. (2013). Social Networking Meets Software Development: Perspectives from GitHub, MSDN, Stack Exchange, and TopCoder. *IEEE Software*, *30*(1), 52–66. doi:10.1109/MS.2013.13

Chandramouli, B., Ali, M., Goldstein, J., Sezgin, B., & Raman, B. S. (2010). Data Stream Management Systems for Computational Finance. *IEEE Computer*, *43*(12), 45–52. doi:10.1109/MC.2010.346

Cipolla-Ficarra, F. (2010a). *Quality and Communicability for Interactive Hypermedia Systems: Concepts and Practices for Design*. Hershey, PA: IGI Global. doi:10.4018/978-1-61520-763-3

Cipolla-Ficarra, F. (2010b). *Persuasion On-Line and Communicability: The Destruction of Credibility in the Virtual Community and Cognitive Models*. New York: Nova Publishers.

Cipolla-Ficarra, F. (2012). *New Horizons in Creative Open Software, Multimedia, Human Factors and Software Engineering*. Bergamo: Blue Herons.

Cipolla-Ficarra, F. (2014). *Advanced Research and Trends in New Technologies, Software, Human-Computer Interaction, and Communicability*. Hershey, PA: IGI Global. doi:10.4018/978-1-4666-4490-8

Cipolla-Ficarra, F., & Cipolla-Ficarra, M. (2008). Interactive Systems, Design and Heuristic Evaluation: The Importance of the Diachronic Vision. In *Proceedings New Directions in Intelligent Interactive Multimedia* (pp. 625–634). Heidelberg, Germany: Springer. doi:10.1007/978-3-540-68127-4_64

Cipolla-Ficarra, F., & Ficarra, V. (2011). Software Management Applications, Textile CAD and Human Factors: A Dreadful Industrial Example for Information and Communication Technology. In *Proceedings First International Conference on Advances in New Technologies, Interactive Interfaces and Communicability*. Heidelberg, Germany: Springer. doi:10.1007/978-3-642-20810-2_13

Colapietro, V. (1993). *Semiotics*. New York: Paragon House.

Debray, R. (1992). *Vie et mort de l'image*. Paris: Gallimard. (in French)

Eco, U. (1977). *A Theory of Semiotics*. Bloomington, IN: Indiana University Press.

Eco, U. (1984). *Semiotics and the Philosophy of Language*. London: Macmillan. doi:10.1007/978-1-349-17338-9

Espasa-Calpe. (1998). *CD-ROM Dictionary of the Spanish Language of the Espasa-Calpe*. Madrid: Espasa-Calpe.

Fairclough, N. (2003). *Analysing Discourse: Textual Analysis for Social Research*. London: Routledge.

Focus Multimedia. (1998). *CD-ROM Artist*. Rugeley: Focus Multimedia.

Larousse. (1998). *CD-ROM Larousse multimedia Encyclopaedia*. Paris: Larousse.

Nöth, W. (1995). *Handbook of Semiotics*. Bloomington, IN: Indiana University Press.

Pons, A. P. (2006). Biometric Marketing: Targeting the Online Consumer. *Communications of the ACM*, *49*(8), 60–65. doi:10.1145/1145287.1145288

Publishing, D. K. (1997). *CD-ROM Encyclopaedia of Science*. London: DK Publishing.

Saussure, F. (1983). *Course in General Lingistics*. New York: McGraw-Hill.

Turgeon. (1995). *CD-ROM Windows '95*. Barcelona: Turgeon. (in Spanish)

Zhong, N., Liu, J., & Yao, Y. (2007). Envisioning Intelligent Information Technologies through the Prism of Web Intelligence. *Communications of the ACM*, *50*(3), 89–94. doi:10.1145/1226736.1226741

ADDITIONAL READING

Ailamaki, A., Katere, V., & Dash, D. (2010). Managing Scientific Data. *Communications of the ACM*, *53*(6), 68–78. doi:10.1145/1743546.1743568

Bauman, Z. (1999). *Culture as Praxis*. London: Sage.

Biber, D., Conrad, S., & Reppen, R. (1998). *Corpus Linguistics: Investigating Language Structure and Use*. Cambridge: Cambridge University. doi:10.1017/CBO9780511804489

Block, D., & Cameron, D. (2001). *Globalization and Language Teaching*. New York: Routledge.

Boehm, B. (1981). *Software Engineering Economics*. Englewood Cliffs: Prentice-Hall.

Card, S., Mackinlay, J., & Shneiderman, B. (1999). *Readings in Information Visualization: Using Vision to Think*. San Francisco: Morgan Kauffman.

Chen, H. (2010). Business and Market Intelligence 2.0. *IEEE Intelligent Systems*, *25*(2), 74–82. doi:10.1109/MIS.2010.43

Cipolla-Ficarra, et al.. (2013). *Scientific Computing, Communicability and Cultural Heritage: Future Trends in Software and Interactive Design. Bergamo: Blue Herons Cipolla-Ficarra, et al. (2014). Strategies for a Creative Future with Computer Science, Quality Design and Communicability*. Bergamo: Blue Herons.

Crystal, D. (2001). *Language and the Internet*. Cambridge: Cambridge University Press. doi:10.1017/CBO9781139164771

Curtis, B., Sappidi, J., & Szynkarski, A. (2012). Estimatine the Principal of an Applications Technical Debt. *IEEE Software*, *29*(6), 34–42. doi:10.1109/MS.2012.156

Douglas, M. (1970). *Natural Symbols*. London: Routledge.

Eco, U. (1979). *The Role of the Reader: Explorations in the Semiotics of Texts*. Bloomington: Indiana University Press.

Fairclough, N. (1995). *Critical Discourse Analysis: The Critical Study of Language*. London: Longman.

Fellbaum, C. (1998). *WordNet: An Electronic Lexical Database*. Cambridge: MIT Press.

Gee, J. (1999). *An Introduction to Discourse Analysis. Theory and Method*. London: Routledge.

Hodge, R., & Kress, G. (1988). *Social Semiotics*. Ithaca: Cornell University Press.

Holmes, N. (2004). Languages and the Computing Profession. *IEEE Computer*, *37*(3), 102–104. doi:10.1109/MC.2004.1274016

Kotler, P., Roberto, N., & Lee, N. (2002). *Social Marketing: Improving The Quality of Life*. London: Sage.

Lotman, Y. (1990). *Universe of the Mind: A Semiotic Theory of Culture*. Bloomington: Indiana University Press.

Lowgren, J. (2013). Annotated Portfolios and Other Forms of Intermediate-Level Knowledge. *Interaction*, *20*(1), 30–34. doi:10.1145/2405716.2405725

Maldonado, T. (1994). *Reale e virtuale*. Milano: Feltrinelli. in Italian

Mills, S. (1997). *Discourse*. London: Routledge.

Nelson, R., & Winter, S. (1982). *An Evolutionary Theory of Economic Change*. Cambridge: Harvard University Press.

Patton, M. Q. (2002). *Qualitative Research and Evaluation Methods*. Thousand Oaks: Sage.

Peck, J., Yeung, H. (2003). *Remaking the Global Economy: Economic-Geographical Perspectives*. London: Sag

Searle, J. (1979). *Expression and Meaning*. Cambridge: Cambridge University Press. doi:10.1017/CBO9780511609213

Sebeok, T. (2001). *Global Semiotics*. Bloomington: Indiana University Press.

Veltman, K. (2014). *Alphabet of Life*. Maastricht: Virtual Maastricht McLuhan Institute.

Vygotsky, L. (1962). *Thought and Language*. Cambridge: MIT Press. doi:10.1037/11193-000

KEY TERMS AND DEFINITIONS

Communicability: A qualitative communication between the user and the interactive system, such as mobile phones, augmented reality, immersion multimedia, hypermedia, among others. The extent to which an interactive system successfully conveys its functionality to the user.

Financial Information: Data used for optimal financial planning and forecasting decisions and outcomes for potential clients, providers, bankers, investors, etc.

Interactive System: A computer device made up by a CPU and peripherals, whose functioning requires a constant interaction with the user. Currently these systems tend to their miniaturization and/or invisibility, the mobility and wireless connectability among them.

Linguistics: The study of language, and includes an analysis of language form, language meaning, and language in context. Some areas of this science of language are phonetics, phonology, morphology, syntax, semantics, pragmatics, and evolution of the linguistics.

Semanteme: An indivisible unit of meaning. In other words, one of the minimum elements of lexical meaning in a language.

Semiotics: The study of signs. It is a systematic study of the nature, properties, and kinds of the signs.

Transparency of Meaning: Analyzes the use of terms (mainly), images and sounds inside the interface.

Chapter 14
Statistics and Graphics Online:
Links Between Information in Newspapers and User Experience Evaluation

Francisco V. Cipolla-Ficarra
Latin Association of Human-Computer Interaction, Spain & International Association of Interactive Communication, Italy

Alejandra Quiroga
Universidad Nacional de La Pampa, Argentina

Jim Carré
University of the Netherlands Antilles, Curaçao

Valeria M. Ficarra
Latin Association of Human-Computer Interaction, Spain & International Association of Interactive Communication, Italy

ABSTRACT

In the chapter are indicated the main links of the isotopies between the static information and the different ways of graphic representation for the readers of online newspapers. Besides, a set of examples of news is presented with statistic data, analyzing those that boost or discourage iconicity and the ease of understanding. Finally, a study is made of the link between the statistic and the use of the comic to draw the attention of the user.

DOI: 10.4018/978-1-5225-3437-2.ch014

INTRODUCTION

For the realization of our study we have used notions stemming from semiotics, descriptive statistics, online interactive design and communicability. From semiotics we use the notion of iconicity (Eco, 1979; Saussure, 1983; Greimas, 1984; Nöth, 1995). Having the status or properties of a icon; fulfilling the function or playing the role of an icon (a sign which represents its object by virtue of a resemblance to that object). We will try to locate that iconicity in each one of the graphics that make up the current work. Our universe of study is made up by statistic graphics of 2012, 2013 and 2014 from an online Spanish paper "El Pais" (www.elpais.es), reducing the change of style to represent the graphic stemming from the statistic data. The sign (+) means that communicability is present, (++) denotes thatt the ease of understanding of the statistic data and the iconicity are present. In contrast, if there is a negative sign (-) or signs (- -), they have an inverse sense, that is, it means the absence of the previously enumerated components.

The graphic representation of statistic information in the newspapers must be regarded as a means or a complementary tool to transfer round-ups, synthesis, conclusions and so on to public opinion. These graphics have acquired great diffusion in the written press of the 20th century, especially for economic and social information. Later on, those graphics were accompanied by pictures, illustrations, etc, thus establishing a link with infographics (Ware, 2013; Smiciklas, 2012). Whereas in Spain the word "infographics" is normally used as a synonymous of a computer animated image, in other countries it is rather related to the explanation graphics and illustrations in general, such images may appear published in a newspaper, accompanied by statistic information (Ficarra, 1993). Now in the graphic arts both uses are correct. In contrast, in some Latin American countries and in several European countries infographics is a synonymous for computer graphics (computer-made static point of view of the image). The truth is that since 1990 the graphic arts transit in the era of digital communication, boosted by the Internet (Cipolla-Ficarra, 2005). Hence it is necessary to speak of the infographic arts: info (for information) and graphics (computer made images in 2D and/or 3D). Here the term infographics is used as synonymous of computer graphics. Besides, in such area are seated the originality and creativity factors of a graphic arts work. In infographics usually converge not only the technological aspect, but besides the creative factor (Lankow, Ritchie, & Crooks, 2012). Now the main activity of the graphic designer is textual communication. That is, he/ she is a "visual communicator through letters". Moreover, the workers of that sector must be experts in setting texts. Texts which may be accompanied by statistic data, static and/or dynamic images, with sound media, such as can be the case of an offline and/or online hypermedia newspaper. In this kind of digital support of the contents many of the traditional limitations of the analogical media have been overcome in graphic representation (Chen, & Paul, 2001). Besides, even if it is true that the graphic method of information represents a more attractive way to draw the attention of the readers in the newspapers, in paper support, those same data grouped and from the technical point of view, can't be regarded as a rigorous way in itself, like an exactness of statistic representation (Ficarra, 1993; Gage, 2000; Riobbo & Pio de Oro, 2000). Some of those classical limitations in the analogical media for the graphic representation are:

- The graphic method can't represent as many data as a statistic table, for instance.
- The appreciation of details is not possible.
- The graphic in itself can't give exact values.
- Deformations are likely to occur because of the scales used.
- The graphics required more time for its realization than the tables.

Aside from those characteristics with a negative sign, the graphics boost, in principle, the user experience evaluation, since it is already possible to have a view of the whole, observing at a single glance what is considered in abstract. Obviously, starting from the numeric data, one can infer the veracity or not of the statistic source of information. William Playfair, the founder of graphical methods of statistics, claimed that the advantage of the proposed method is not to give the most accurate expression than that of figures, but giving a more simple and permanent of the gradual progress and of comparable amounts in different periods, presenting at sight a figure (graphics) whose proportions match the amount of realities that it attempts to express (Playfair, 2005). In this sense, infographics and iconicity have contributed to boost Playfair's notions in the digital papers. Next two examples of infographics.

THE GRAPHIC REPRESENTATION OF STATISTIC DATA

Some of the rules to bear in mind in the graphic representation of statistic data are summed-up in the following way (Cleveland, 1993; Cleveland, 1994; Tufte, 2001; Cipolla-Ficarra, 2014):

- The general disposition of a diagram must advance from left to right.
- It is convenient to depict the amounts through lineal magnitudes, curves and bars, since the surfaces and the volumes may lead to mistaken interpretations.
- Whenever possible, the vertical scale of the curve must be selected in such a way that the line of zero appears in the diagram. The visual impression is incorrect in case there is no such line.
- The zero line must be differentiated through a thicker drawing than the lines that depict the coordinates.
- When the curves depict percentages, it is advisable to stress the 100% line or any other used as basis of comparison.
- If the scale of a diagram is related to dates and the depicted period is not a complete unit, it is better to show the first and the last coordinate, since the diagram does not depict the beginning or the end of time.
- No more coordinate lines (frames) must be drawn than those necessary to help the reading of the graphic.
- The curves of a diagram must be thicker than the lines of the coordinates (frames).
- In the curves representing a series of observations, it is advisable, whenever possible, to indicate clearly in the diagram all the points that are depicted by the separate observations.
- The numbers indicating the scale of a diagram must be placed to the left of the lower part along the respective axes.
- It is advisable to include in the diagram the numeric data or formula represented.
- If the numeric data are not included in the diagram, it is advisable to give them in the form of a table accompanying said diagram.
- All the titles and figures of the diagram must be placed in such a way that they are easy to read starting from the lower horizontal or from the left margin, and as far as possible, the captions, signs etc. must be placed in a horizontal way and exceptionally in a vertical way.

Figure 1. Correct use of infographics in a high speed train accident where the map of the calamity [+], the sketch of how the event developed, the use of the arrows, circles, etc, indicators, the pictures, the 2D and 3D figures for the details of the train and the texts make up a visual unit with little margin for ambiguity or vagueness of the presented information [-].

(Approximate Translation: Article of the Spanish paper El País with the title "First deadly accident in Spain in high speed railway". In the graphics it can be read the route of the train "Alvia Madrid-Ferrol": the place of the accident [circular graphic]. The characteristics of the train and the model: Alvia series 730; and the graphic in 3D of the bend of A Grandeira with the time of the accident: 20:41 PM.)

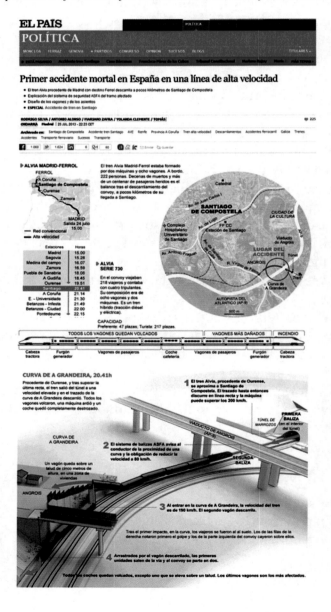

Figure 2. An incorrect use of infographics in the Olympic sport [- -]. The error is located in the high amount of the data presented in tables, graphics, photographies, etc, and their disposition make every reader go into an endless semiosis between signification and significant generates a disorientation (Veron, 2004). Some of the rules to be taken into account in the graphic representation of statistic data.
(Approximate Translation: Article of the Spanish newspaper El País, with the title: "New Olympic record by Bolt" and with the subtitle "the Jamaican athlete achieves the second best mark of all times in the 100 meters".)

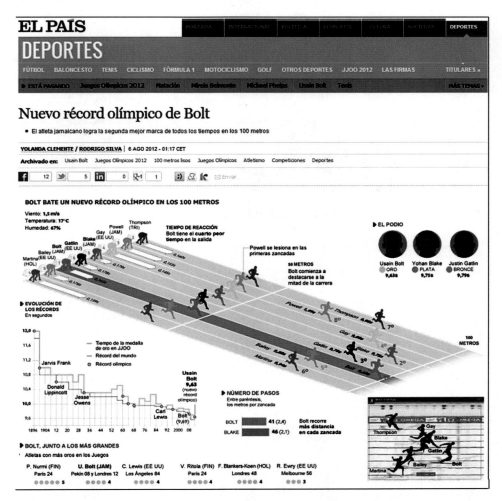

- If a diagram requires the drawing of two or more curves, this must be of different color or of a different type of line. The crossing of lines must be avoided in order to prevent confusion.

Those are statistic data which at the moment of the representation may have or not a mathematic basis, and between both are those which in the current work are called hybrids. The statistic foundation will be different depending on whether they are flat graphic representations, cartographic or special (pictograms or sketches). In this senses, traditionally there are two great sets, and in them there are 7 subsets. The set of those which have a mathematic basis are mainly: dots graphics, lineal (straight and curved),

Figure 3. Accounting information about the corruption in Spain
(Approximate Translation: Article of the Spanish newspaper El País with the title: "55 jottings of the B accountancy of Barcenas confirmed".)

Figure 4. Banking and accounting information of a corruption network in Spain
(Approximate Translation: Article of the Spanish paper El País with the title: "Payments of the PP to José María Aznar in 1996". Bar graphic with the Aznar representation expenses [left area]. Representation expenses in the year 1996 and statement sent by the PP to the Finance ministry with the payments to Aznar in 1996 [right and lower part].)

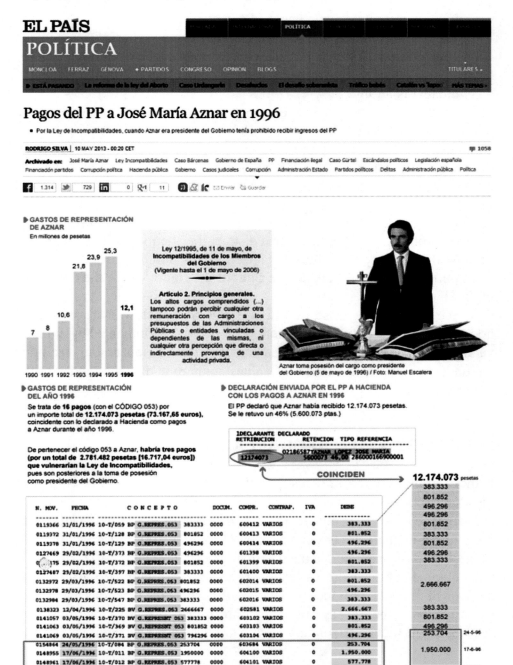

surface (rectangles, circular, triangular, etc.), stereometric (pyramidal, cubic, etc.). Those which do not have a mathematic basis are made up by three subsets: cartograms, (statistic maps, for instance), pictograms, free or special graphics. Between both there are the hybrids, that is, a combination of data with and without mathematic basis, like in the Figure 7.

In the graphic hybrids, the surface graphics can be grouped (rectangles), tables and columns of those tables, like other elements to be visually highlighted (arrows, lines, squares, etc, generally in red color), and even photographs of what the text is telling.

In the Figure 3, the graphic representation in the shape of bars has as a purpose to indicate double values which have been allocated each one of the columns, where there is a picture on the axis of the abscises [+]. However, the group of columns on the left margin of the graphics turns out to be unreadable, since there is not match between the numeric information and its representation [-].

In the Figure 5 there is a combination of graphics in the shape of vertical and horizontal bars and tables which distract the attention of the reader [- -] because the lower bars in a horizontal format from left to right are presented as a continuation in the zone of the right of the figure where the data stand in the shape of a table.

In the Figure 6 they resort to the use of a kind of flow chart, where the nodes of the different links have pictures of people accompanied by numeric values. The use of continuous, dotted lines, and the different colours facilitate the understanding of the traffic of values among the different nodes of the structure [+ +].

STATISTIC MAPS AND GRAPHICS

In the example of the Figure 1, can be seen the correct use of a map to illustrate the exact spot of an accident. It is in the thematic cartography where the convergence with the graphic representation of statistic data takes place, with our without mathematic basis (Kraak, & Ormeling, 2003). A good example of these maps is generated in the presidential elections (Figure 7), where the votes obtained by the main candidates are depicted in relation to the territorial division of the state, province or municipality where the elections have taken place. However, there are symbols which are used incorrectly, since the reader can not count them horizontally, as it can be seen in the Figure 8 (Bertin,

Figure 5. Graphic representation of the results of a survey with regard to the teaching of religion and the position that the main Spanish political parties have on the issue [+]
(*Approximate Translation: Title: "The religion subject" and with the subtitle "poll over the religion teaching in the classroom".*)

Figure 6. Accounting information about a Spanish entrepreneurial network not transparent with the tax revenue office by relating activities both profit and non-profit [-]
(Approximate Translation: Graphic of the Spanish paper El País with an entrepreneurial criminal plot. Kind of business: non-profit [blue colour], and for profit [yellow colour].)

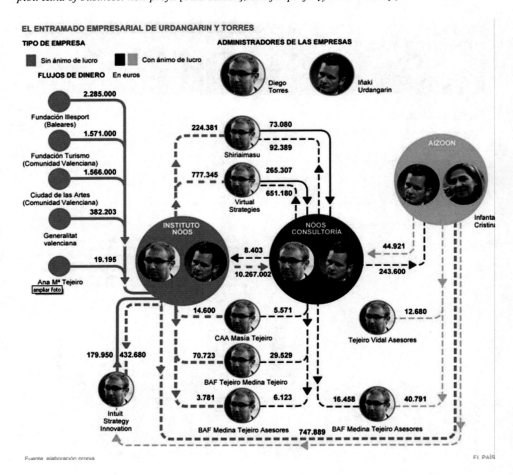

1983; Hampshire & Stephenson, 2008). In the Figure 8, the designer of the graphic has included their total in a parenthesis. Besides, in that figure the use of the lineal graphics as rings prompts a visual confusion, in principle, to understand the information about the two main groups of the statistic data. In contrast, that same combination of graphic representations with a map of the Spanish autonomous regions have a higher level of understanding and iconicity in the Figure 9.

Figure 7. Results of the elections in the USA [+ +]
(Approximate Translation: "The best is yet to come", and with the first subtitle "The president achieves a second term by winning in most of the key states and gains the popular vote for over two million votes".)

An excellent graphic where is depicted with a map the level of employment in the world is in the Figure 10. On it, flag, text and figures boost the iconicity of each one of the countries which are referred. In contrast, in the Figure 11, the combination of bars, lines, in the upper part of the figure, with a map of the EU in the lower part, whereas comparatives are made between the member countries of the EU, Japan and the USA, of which two countries do not have their corresponding maps. This representation prompts a high level of confusion in the lines of the isotopies of the signification and the significant between the visual and textual information.

Now by using a map the designer is bolstering the geographical idea to which referred the data of descriptive statistics, for instance and includes the cartogram with icons, such as can be the use objects, people, etc. In the figure there are examples of those icons whereas in the Figure 13 can be seen how there is a use of people as if they were vertical bars, with statistic information. However, the categories depicted in a joint and disorderly way

Figure 8. Incorrect use of the stars to count the total of votes obtained [– –]
(Approximate Translation: Graphics with the results of the votes in blue color [Obama] and in red color [Romney]. The intention of vote is with lineal graphics in the left area, the house of representatives in the right area with graphics in the shape of semicircles, and the total of governors in the lower part counted with stars.)

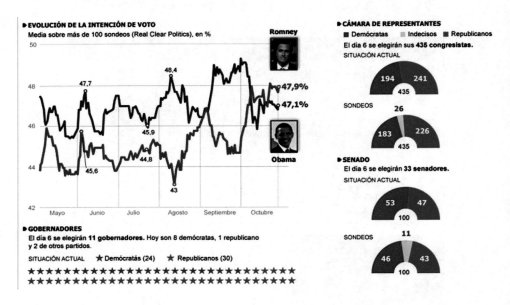

(autonomous region, sex, civil status, date of birth, level of training, time looking for a job, last occupation breed confusion in the isotopic lines.

ONLINE DYNAMIC STATISTIC INFORMATION AND THE USE OF COMICS TO DRAW ATTENTION

One of the main advantages of the digital papers and which have meant a real "r"evolution in the printed press is the possibility of offering static and dynamic information in real time. Statistic information is no exception to this rule. We have an example in the Figures 15 and 16 where a new about the rise of the Spanish risk premium is reflected in two different moments along the day –18th of July 2012– and with a historic summary of its evolution on the 20th July 2012 (Figure 17), of the last two decades (1990–2010). In all these figures, by using a same kind of lineal graphic and with the same maroon color, it has generated an isotopy that has quickly facilitated the understanding of the news.

Figure 9. Correct use of the hybrid representation in the map of unemployed in Spain [+]

(Approximate Translation: "Evolution of unemployment" Lineal graphic with the number of unemployed and the unemployment rate [upper area]. Map of the unemployed by communities and in total of thousands [lower left area]. In the lower right area, the circular graphic, where is the information by sex, that is, men [red] and women [grey] and by sectors [vertical bar]: services, industry and agriculture.)

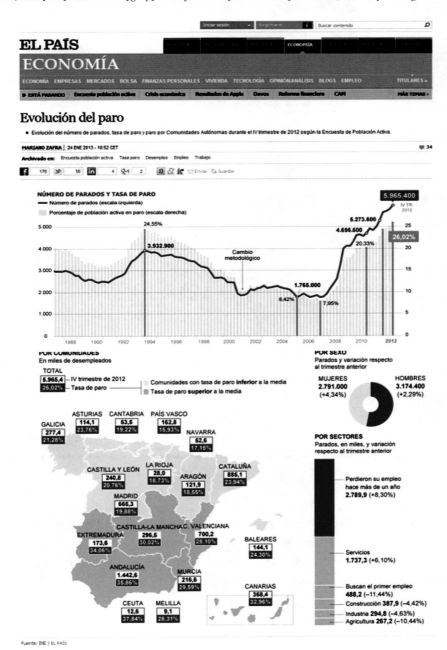

Figure 10. Correct use in the thematic cartographic representation and the statistic information [+ +]
(Approximate Translation: The atlas of employment. Countries with a larger job offer and more demanded profiles. Unemployment rate in %.)

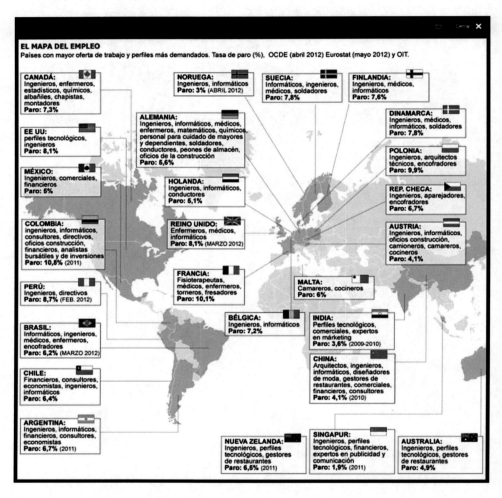

Gremais defines isotopy as the principle that allows the semantic concatenation of utterances (Greimas, 1984; Nöth, 1995). Greimas develops the theory of textual coherence on the basis of his concept of contextual semes. The iterativity (recurrence) of contextual semes, which connect the semantic elements of discourse (sememes), assures its textual homogeneity and coherence.

Figure 11. Incorrect use of the cartographic and statistic representation with a mathematic basis (lines and bars) [– –]

(*Approximate Translation: Lineal graphic of the GNP in Europe [euro zone], USA and Japan. In red colour the yearly variation and in grey colour the quarterly variation. In the lower part, the GNP by UE countries. In grey colour, better or the same that the UE average, in pink colour, worse than the European average.*)

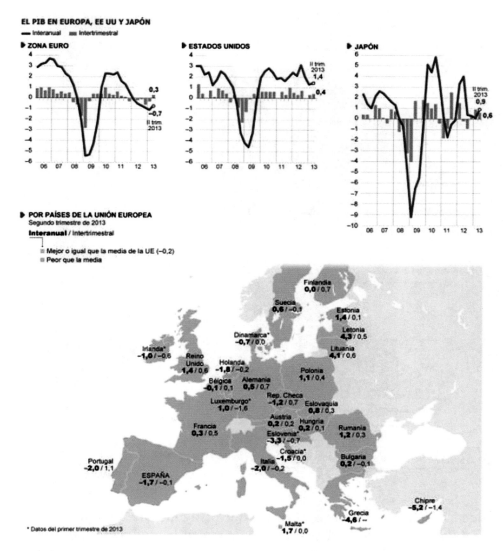

Another of the resources which quickly facilitate the understanding of the information are the comics, especially in the educational environment, as it has been seen in the origins of the interactive systems for the connection and

Figure 12. Correct use of the symbols in statistics with touristic purposes [+]
(Approximate Translation: Graphic of the tourism market in Spain. In the upper left side. Arrival of
international tourists in millions of people. In the left lower side: Expense of the tourists in thousands
of millions of euros. In the upper right side: Pathways of access of the international tourists [until
November 2013]. In the right lower part: Evolution of tourism inside Spain [yearly change in the
number of trips].)

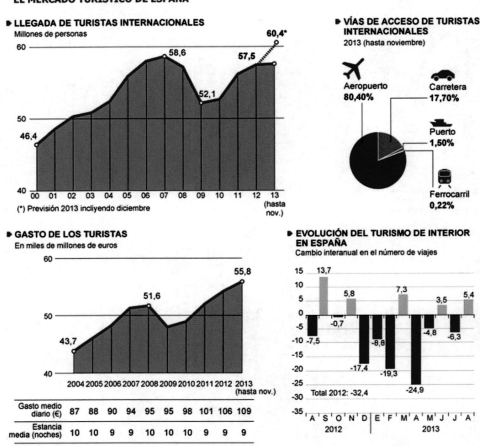

attendance to the subjects of a virtual university in Barcelona, for instance (Cipolla-Ficarra, 1996). Basically, a comic can be defined at operational level as a story told through interrelated drawings and text which depict a progressive series of meaningful moments of said story, according to the selection made by a narrator (Baur, 1978). Each moment, expressed by an illustration, receives the generic number of vignette. The main characteristics

Figure 13. Incorrect use of real human figures, with the effect of blurring and in a vertical rectangles format [– –]
(Approximate Translation: "Robot portrait of the unemployed", and with the subtitle "Percentage of unemployed by different groups [sex, age…] in relation to the total of the unemployed. From left to right in the photo [of the total of unemployed]. By region, by sex, by marital status, by age group, level of training, time searching for a job, and lastly occupation.)

of the comic, from a didactic point of view, for instance, can be summed up in the following way: the diachronic storytelling of the message; integration of verbal or iconic elements; use of a well defined series in its basic aspects, of

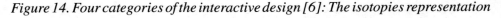

Figure 14. Four categories of the interactive design [6]: The isotopies representation

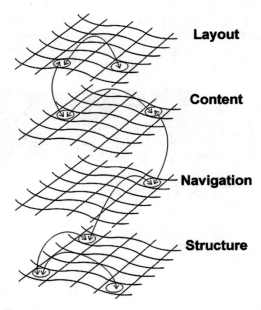

codes and conventions; its realization is made tending to a wide circulation, to which its creation is usually subordinated, and its purpose is predominantly entertaining. However, this set of elements does not exclude the presence of others. The texts, which may exist or not according to the storytelling needs, allow to signify all that which the protagonists of the plot feel, think or verbalize. In our universe of study has been detected the presence of verbalized messages where data are used and statistic representation in the shape of 3D rectangular and vertical bars, where some hippopotamus try to attract the attention of the reader about the climatic change in Spain, the rest of the world and the emission of CO_2, for instance. They do it through a single vignette and correctly, the author of the comic resorts to the sources to certify the veracity of the statistic data based on the mathematics.

The hybrid graphics such as infographics are those which need a greater attention of the interactive designers because communicability can be nil in the multimedia phones devices (Nielsen & Budiu, 2013). In our study have been incorporated each one of the graphics of the current work in different supports to be evaluated by adult users, whose results are presented in the Figures 21 and 22. The group of users is made up by 20 people, who daily read the press in digital support. Their ages range from 24-31 years. They

Figure 15. Lineal graphic representation and of mathematic basis at the hour 10:30 (06.18.2012) [+]
(Approximate Translation: The doubts about the solvency of Spain sharpen in spite of the results in Greece". Graphic of the evolution of the risk premium in red color and the mark of the evolution of the markets live (orange color). In the box of the upper right side is the value of 569 at 10:30 AM.)

have evaluated the ease of interpretation of the information in the interface in a scale from 0 to 10, 10 being the highest value, and zero is the minimum value.

The results obtained make apparent the preference for the vertical bars over the horizontal ones, the segmented circles over the circles or semicircles. Also the maps still fulfil an important function to focus quickly the visual over the rest of the information. However, in the hybrid graphics, the understating of the information is practically nil in the multimedia mobile phone supports. The use of comics for the presentation of the statistic information is widely accepted by all the users, irrespective of the digital support used, such as: PC, tablet PC, iPhone, etc.

Figure 16. Lineal graphic representation and of mathematic basis at the hour 14.46 (06.18.2012) [+]

(Approximate Translation: "The doubts about the solvency of Spain sharpen in spite of the results in Greece". Graphic of the evolution of the risk premium in red color and the mark of the evolution of the markets live [orange color]. In the box of the upper right side is the value of 589 at 14:46 PM.)

Dynamic and static means of information structures, in the digital press format tend to include statistics in their contents, and in a non-neutral way in the current universe of study. The attribute of wealth in the interactive design, that is, the possibility that the user has of accessing the same information through different media (pictures, outlines, comics, etc.) or alternatives of the structure of access to the information (guided links, indexes, listings, etc.) do not always boost the interrelation between the user and the multimedia device, due to failures in communicability. The visual information of the printed media in digital supports, whether it is the normal screens of the personal computers or the mobile phones; still have a very active role to draw the attention and ease the speed of the textual decoding.

Figure 17. An evolution summary of the information through a lineal graphic representation with a mathematic base [+]

(Approximate Translation: "Historic evolution of the risk premium". Two decades in the risk premium (differential of the performance of the bonus in ten years with the German bonus in basic points). In the lower part the different governments in the historic evolution of the Spanish risk premium.)

LESSONS LEARNED

The isotopic lines link different components of the interactive design categories. The categories of layout and content are the most important in the current work. They have indicated that the hybrid graphic representation is used prevailingly in the political contents. In our case, contemporary Spanish ones.

Figure 18. Lineal graphic representation of the concentration of CO$_2$ (ppm-400 parts per million) during the last 800,000 years, indicating when the homo sapiens appeared and currently how the 400 ppm have been surpassed [++]
(*Approximate Translation: CO$_2$ concentration during the last years. Data obtained from the ice core until 1958 when the measurements started in the Manua Loa observatory in Hawaii.*)

Figure 19. Representation through bars of the rise with Spanish temperatures, in the month of july 2012, a +0,5% in comparison with the period 1971–2000 [++]
(*Approximate Translation: Increase of the average temperature in the month of July. In the balloons of the comic it can be read the dialogue between the hippopotamus [popo –light blue and Pota –pink]. "July has been just a bit hotter than usual" [Popo]. "Yes, but it has rained half as much as usual", Pota.*)

Figure 20. Representation through 3D bars of the rise of the average temperature of the planet and a humor note for the forecast of 2100 when the character of the vignette uses binoculars [++]
(*Approximate Translation: Average temperatura of the planet: 1880 [13.2 C], 1950 [14.0 C], 2012 [14.6 C], forecast 2100 [without data because "Pota" character needs binoculars to find the number].*)

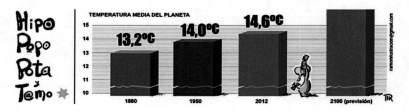

The purpose is to boost the public opinion, through the readers of the digital and/or analogical papers. That is to say, a hybrid graphic representation aimed at the failings in the controls in the economic, financial and fiscal systems,

Figure 21. Comics with statistical information: the users evaluation

Comics

	U1	U2	U3	U4	U5	U6	U7	U8	U9	U10	U11	U12	U13	U14	U15	U16	U17	U18	U19	U20
▪Series1	9	10	9	10	9	8	10	9	9	8	9	8	9	10	9	8	10	9	9	8

Figure 22. Three multimedia devices with statistical information –PCs, Tablet PC, and iPhone: Results of the evaluation

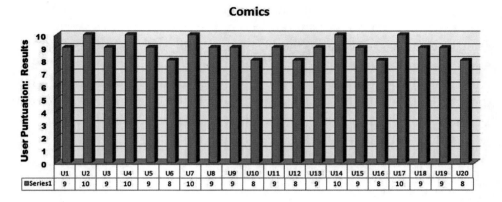

Graphics, Communicability and Multimedia Devices: Results

	PC	Tablet PC	iPhone
▪Traditional	9	10	8
▪Hybrid	7	7	4
▪Comics	10	9	7

and which activate the judiciary system. The numeric data, coherently and correctly presented among themselves, allow the intersection between dynamic and static means, thus raising the level of communicability. In contrast, in the combination of graphic representations of the economic and/or financial contents, that is, with or without basis in the mathematics, as it has been seen, ambiguity, vagueness, etc., are common denominators. This denominator generates an intentional chaos in the visual and textual information. The goal is to prevent an easy understanding of the local, provincial, regional, estate-wide reality by the potential readers of Spanish digital and/or analogical papers. Besides, in many cases, those contents and their modelling coincide 100% between the paper support and the digital one. Simultaneously, it has been verified that the analyzed comics, with statistic data, are an exception to that reality. Those comics boost the attention of the user towards current pressing issues, such as those related to the ecology, environmental contamination, climate change, etc. Finally, the classical graphics of statistic data which are related to the Spanish unemployed usually have an excellent level of communicability. In contrast, in those statistical data where a comparison of the local reality with the global reality is sought, the intersection of different kinds of representation only serve to increase the confusion about the topic dealt with in the online article.

CONCLUSION

Although in the 20th century there was a clear division between statistic representation with a mathematic base and not mathematic, with digital infographics a new modality to depict that information has been generated, such as the hybrid. In it an intersection of techniques of the graphic computer science takes place, such as can be the graphics that emulate or simulate 3D bars, blurring effects, transparencies, etc, statistic information, thematic cartography, comics, as it has been verified in our universe of study. In the presented examples, when there is a high presence of iconicity, the isotopic lines increase, thus facilitating the fast interpretation of the content of the hybrid information, for example. Now an inappropriate use of statistic graphics may bring about a demotivation and dropping the reading of the article. Some of those examples belong to the graphic representation which have called hybrid in the current work, but others belong exclusively to the classical environment of the representation of the information. The former are more recent and they are in the experimentation stage to generate a new way or representation of the statistic data. Nevertheless, the latter go back to the times of Willian Playfair (18th–19th centuries). Consequently, the failings detected in the current work are not accepted by the readers of the digital and analogical papers of the 21st century. That is, those are failings that affect the communicability of the online contents, among local and global users, such as the reading of a newspaper, for instance. In the future, we will broaden the current universe of study, with new examples, towards the bidirectional eric-etic relationship between the local and global reader of statistic information in the digital papers, which allow the potential users to have a free access to online information.

ACKNOWLEDGMENT

Our very special thanks go to Maria Ficarra. Besides, we should like to address a few words of thanks to Luisa Varela, Mary Brie, Sonia Flores, Giselda Verdone, Inés Bernardi, Jacqueline Alma, Donald Nilson, and Carlos, who contribute with their work, opinions and remarks.

REFERENCES

Baur, E. (1978). *La historieta como experiencia didáctica*. Editorial Nueva Imagen. (in Spanish)

Bertin, J. (1983). *Semiology of Graphics: Diagrams, Networks, Maps*. Madison, WI: The University of Wisconsin Press.

Chen, C., & Paul, R. (2001). Visualizing a Knowledge Domains Intellectual Structure. *IEEE Computer*, *34*(3), 65–71. doi:10.1109/2.910895

Cipolla-Ficarra, F. (1996). *Evaluation and communication techniques in multimedia product design for on the net university education. In Multimedia on the Net* (pp. 151–165). Heidelberg, Germany: Springer. doi:10.1007/978-3-7091-9472-0_14

Cipolla-Ficarra, F. (2005). *Interazione uomo-computer nel XXI secolo: Analisi e valutazione euristica della qualità per la comunicazione e l'usabilità*. Bergamo: Blue Herons. (in Italian)

Cipolla-Ficarra, F. (2014). *Advanced Research and Trends in New Technologies, Software, Human-Computer Interaction, and Communicability*. Hershey, PA: IGI Global. doi:10.4018/978-1-4666-4490-8

Cleveland, W. (1993). *Visualizing Data*. Hobart Press.

Cleveland, W. (1994). *The Elements of Graphing Data. Summit*. Hobart Press.

Eco, U. (1979). *A Theory of Semiotics*. Indiana University Press.

Ficarra, F.V.C. (1993). Ciencia, comunicacion cientifica e infografia: Una triada exquisita. *Imaging*, (16), 27-31. (in Spanish)

Ficarra, F. V. C. (1999). Artes gráficas e infográficas en el siglo XXI. [In Spanish]. *Chasqui*, (68), 30–33.

Gage, J. (2000). *Color and Meaning: Art, Science, and Symbolism*. Berkeley, CA: University of California Press.

Greimas, A. (1984). *Structural Semantics: An Attempt at a Method*. University of Nebraska Press.

Hampshire, M., & Stephenson, K. (2008). *Signs and Symbols*. Rockport Publishers.

Kraak, M., & Ormeling, F. (2003). *Cartography: Visualization of Spatial Data Paperback*. New York: Pearson Education.

Lankow, J., Ritchie, J., & Crooks, R. (2012). *Infographics: The Power of Visual Storytelling*. Hoboken, NJ: John Wiley.

Modesto-Escobar, R. (1999). *Análisis Gráfico Exploratorio*. Madrid: La Muralla. (in Spanish)

Nielsen, J. & Budiu, R. (2013). *Mobile Usability*. Berkeley, CA: New Riders.

Nöth, W. (1995). *Handbook of Semiotics*. Bloomington, IN: Indiana University Press.

Playfair, W. (2005). *Playfair's Commercial and Political Atlas and Statistical Breviary*. Cambridge, UK: Cambridge University Press.

Rioboo, J., & Pío de Oro, C. (2000). *Representaciones gráficas de datos estadísticos*. Madrid: Alfa Centauro. (in Spanish)

Saussure, F. (1983). *Course in General Lingistics*. New York: McGraw-Hill.

Smiciklas, M. (2012). *The Power of Infographics: Using Pictures to Communicate and Connect With Your Audience*. Bergen: Person Education.

Tufte, E. (2001). *The Visual Display of Quantitative Information Hardcover*. Cheshire, UK: Graphics Press.

Veron, E. (2004). *La semiosis social. Fragmentos de una teoría de la discursividad*. Barcelona: Gedisa. (in Spanish)

Ware, C. (2013). *Information Visualization: Perception for Design*. Waltham, MA: Morgan Kaufmann.

ADDITIONAL READING

Barthes, R. (1985). *L'aventure sémiologique*. Paris: Seuil. In French

Baudisch, P., DeCarlo, D., Duchowski, A. T., & Geisler, W. S. (2003). Focusing on the Essential: Considering Attention in Display Design. *Communications of the ACM, 46*(3), 60–66. doi:10.1145/636772.636799

Brown, D. C., Burbano, E., Minski, J., & Cruz, I. E. (2002). Evaluating Web Page Color and Layout Adaptations. *IEEE MultiMedia, 9*(1), 86–89. doi:10.1109/93.978356

Bryson, S., Kenwright, D., Cox, M., Ellsworth, D., & Haimes, R. (1999). Visually Exploring Gigabyte Data Sets in Real Time. *Communications of the ACM, 42*(8), 82–90. doi:10.1145/310930.310977

Cipolla-Ficarra, F. (1996). A User Evaluation of Hypermedia Iconography. In Proceedings Compugraphics. Paris: GRASP, 182-191

Cipolla-Ficarra, F. (1999). Evaluation Heuristic of the Richness. In *Proceedings International Conference on Information Analysis and Synthesis, ISAS '99*, 23-30. Orlando: ISAS

Cipolla-Ficarra, F. (2013). *Advanced Research and Trends in New Technologies, Software, Human-Computer Interaction, and Communicability*. Hershey: IGI Global.

Cipolla-Ficarra, F. et al.. (2011). *Computational Informatics, Social Factors and New Information Technologies: Hypermedia Perspectives and Avant-Garde Experiences in the Era of Communicability Expansion*. Bergamo: Blue Herons.

Cipolla-Ficarra, F. et al.. (2011). *Advances in Dynamic and Static Media for Interactive Systems: Communicability, Computer Science and Design* (pp. 165–189). Bergamo: Blue Herons Editions.

Cipolla-Ficarra, F., & Cipolla-Ficarra, M. (2009). Computer Animation and Communicability in Multimedia System and Services: A Trichotomy Evaluation. In *Proceedings New Directions in Intelligent Interactive Multimedia* (pp. 103–115). Berlin: Springer.

Dalmasso, M. (1992). *La imagen y el sentido. Las paradojas de lo verosímil. Teoría y Crítica de la Manipulación, 2*. Córdoba: Universidad Nacional de Córdoba. In Spanish

Haining, R. (2003). *Spatial Data Analysis: Theory and Practice*. Cambridge: Cambridge University Press. doi:10.1017/CBO9780511754944

Hampshire, M., & Stephenson, K. (2006). *Stripes. Have*. Rockport Publishers.

Haralick, R. (1990). Investigating the Effects of Color. *Communications of the ACM, 33*(2), 120–124. doi:10.1145/75577.75578

Hinman, R. (2009). 90 Mobiles in 90 Days: A Celebration of Ideas for Mobile User Experience. *Interaction, 16*(1), 11–13.

Louridas, P., & Ebert, C. (2013). Embedded Analytics and Statistics for Big Data. *IEEE Software, 30*(6), 33–39. doi:10.1109/MS.2013.125

Lucero, A., Jones, M., Jokela, T., & Robinson, S. (2013). Mobile Collocated Interactions: Taking an Offline Break Together. *Interaction, 20*(2), 26–32. doi:10.1145/2427076.2427083

Ma, K., & Muelder, C. (2013). Large-Scale Graph Visualization and Analytics. *IEEE Computer, 46*(7), 39–45. doi:10.1109/MC.2013.242

Marcus, A. (1993). Human Communications Issues in Advanced UIs. *Communications of the ACM, 36*(4), 101–109. doi:10.1145/255950.153670

Moles, A. (1970). *L'Affiche dans la societé urbaine*. Paris: Dunod. In French

Orzan, A., Bousseau, A., Barla, P., Winnemöller, H., Thollot, J., & Salesin, D. (2013). Diffusion Curves: A Vector Representation for Smooth-Shaded Images. *Communications of the ACM, 56*(7), 101–108. doi:10.1145/2483852.2483873

Robinson, et al.. (1995). *Elements of Cartography*. Hoboken: John Wiley.

Rodríguez-Diéguez, J. (1988). *El comic y su utilización didáctica: Los tebeos en la enseñanza*. Barcelona: Gustavo Gili. In Spanish

Steimberg, O. (1977). *Leyendo historietas. Estilos y sentidos de un arte menor*. Buenos Aires: Ediciones Nueva Vison. In Spanish

Ullmer, B. (2012). Entangling Space, Form, Light, Time, Computational STEAM, and Cultural Artifacts. *Interaction, 19*(4), 32–39. doi:10.1145/2212877.2212887

Zhang, D. et al.. (2012). Social and Community Intelligence: Technologies and Trends. *IEEE Computer, 29*(4), 88–92.

KEY TERMS AND DEFINITIONS

Communicability: A qualitative communication between the user and the interactive system, such as mobile phones, augmented reality, immersion multimedia, hypermedia, among others. The extent to which an interactive system successfully conveys its functionality to the user.

Descriptive Statistics: Traditionally are statistics that quantitatively describe or summarize features of a collection of information. They are used to describe the basic features of the data in a research study, for example, in a communicability lab., usability lab., etc. Besides, they provide simple summaries about the sample and the measures, for example, the user interaction with interactive systems. Together with simple graphics analysis, they form the basis of virtually every quantitative analysis of data.

Interactive System: A computer device made up by a CPU and peripherals, whose functioning requires a constant interaction with the user. Currently these systems tend to their miniaturization and/or invisibility, the mobility and wireless connectability among them.

Isotopy: The principle that allows the semantic concatenation of utterances (definition from Algirdas Julien Greimas).

Semiosis: A triadic process in which an object generates a sign of itself, and in turn, the sign generates an interpretant of itself (definition from Charles Sanders Peirce). In other words, it is a process in which a potentially endless series of interpretants is generated.

Semiotics or Semiology: A name for the general theory of signs, sometimes supposed to be a science of sings.

User Experience: It includes the human emotions about using a product, system or service. It is not a synonymous of communicability or usability. Besides, generally, it includes the practical, experiential, affective, meaningful and valuable aspects of human–computer interaction and product ownership.

Conclusion

A diachronic vision about reality is a positive exercise to better understand how the technology-enhanced human interaction in modern society. In each one of the presented chapters there is an attempt at looking to the past to remember and transfer the accumulated knowledge towards new challenges and horizons. Besides, those chapters contain true cases, experiments, examples, etc. of how the human being can damage the noble nature of certain discoveries and inventions inside the framework of computer sciences and all its derivations. They are the so called human factors and social factors. In the quality of the software it is logical and normal to find them. However, their degeneration is what we usually include in the Garduña factor. A factor that slows down considerably all the achievements of human kind by discouraging groups of professionals who work anonymously for the common good. It is striking how some of those individuals who boycott the areas of knowledge such as the human-computer interaction call themselves disinterested workers.

If they aren't interested they might work in something else, instead of blocking the mechanism of transparent scientific progress. In reality they are disinterested workers. Many of them are allowed to manage considerable financial resources stemming from the public and private subsidies. As well as to keep the benefits that this entails, in administering that money with bank or financial bodies. Some of these institutions have been literally saved with the hunger and even with the life of thousands of citizens, in the new millennium and surrounded by the latest technologies. Without mentioning the benefits received from that service sectors, because of the sponsoring to activities inside or outside the training centres, or the personal help. We are in times where it is forbidden to tell truths in certain environments. That who tells them is automatically marginalized and burned up, as they were in the medieval human bonfires. Not for nothing making a PhD in some universities as a foreigner may entail a decade, that is, three times as much as the local students and where the group of tutors of the student become their enemies along his professional life.

Aside from that reality that is included in the garduña factor, the formal and factual sciences still advance by giant steps every passing second. It suffices to see the evolution of the operative systems of the PCs and the influence exerted in the development of the contents for the online and offline interactive systems. Advances where computer science has streamlined the education and the sciences in myriad places in the planet in a harmonious and constant way. Now the new challenges come from artificial intelligence, with robotics: the quantum computers; the nanotechnology applied to healthcare: the drones and the air transportation of people, communicability and the mobile devices of multimedia phones, among other interesting scientific challenges: in a new area which can be called: "Quantic-Nanotechnological-Self- Sufficient Era". An era in which the quality of communication, that is, communicability, will be essential for the interrelations among the human beings and the intelligent machines.

Before finishing with a set of famous quotes, I send a new thank you very much to the splendid human team in IGI Global, in a particular way to Colleen Moore, for all the support given in these months, together with each one of her colleagues in Chocolate Ave.

"Truth never damages a cause that is just" (Mahatma Gandhi); "Keep your face to the sunshine and you cannot see a shadow" (Helen Keller); "The good news about computers is that they do what you tell them to do. The bad news is that they do what you tell them to do" (Ted Nelson); "The internet could be a very positive step towards education, organisation and participation in a meaningful society" (Noam Chomsky); and "How is it that little children are so intelligent and men so stupid? It must be education that does it" (Alexandre Dumas).

About the Authors

Francisco V. Cipolla-Ficarra is a professor, reaserh and writer. PhD-Ing. Area: Multimedia (1999). B.A. in Social Communication (1988). B.A. in Computer Programming and Systems Analysis (1983). Manager and coordinator of the first Human-Computer Interaction Lab. in Barcelona, Spain (1997 – 1999). Professor in American and European universities, technical and professional colleges (1981 – present), subjects: computer science, computer graphics and animation, human-computer interaction, design and multimedia. Scientific journalist and writer (1989 – present). CEO: Blue Herons Editions. Coordinator of AInCI (*International Association of Interactive Communication* –www.ainci.com) and ALAIPO (*Latin Association International of Human-Computer Interaction* –www.alaipo. com). Main research interests: HCI, communicability, quality, auditory and evaluation of interactive systems, computer graphics and animation, social communication, semiotics, e-learning, video games, ecological and cultural heritage. ACM and IEEE member.

Maria Valeria Ficarra is a lawyer. B.A. Union lawyer (2003). Master in International Legal Practice (2008). Public Relations: AInCI (*International Association of Interactive Communication*) and ALAIPO (*Latin Association International of Human-Computer Interaction*) Barcelona, Spain. Main research interests: labour and international law, legal and business strategies, problem-solving techniques, leadership, psychology, sociology, communication, cultural understanding and cooperation.

Miguel Cipolla-Ficarra is a professor and research. PhD. Area: Power Electronic Engineering (1996). B.A. Electronic Engineering – Telecommunications (1990). B.A. Electric Engineering (1999). Professor in European universities, technical and professional colleges (1987 – present). Software project manager: design, development and implementation of algorithms. Product manager, application engineer and technical sales engineer in international projects. Director of laboratory in F&F Multimedia Communic@tions Corp. Technical manager in AInCI (*International Association of Interactive Communication* –www.ainci.com) and ALAIPO (*Latin Association International of Human-Computer Interaction* –www.alaipo.com). Main research interests: interfaces, usability engineering, interactive systems, telecommunication, computer sciences, networks, industrial design, programmation, automation, motors on microprocessor, ecological energy, e-commerce and computer aided education.

Alejandra Quiroga received a Bachelor's Degree in Computer Sciences in 1983 (Bahia Blanca, Argentina). She has a Educational Bachelor in 1988 (Buenos Aires, Argentina) and a Master's Degree in Computer Engineering in 2004 (Sweden). She is currently a teaching assistant (La Pampa, Argentina) and PhD student. Her current research subjects are education, user-centered design, open source software, software engineering and robotics. New fields of interest are computer graphics, computer-aided design, computer vision, semantic web and cloud computing.

Jacqueline Alma lives and works in Vancouver (BC), Canada. She was a professor at the HEC Montréal École de Gestion, British Columbia Institute of Technology, and Vancouver Film School. She received her B.A., master's and doctorate degree in Computing & IT from the Simon Fraser University and University of British Columbia. The main areas of the interest are computer science, database, interactive design, video games, computer animation, cinema digital and business technology management.

Jim Carré is a teacher in Curaçao Island. He received his master's degree in Psychology in Florida (USA). He has a B.A. in Computer Science (Brazil). Furthermore, he had studied in Faculty of Societal and Behavioral (Curaçao) and Informatics (Venezuela). His recent topics of interest are: psychology, psychiatry, cognitive models, marketing and commerce, e-learning models, learning systems, artificial intelligence, systems security and augmented reality.

Index

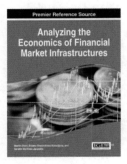

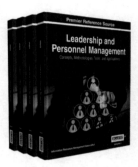
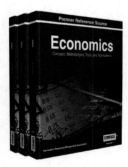
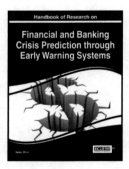

Stay Current on the Latest Emerging Research Developments

Become an IGI Global Reviewer for Authored Book Projects

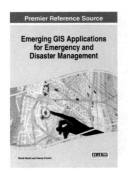
Premier Reference Source

Emerging GIS Applications for Emergency and Disaster Management

Premier Reference Source

Managerial Strategies and Green Solutions for Project Sustainability

Premier Reference Source

Comparative Approaches to Using R and Python for Statistical Data Analysis

Premier Reference Source

Solutions for High-Touch Communications in a High-Tech World

The overall success of an authored book project is dependent on quality and timely reviews.

In this competitive age of scholarly publishing, constructive and timely feedback significantly decreases the turnaround time of manuscripts from submission to acceptance, allowing the publication and discovery of progressive research at a much more expeditious rate. Several IGI Global authored book projects are currently seeking highly qualified experts in the field to fill vacancies on their respective editorial review boards:

Applications may be sent to:
development@igi-global.com

Applicants must have a doctorate (or an equivalent degree) as well as publishing and reviewing experience. Reviewers are asked to write reviews in a timely, collegial, and constructive manner. All reviewers will begin their role on an ad-hoc basis for a period of one year, and upon successful completion of this term can be considered for full editorial review board status, with the potential for a subsequent promotion to Associate Editor.

If you have a colleague that may be interested in this opportunity, we encourage you to share this information with them.

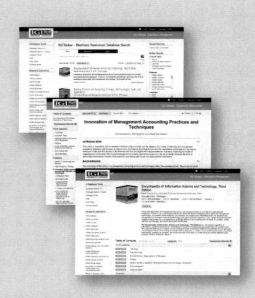

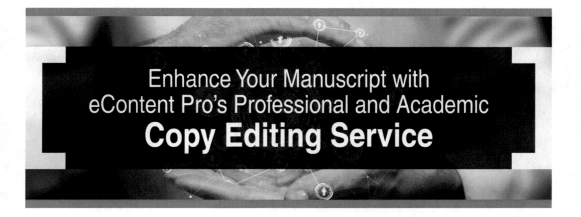